# BOB DYLAN
## THE LYRICS 1961–2012

Simon & Schuster

New York  London  Toronto  Sydney  New Delhi

# BOB DYLAN

## THE LYRICS 1961–2012

# Bob Dylan

Big City Blues by Bob Dylan 1961

I been thinkin' a out you darlin'
You been on my mind
But i cant stay long in this here town
I ain't the settlin' kind
Rain is crashin on the roof
My boots ~~are~~ feel hot as coals
Got to keep movin' on
You know i got to go

Goin' to New York city
Gonna find my way
Gonna play in the biggest nightclu
underneath the lights of ol'Broadway
Heard lots a things about that big town
Heard the streets are ~~l~~ full of gold
Gonna dig me up a brick take it to the bank
gonna roll, jelly roll

# Talking New York

Ramblin' outa the wild West
Leavin' the towns I love the best
Thought I'd seen some ups and downs
'Til I come into New York town
People goin' down to the ground
Buildings goin' up to the sky

Wintertime in New York town
The wind blowin' snow around
Walk around with nowhere to go
Somebody could freeze right to the bone
I froze right to the bone
*New York Times* said it was the coldest winter in seventeen years
I didn't feel so cold then

I swung onto my old guitar
Grabbed hold of a subway car
And after a rocking, reeling, rolling ride
I landed up on the downtown side
Greenwich Village

I walked down there and ended up
In one of them coffee-houses on the block
Got on the stage to sing and play
Man there said, "Come back some other day
You sound like a hillbilly
We want folk singers here"

Well, I got a harmonica job, begun to play
Blowin' my lungs out for a dollar a day
I blowed inside out and upside down
The man there said he loved m' sound
He was ravin' about how he loved m' sound
Dollar a day's worth

And after weeks and weeks of hangin' around
I finally got a job in New York town
In a bigger place, bigger money too
Even joined the union and paid m' dues

Now, a very great man once said
That some people rob you with a fountain pen
It didn't take too long to find out
Just what he was talkin' about
A lot of people don't have much food on their table
But they got a lot of forks 'n' knives
And they gotta cut somethin'

So one mornin' when the sun was warm
I rambled out of New York town
Pulled my cap down over my eyes
And headed out for the western skies
So long, New York
Howdy, East Orange

# Song to Woody

I'm out here a thousand miles from my home
Walkin' a road other men have gone down
I'm seein' your world of people and things
Your paupers and peasants and princes and kings

Hey, hey, Woody Guthrie, I wrote you a song
'Bout a funny ol' world that's a-comin' along
Seems sick an' it's hungry, it's tired an' it's torn
It looks like it's a-dyin' an' it's hardly been born

Hey, Woody Guthrie, but I know that you know
All the things that I'm a-sayin' an' a-many times more
I'm a-singin' you the song, but I can't sing enough
'Cause there's not many men that done the things that you've done

Here's to Cisco an' Sonny an' Leadbelly too
An' to all the good people that traveled with you
Here's to the hearts and the hands of the men
That come with the dust and are gone with the wind

I'm a-leavin' tomorrow, but I could leave today
Somewhere down the road someday
The very last thing that I'd want to do
Is to say I've been hittin' some hard travelin' too

# Hard Times in New York Town

Come you ladies and you gentlemen, a-listen to my song
Sing it to you right, but you might think it's wrong
Just a little glimpse of a story I'll tell
'Bout an East Coast city that you all know well
It's hard times in the city
Livin' down in New York town

Old New York City is a friendly old town
From Washington Heights to Harlem on down
There's a-mighty many people all millin' all around
They'll kick you when you're up and knock you when you're down
It's hard times in the city
Livin' down in New York town

It's a mighty long ways from the Golden Gate
To Rockefeller Plaza 'n' the Empire State
Mister Rockefeller sets up as high as a bird
Old Mister Empire never says a word
It's hard times from the country
Livin' down in New York town

Well, it's up in the mornin' tryin' to find a job of work
Stand in one place till your feet begin to hurt
If you got a lot o' money you can make yourself merry
If you only got a nickel, it's the Staten Island Ferry
And it's hard times in the city
Livin' down in New York town

Mister Hudson come a-sailin' down the stream
And old Mister Minuet paid for his dream
Bought your city on a one-way track
'F I had my way I'd sell it right back
And it's hard times in the city
Livin' down in New York town

I'll take all the smog in Cal-i-for-ne-ay
'N' every bit of dust in the Oklahoma plains
'N' the dirt in the caves of the Rocky Mountain mines
It's all much cleaner than the New York kind
And it's hard times in the city
Livin' down in New York town

So all you newsy people, spread the news around
You c'n listen to m' story, listen to m' song
You c'n step on my name, you c'n try 'n' get me beat
When I leave New York, I'll be standin' on my feet
And it's hard times in the city
Livin' down in New York town

# Talking Bear Mountain Picnic Massacre Blues

I saw it advertised one day
Bear Mountain picnic was comin' my way
"Come along 'n' take a trip
We'll bring you up there on a ship
Bring the wife and kids
Bring the whole family"
Yippee!

Well, I run right down 'n' bought a ticket
To this Bear Mountain Picnic
But little did I realize
I was in for a picnic surprise
Had nothin' to do with mountains
I didn't even come close to a bear

Took the wife 'n' kids down to the pier
Six thousand people there
Everybody had a ticket for the trip
"Oh well," I said, "it's a pretty big ship
Besides, anyway, the more the merrier"

Well, we all got on 'n' what d'ya think
That big old boat started t' sink
More people kept a-pilin' on
That old ship was a-slowly goin' down
Funny way t' start a picnic

Well, I soon lost track of m' kids 'n' wife
So many people there I never saw in m' life
That old ship sinkin' down in the water
Six thousand people tryin' t' kill each other
Dogs a-barkin', cats a-meowin'
Women screamin', fists a-flyin', babies cryin'
Cops a-comin', me a-runnin'
Maybe we just better call off the picnic

I got shoved down 'n' pushed around
All I could hear there was a screamin' sound
Don't remember one thing more
Just remember wakin' up on a little shore
Head busted, stomach cracked
Feet splintered, I was bald, naked . . .
Quite lucky to be alive though

Feelin' like I climbed outa m' casket
I grabbed back hold of m' picnic basket
Took the wife 'n' kids 'n' started home
Wishin' I'd never got up that morn

Now, I don't care just what you do
If you wanta have a picnic, that's up t' you
But don't tell me about it, I don't wanta hear it
'Cause, see, I just lost all m' picnic spirit
Stay in m' kitchen, have m' own picnic . . .
In the bathroom

Now, it don't seem to me quite so funny
What some people are gonna do f'r money
There's a bran' new gimmick every day
Just t' take somebody's money away
I think we oughta take some o' these people
And put 'em on a boat, send 'em up to Bear Mountain . . .
For a picnic

# Rambling, Gambling Willie

Come around you rovin' gamblers and a story I will tell
About the greatest gambler, you all should know him well
His name was Will O'Conley and he gambled all his life
He had twenty-seven children, yet he never had a wife
And it's ride, Willie, ride
Roll, Willie, roll
Wherever you are a-gamblin' now, nobody really knows

He gambled in the White House and in the railroad yards
Wherever there was people, there was Willie and his cards
He had the reputation as the gamblin'est man around
Wives would keep their husbands home when Willie came to town
And it's ride, Willie, ride
Roll, Willie, roll
Wherever you are a-gamblin' now, nobody really knows

Sailin' down the Mississippi to a town called New Orleans
They're still talkin' about their card game on that Jackson River Queen
"I've come to win some money," Gamblin' Willie says
When the game finally ended up, the whole damn boat was his
And it's ride, Willie, ride
Roll, Willie, roll
Wherever you are a-gamblin' now, nobody really knows

Up in the Rocky Mountains in a town called Cripple Creek
There was an all-night poker game, lasted about a week
Nine hundred miners had laid their money down
When Willie finally left the room, he owned the whole damn town
And it's ride, Willie, ride
Roll, Willie, roll
Wherever you are a-gamblin' now, nobody really knows

But Willie had a heart of gold and this I know is true
He supported all his children and all their mothers too
He wore no rings or fancy things, like other gamblers wore
He spread his money far and wide, to help the sick and the poor
And it's ride, Willie, ride
Roll, Willie, roll
Wherever you are a-gamblin' now, nobody really knows

When you played your cards with Willie, you never really knew
Whether he was bluffin' or whether he was true
He won a fortune from a man who folded in his chair
The man, he left a diamond flush, Willie didn't even have a pair
And it's ride, Willie, ride
Roll, Willie, roll
Wherever you are a-gamblin' now, nobody really knows

It was late one evenin' during a poker game
A man lost all his money, he said Willie was to blame
He shot poor Willie through the head, which was a tragic fate
When Willie's cards fell on the floor, they were aces backed with eights
And it's ride, Willie, ride
Roll, Willie, roll
Wherever you are a-gamblin' now, nobody really knows

So all you rovin' gamblers, wherever you might be
The moral of the story is very plain to see
Make your money while you can, before you have to stop
For when you pull that dead man's hand, your gamblin' days are up
And it's ride, Willie, ride
Roll, Willie, roll
Wherever you are a-gamblin' now, nobody really knows

# Standing on the Highway

Well, I'm standin' on the highway
Tryin' to bum a ride, tryin' to bum a ride
Tryin' to bum a ride
Well, I'm standin' on the highway
Tryin' to bum a ride, tryin' to bum a ride
Tryin' to bum a ride
Nobody seem to know me
Everybody pass me by

Well, I'm standin' on the highway
Tryin' to hold up, tryin' to hold up
Tryin' to hold up and be brave
Well, I'm standin' on the highway
Tryin' to hold up, tryin' to hold up and be brave
One road's goin' to the bright lights
The other's goin' down to my grave

Well, I'm lookin' down at two cards
They seem to be handmade
Well, I'm lookin' down at two cards
They seem to be handmade
One looks like it's the ace of diamonds
The other looks like it is the ace of spades

Well, I'm standin' on the highway
Watchin' my life roll by
Well, I'm standin' on the highway
Watchin' my life roll by
Well, I'm standin' on the highway
Tryin' to bum a ride

Well, I'm standin' on the highway
Wonderin' where everybody went,
    wonderin' where everybody went
Wonderin' where everybody went
Well, I'm standin' on the highway
Wonderin' where everybody went,
    wonderin' where everybody went
Wonderin' where everybody went
Please mister, pick me up
I swear I ain't gonna kill nobody's kids

I wonder if my good gal
I wonder if she knows I'm here
Nobody else seems to know I'm here
I wonder if my good gal
I wonder if she knows I'm here
Nobody else seems to know I'm here
If she knows I'm here, Lawd
I wonder if she said a prayer

# Poor Boy Blues

Mm, tell mama
Where'd ya sleep last night?
Cain't ya hear me cryin'?
Hm, hm, hm

Hey, tell me baby
What's the matter here?
Cain't ya hear me cryin'?
Hm, hm, hm

Hey, stop you ol' train
Let a poor boy ride
Cain't ya hear me cryin'?
Hm, hm, hm

Hey, Mister Bartender
I swear I'm not too young
Cain't ya hear me cryin'?
Hm, hm, hm

Blow your whistle, policeman
My poor feet are trained to run
Cain't ya hear me cryin'?
Hm, hm, hm

Long-distance operator
I hear this phone call is on the house
Cain't ya hear me cryin'?
Hm, hm, hm

Ashes and diamonds
The diff'rence I cain't see
Cain't ya hear me cryin'?
Hm, hm, hm

Mister Judge and Jury
Cain't you see the shape I'm in?
Don't ya hear me cryin'?
Hm, hm, hm

Mississippi River
You a-runnin' too fast for me
Cain't ya hear me cryin'?
Hm, hm, hm

# Ballad for a Friend

Sad I'm a-sittin' on the railroad track
Watchin' that old smokestack
Train is a-leavin' but it won't be back

Years ago we hung around
Watchin' trains roll through the town
Now that train is a-graveyard bound

Where we go up in that North Country
Lakes and streams and mines so free
I had no better friend than he

Something happened to him that day
I thought I heard a stranger say
I hung my head and stole away

A diesel truck was rollin' slow
Pullin' down a heavy load
It left him on a Utah road

They carried him back to his home town
His mother cried, his sister moaned
Listenin' to them church bells tone

# Man on the Street

I'll sing you a song, ain't very long
'Bout an old man who never done wrong
How he died nobody can say
They found him dead in the street one day

Well, the crowd, they gathered one fine morn
At the man whose clothes 'n' shoes were torn
There on the sidewalk he did lay
They stopped 'n' stared 'n' walked their way

Well, the p'liceman come and he looked around
"Get up, old man, or I'm a-takin' you down"
He jabbed him once with his billy club
And the old man then rolled off the curb

Well, he jabbed him again and loudly said
"Call the wagon; this man is dead"
The wagon come, they loaded him in
I never saw the man again

I've sung you my song, it ain't very long
'Bout an old man who never done wrong
How he died no one can say
They found him dead in the street one day

# Talkin' John Birch Paranoid Blues

Well, I was feelin' sad and feelin' blue
I didn't know what in the world I wus gonna do
Them Communists they wus comin' around
They wus in the air
They wus on the ground
They wouldn't gimme no peace . . .

So I run down most hurriedly
And joined up with the John Birch Society
I got me a secret membership card
And started off a-walkin' down the road
Yee-hoo, I'm a real John Bircher now!
Look out you Commies!

Now we all agree with Hitler's views
Although he killed six million Jews
It don't matter too much that he was a Fascist
At least you can't say he was a Communist!
That's to say like if you got a cold you take a shot of malaria

Well, I wus lookin' everywhere for them gol-darned Reds
I got up in the mornin' 'n' looked under my bed
Looked in the sink, behind the door
Looked in the glove compartment of my car
Couldn't find 'em . . .

I wus lookin' high an' low for them Reds everywhere
I wus lookin' in the sink an' underneath the chair
I looked way up my chimney hole
I even looked deep down inside my toilet bowl
They got away . . .

Well, I wus sittin' home alone an' started to sweat
Figured they wus in my T.V. set
Peeked behind the picture frame
Got a shock from my feet, hittin' right up in the brain
Them Reds caused it!
I know they did . . . them hard-core ones

Well, I quit my job so I could work all alone
Then I changed my name to Sherlock Holmes
Followed some clues from my detective bag
And discovered they wus red stripes on the American flag!
That ol' Betsy Ross . . .

Well, I investigated all the books in the library
Ninety percent of 'em gotta be burned away
I investigated all the people that I knowed
Ninety-eight percent of them gotta go
The other two percent are fellow Birchers . . . just like me

Now Eisenhower, he's a Russian spy
Lincoln, Jefferson and that Roosevelt guy
To my knowledge there's just one man
That's really a true American: George Lincoln Rockwell
I know for a fact he hates Commies cus he picketed the movie *Exodus*

Well, I fin'ly started thinkin' straight
When I run outa things to investigate
Couldn't imagine doin' anything else
So now I'm sittin' home investigatin' myself!
Hope I don't find out anything . . . hmm, great God!

# The Death of Emmett Till

'Twas down in Mississippi not so long ago
When a young boy from Chicago town stepped through a Southern door
This boy's dreadful tragedy I can still remember well
The color of his skin was black and his name was Emmett Till

Some men they dragged him to a barn and there they beat him up
They said they had a reason, but I can't remember what
They tortured him and did some things too evil to repeat
There were screaming sounds inside the barn, there was laughing sounds
    out on the street

Then they rolled his body down a gulf amidst a bloody red rain
And they threw him in the waters wide to cease his screaming pain
The reason that they killed him there, and I'm sure it ain't no lie
Was just for the fun of killin' him and to watch him slowly die

And then to stop the United States of yelling for a trial
Two brothers they confessed that they had killed poor Emmett Till
But on the jury there were men who helped the brothers commit this
    awful crime
And so this trial was a mockery, but nobody seemed to mind

I saw the morning papers but I could not bear to see
The smiling brothers walkin' down the courthouse stairs
For the jury found them innocent and the brothers they went free
While Emmett's body floats the foam of a Jim Crow southern sea

If you can't speak out against this kind of thing, a crime that's so unjust
Your eyes are filled with dead men's dirt, your mind is filled with dust
Your arms and legs they must be in shackles and chains, and your blood it
    must refuse to flow
For you let this human race fall down so God-awful low!

This song is just a reminder to remind your fellow man
That this kind of thing still lives today in that ghost-robed Ku Klux Klan
But if all of us folks that thinks alike, if we gave all we could give
We could make this great land of ours a greater place to live

# Let Me Die in My Footsteps

I will not go down under the ground
'Cause somebody tells me that death's comin' 'round
An' I will not carry myself down to die
When I go to my grave my head will be high
Let me die in my footsteps
Before I go down under the ground

There's been rumors of war and wars that have been
The meaning of life has been lost in the wind
And some people thinkin' that the end is close by
'Stead of learnin' to live they are learnin' to die
Let me die in my footsteps
Before I go down under the ground

I don't know if I'm smart but I think I can see
When someone is pullin' the wool over me
And if this war comes and death's all around
Let me die on this land 'fore I die underground
Let me die in my footsteps
Before I go down under the ground

There's always been people that have to cause fear
They've been talking of the war now for many long years
I have read all their statements and I've not said a word
But now Lawd God, let my poor voice be heard
Let me die in my footsteps
Before I go down under the ground

If I had rubies and riches and crowns
I'd buy the whole world and change things around
I'd throw all the guns and the tanks in the sea
For they are mistakes of a past history
Let me die in my footsteps
Before I go down under the ground

Let me drink from the waters where the mountain streams flood
Let the smell of wildflowers flow free through my blood
Let me sleep in your meadows with the green grassy leaves
Let me walk down the highway with my brother in peace
Let me die in my footsteps
Before I go down under the ground

Go out in your country where the land meets the sun
See the craters and the canyons where the waterfalls run
Nevada, New Mexico, Arizona, Idaho
Let every state in this union seep down deep in your souls
And you'll die in your footsteps
Before you go down under the ground

# Baby, I'm in the Mood for You

Sometimes I'm in the mood, I wanna leave my lonesome home
And sometimes I'm in the mood, I wanna hear my milk cow moan
And sometimes I'm in the mood, I wanna hit that highway road
But then again, but then again, I said oh, I said oh, I said
Oh babe, I'm in the mood for you

Sometimes I'm in the mood, Lord, I had my overflowin' fill
Sometimes I'm in the mood, I'm gonna make out my final will
Sometimes I'm in the mood, I'm gonna head for the walkin' hill
But then again, but then again, I said oh, I said oh, I said
Oh babe, I'm in the mood for you

Sometimes I'm in the mood, I wanna lay right down and die
Sometimes I'm in the mood, I wanna climb up to the sky
Sometimes I'm in the mood, I'm gonna laugh until I cry
But then again, I said again, I said again, I said
Oh babe, I'm in the mood for you

Sometimes I'm in the mood, I'm gonna sleep in my pony's stall
Sometimes I'm in the mood, I ain't gonna do nothin' at all
Sometimes I'm in the mood, I wanna fly like a cannonball
But then again, but then again, I said oh, I said oh, I said
Oh babe, I'm in the mood for you

Sometimes I'm in the mood, I wanna back up against the wall
Sometimes I'm in the mood, I wanna run till I have to crawl
Sometimes I'm in the mood, I ain't gonna do nothin' at all
But then again, but then again, I said oh, I said oh, I said
Oh babe, I'm in the mood for you

Sometimes I'm in the mood, I wanna change my house around
Sometimes I'm in the mood, I'm gonna make a change in this here town
Sometimes I'm in the mood, I'm gonna change the world around
But then again, but then again, I said oh, I said oh, I said
Oh babe, I'm in the mood for you

# Long Ago, Far Away

To preach of peace and brotherhood
Oh, what might be the cost!
A man he did it long ago
And they hung him on a cross
Long ago, far away
These things don't happen
No more, nowadays

The chains of slaves
They dragged the ground
With heads and hearts hung low
But it was during Lincoln's time
And it was long ago
Long ago, far away
Things like that don't happen
No more, nowadays

The war guns they went off wild
The whole world bled its blood
Men's bodies floated on the edge
Of oceans made of mud
Long ago, far away
Those kind of things don't happen
No more, nowadays

One man had much money
One man had not enough to eat
One man he lived just like a king
The other man begged on the street
Long ago, far away
Things like that don't happen
No more, nowadays

One man died of a knife so sharp
One man died from the bullet of a gun
One man died of a broken heart
To see the lynchin' of his son
Long ago, far away
Things like that don't happen
No more, nowadays

Gladiators killed themselves
It was during the Roman times
People cheered with bloodshot grins
As eyes and minds went blind
Long ago, far away
Things like that don't happen
No more, nowadays

And to talk of peace and brotherhood
Oh, what might be the cost!
A man he did it long ago
And they hung him on a cross
Long ago, far away
Things like that don't happen
No more, nowadays, do they?

# Ain't Gonna Grieve

Well, I ain't a-gonna grieve no more, no more
Ain't a-gonna grieve no more, no more
Ain't a-gonna grieve no more, no more
And ain't a-gonna grieve no more

Come on brothers, join the band
Come on sisters, clap your hands
Tell everybody that's in the land
You ain't a-gonna grieve no more

Well, I ain't a-gonna grieve no more, no more
Ain't a-gonna grieve no more, no more
Ain't a-gonna grieve no more, no more
And ain't a-gonna grieve no more

Brown and blue and white and black
All one color on the one-way track
We got this far and ain't a-goin' back
And I ain't a-gonna grieve no more

Well, I ain't a-gonna grieve no more, no more
Ain't a-gonna grieve no more, no more
Ain't a-gonna grieve no more, no more
I ain't a-gonna grieve no more

We're gonna notify your next of kin
You're gonna raise the roof until the house falls in
If you get knocked down get up again
We ain't a-gonna grieve no more

Well, I ain't a-gonna grieve no more, no more
Ain't a-gonna grieve no more, no more
Ain't a-gonna grieve no more, no more
I ain't a-gonna grieve no more

We'll sing this song all night long
Sing it to my baby from midnight on
She'll sing it to you when I'm dead and gone
Ain't a-gonna grieve no more

Well, I ain't a-gonna grieve no more, no more
Ain't a-gonna grieve no more, no more
Ain't a-gonna grieve no more, no more
I ain't a-gonna grieve no more

# Gypsy Lou

If you getcha one girl, better get two
Case you run into Gypsy Lou
She's a ramblin' woman with a ramblin' mind
Always leavin' somebody behind
Hey, 'round the bend
Gypsy Lou's gone again
Gypsy Lou's gone again

Well, I seen the whole country through
Just to find Gypsy Lou
Seen it up, seen it down
Followin' Gypsy Lou around
Hey, 'round the bend
Gypsy Lou's gone again
Gypsy Lou's gone again

Well, I gotta stop and take some rest
My poor feet are second best
My poor feet are wearin' thin
Gypsy Lou's gone again
Hey, gone again
Gypsy Lou's 'round the bend
Gypsy Lou's 'round the bend

Well, seen her up in old Cheyenne
Turned my head and away she ran
From Denver Town to Wichita
Last I heard she's in Arkansas
Hey, 'round the bend
Gypsy Lou's gone again
Gypsy Lou's gone again

Well, I tell you what if you want to do
Tell you what, you'll wear out your shoes
If you want to wear out your shoes
Try and follow Gypsy Lou
Hey, gone again
Gypsy Lou's 'round the bend
Gypsy Lou's 'round the bend

Well, Gypsy Lou, I been told
Livin' down on Gallus Road
Gallus Road, Arlington
Moved away to Washington
Hey, 'round the bend
Gypsy Lou's gone again
Gypsy Lou's gone again

Well, I went down to Washington
Then she went to Oregon
I skipped the ground and hopped a train
She's back in Gallus Road again
Hey, I can't win
Gypsy Lou's gone again
Gypsy Lou's gone again

Well, the last I heard of Gypsy Lou
She's in a Memphis calaboose
She left one too many a boy behind
He committed suicide
Hey, you can't win
Gypsy Lou's gone again
Gypsy Lou's gone again

# Long Time Gone

My parents raised me tenderly
I was their only son
My mind got mixed with ramblin'
When I was all so young
And I left my home the first time
When I was twelve and one
I'm a long time a-comin', Maw
An' I'll be a long time gone

On the western side of Texas
On the Texas plains
I tried to find a job o' work
But they said I's young of age
My eyes they burned when I heard
"Go home where you belong!"
I'm a long time a-comin'
An' I'll be a long time gone

I remember when I's ramblin'
Around with the carnival trains
Different towns, different people
Somehow they're all the same
I remember children's faces best
I remember travelin' on
I'm a long time a-comin'
I'll be a long time gone

I once loved a fair young maid
An' I ain't too big to tell
If she broke my heart a single time
She broke it ten or twelve
I walked and talked all by myself
I did not tell no one
I'm a long time a-comin', babe
An' I'll be a long time gone

Many times by the highwayside
I tried to flag a ride
With bloodshot eyes and gritting teeth
I'd watch the cars roll by
The empty air hung in my head
I's thinkin' all day long
I'm a long time a-comin'
I'll be a long time gone

You might see me on your crossroads
When I'm a-passin' through
Remember me how you wished to
As I'm a-driftin' from your view
I ain't got the time to think about it
I got too much to get done
Well, I'm a long time comin'
An' I'll be a long time gone

If I can't help somebody
With a word or song
If I can't show somebody
They are travelin' wrong
But I know I ain't no prophet
An' I ain't no prophet's son
I'm just a long time a-comin'
An' I'll be a long time gone

So you can have your beauty
It's skin deep and it only lies
And you can have your youth
It'll rot before your eyes
Just give to me my gravestone
With it clearly carved upon:
"I's a long time a-comin'
An' I'll be a long time gone"

# Walkin' Down the Line

Well, I'm walkin' down the line
I'm walkin' down the line
An' I'm walkin' down the line
My feet'll be a-flyin'
To tell about my troubled mind

I got a heavy-headed gal
I got a heavy-headed gal
I got a heavy-headed gal
She ain't a-feelin' well
When she's better only time will tell

Well, I'm walkin' down the line
I'm walkin' down the line
An' I'm walkin' down the line
My feet'll be a-flyin'
To tell about my troubled mind

My money comes and goes
My money comes and goes
My money comes and goes
And rolls and flows and rolls and flows
Through the holes in the pockets in my clothes

Well, I'm walkin' down the line
I'm walkin' down the line
An' I'm walkin' down the line
My feet'll be a-flyin'
To tell about my troubled mind

I see the morning light
I see the morning light
Well, it's not because
I'm an early riser
I didn't go to sleep last night

Well, I'm walkin' down the line
I'm walkin' down the line
An' I'm walkin' down the line
My feet'll be a-flyin'
To tell about my troubled mind

I got my walkin' shoes
I got my walkin' shoes
I got my walkin' shoes
An' I ain't a-gonna lose
I believe I got the walkin' blues

Well, I'm walkin' down the line
I'm walkin' down the line
An' I'm walkin' down the line
My feet'll be a-flyin'
To tell about my troubled mind

# Train A-Travelin'

There's an iron train a-travelin' that's been a-rollin' through the years
With a firebox of hatred and a furnace full of fears
If you ever heard its sound or seen its blood-red broken frame
Then you heard my voice a-singin' and you know my name

Did you ever stop to wonder 'bout the hatred that it holds?
Did you ever see its passengers, its crazy mixed-up souls?
Did you ever start a-thinkin' that you gotta stop that train?
Then you heard my voice a-singin' and you know my name

Do you ever get tired of the preachin' sounds of fear
When they're hammered at your head and pounded in your ear?
Have you ever asked about it and not been answered plain?
Then you heard my voice a-singin' and you know my name

I'm a-wonderin' if the leaders of the nations understand
This murder-minded world that they're leavin' in my hands
Have you ever laid awake at night and wondered 'bout the same?
Then you've heard my voice a-singin' and you know my name

Have you ever had it on your lips or said it in your head
That the person standin' next to you just might be misled?
Does the raving of the maniacs make your insides go insane?
Then you've heard my voice a-singin' and you know my name

Do the kill-crazy bandits and the haters get you down?
Does the preachin' and the politics spin your head around?
Does the burning of the buses give your heart a pain?
Then you've heard my voice a-singin' and you know my name

# Ballad of Donald White

My name is Donald White, you see
I stand before you all
I was judged by you a murderer
And the hangman's knot must fall
I will die upon the gallows pole
When the moon is shining clear
And these are my final words
That you will ever hear

I left my home in Kansas
When I was very young
I landed in the old Northwest
Seattle, Washington
Although I'd a-traveled many miles
I never made a friend
For I could never get along in life
With people that I met

If I had some education
To give me a decent start
I might have been a doctor or
A master in the arts
But I used my hands for stealing
When I was very young
And they locked me down in jailhouse cells
That's how my life begun

Oh, the inmates and the prisoners
I found they were my kind
And it was there inside the bars
I found my peace of mind
But the jails they were too crowded
Institutions overflowed
So they turned me loose to walk upon
Life's hurried tangled road

And there's danger on the ocean
Where the salt sea waves split high
And there's danger on the battlefield
Where the shells of bullets fly
And there's danger in this open world
Where men strive to be free
And for me the greatest danger
Was in society

So I asked them to send me back
To the institution home
But they said they were too crowded
For me they had no room
I got down on my knees and begged
"Oh, please put me away"
But they would not listen to my plea
Or nothing I would say

And so it was on Christmas Eve
In the year of '59
It was on that night I killed a man
I did not try to hide
The jury found me guilty
And I won't disagree
For I knew that it would happen
If I wasn't put away

And I'm glad I've had no parents
To care for me or cry
For now they will never know
The horrible death I die
And I'm also glad I've had no friends
To see me in disgrace
For they'll never see that hangman's hood
Wrap around my face

Farewell unto the old north woods
Of which I used to roam
Farewell unto the crowded bars
Of which've been my home
Farewell to all you people
Who think the worst of me
I guess you'll feel much better when
I'm on that hanging tree

But there's just one question
Before they kill me dead
I'm wondering just how much
To you I really said
Concerning all the boys that come
Down a road like me
Are they enemies or victims
Of your society?

# Quit Your Low Down Ways

Oh, you can read out your Bible
You can fall down on your knees, pretty mama
And pray to the Lord
But it ain't gonna do no good.

You're gonna need
You're gonna need my help someday
Well, if you can't quit your sinnin'
Please quit your low down ways

Well, you can run down to the White House
You can gaze at the Capitol Dome, pretty mama
You can pound on the President's gate
But you oughta know by now it's gonna be too late

You're gonna need
You're gonna need my help someday
Well, if you can't quit your sinnin'
Please quit your low down ways

Well, you can run down to the desert
Throw yourself on the burning sand
You can raise up your right hand, pretty mama
But you better understand you done lost your one good man

You're gonna need
You're gonna need my help someday
Well, if you can't quit your sinnin'
Please quit your low down ways

And you can hitchhike on the highway
You can stand all alone by the side of the road
You can try to flag a ride back home, pretty mama
But you can't ride in my car no more

You're gonna need
You're gonna need my help someday
Well, if you can't quit your sinnin'
Please quit your low down ways

Oh, you can read out your Bible
You can fall down on your knees, pretty mama
And pray to the Lord
But it ain't gonna do no good

You're gonna need
You're gonna need my help someday
Well, if you can't quit your sinnin'
Please quit your low down ways

# I'd Hate to Be You on That Dreadful Day

Well, your clock is gonna stop
At Saint Peter's gate
Ya gonna ask him what time it is
He's gonna say, "It's too late"
Hey, hey!
I'd sure hate to be you
On that dreadful day

You're gonna start to sweat
And you ain't gonna stop
You're gonna have a nightmare
And never wake up
Hey, hey, hey!
I'd sure hate to be you
On that dreadful day

You're gonna cry for pills
And your head's gonna be in a knot
But the pills are gonna cost more
Than what you've got
Hey, hey!
I'd sure hate to be you
On that dreadful day

You're gonna have to walk naked
Can't ride in no car
You're gonna let ev'rybody see
Just what you are
Hey, hey!
I'd sure hate to be you
On that dreadful day

Well, the good wine's a-flowin'
For five cents a quart
You're gonna look in your moneybags
And find you're one cent short
Hey, hey, hey!
I'd sure hate to be you
On that dreadful day

You're gonna yell and scream
"Don't anybody care?"
You're gonna hear out a voice say
"Shoulda listened when you heard the word down there"
Hey, hey!
I'd sure hate to be you
On that dreadful day

# Mixed Up Confusion

I got mixed up confusion
Man, it's a-killin' me
Well, there's too many people
And they're all too hard to please

Well, my hat's in my hand
Babe, I'm walkin' down the line
An' I'm lookin' for a woman
Whose head's mixed up like mine

Well, my head's full of questions
My temp'rature's risin' fast
Well, I'm lookin' for some answers
But I don't know who to ask

But I'm walkin' and wonderin'
And my poor feet don't ever stop
Seein' my reflection
I'm hung over, hung down, hung up!

# Hero Blues

Yes, the gal I got
I swear she's the screaming end
She wants me to be a hero
So she can tell all her friends

Well, she begged, she cried
She pleaded with me all last night
Well, she begged, she cried
She pleaded with me all last night
She wants me to go out
And find somebody to fight

She reads too many books
She got new movies inside her head
She reads too many books
She got movies inside her head
She wants me to walk out running
She wants me to crawl back dead

You need a different kinda man, babe
One that can grab and hold your heart
Need a different kind of man, babe
One that can hold and grab your heart
You need a different kind of man, babe
You need Napoleon Boneeparte

Well, when I'm dead
No more good times will I crave
When I'm dead
No more good times will I crave
You can stand and shout hero
All over my lonesome grave

# Tomorrow Is a Long Time

If today was not an endless highway
If tonight was not a crooked trail
If tomorrow wasn't such a long time
Then lonesome would mean nothing to you at all
Yes, and only if my own true love was waitin'
Yes, and if I could hear her heart a-softly poundin'
Only if she was lyin' by me
Then I'd lie in my bed once again

I can't see my reflection in the waters
I can't speak the sounds that show no pain
I can't hear the echo of my footsteps
Or can't remember the sound of my own name
Yes, and only if my own true love was waitin'
Yes, and if I could hear her heart a-softly poundin'
Only if she was lyin' by me
Then I'd lie in my bed once again

There's beauty in the silver, singin' river
There's beauty in the sunrise in the sky
But none of these and nothing else can touch the beauty
That I remember in my true love's eyes
Yes, and only if my own true love was waitin'
Yes, and if I could hear her heart a-softly poundin'
Only if she was lyin' by me
Then I'd lie in my bed once again

# Bob Dylan's New Orleans Rag

I was sittin' on a stump
Down in New Orleans
I was feelin' kinda low down
Dirty and mean
Along came a fella
And he didn't even ask
He says, "I know of a woman
That can fix you up fast"
I didn't think twice
I said like I should
"Let's go find this lady
That can do me some good"
We walked across the river
On a sailin' spree
And we came to a door
Called one-oh-three

I was just about ready
To give it a little knock
When out comes a fella
Who couldn't even walk
He's linkin' and a-slinkin'
Couldn't stand on his feet
And he moaned and he groaned
And he shuffled down the street
Well, out of the door
There comes another man
He wiggled and he wobbled
He couldn't hardly stand
He had this frightened
Look in his eyes
Like he just fought a bear
He was ready to die

Well, I peeked through the key crack
Comin' down the hall
Was a long-legged man
Who couldn't hardly crawl
He muttered and he uttered
In broken French
And he looked like he'd been through
A monkey wrench

Well, by this time
I was a-scared to knock
I was a-scared to move
I's in a state of shock
I hummed a little tune
And I shuffled my feet
And I started walkin' backwards
Down that broad street
Well, I got to the corner
I tried my best to smile
I turned around the corner
And I ran a bloody mile
Man, I wasn't runnin'
'Cause I was sick
I was just a-runnin'
To get out of there quick

Well, I tripped right along
And I'm a-wheezin' in my chest
I musta run a mile
In a minute or less
I walked on a log
And I tripped on a stump
I caught a fast freight
With a one-arm jump
So, if you're travelin' down
Louisiana way
And you feel kinda lonesome
And you need a place to stay
Man, you're better off
In your misery
Than to tackle that lady
At one-oh-three

# All Over You

Well, if I had to do it all over again
Babe, I'd do it all over you
And if I had to wait for ten thousand years
Babe, I'd even do that too
Well, a dog's got his bone in the alley
A cat, she's got nine lives
A millionaire's got a million dollars
King Saud's got four hundred wives
Well, ev'rybody's got somethin'
That they're lookin' forward to
I'm lookin' forward to when I can do it all again
And babe, I'll do it all over you

Well, if I had my way tomorrow or today
Babe, I'd run circles all around
I'd jump up in the wind, do a somersault and spin
I'd even dance a jig on the ground
Well, everybody gets their hour
Everybody gets their time
Little David when he picked up his pebbles
Even Sampson after he went blind
Well, everybody gets the chance
To do what they want to do
When my time arrives you better run for your life
'Cause babe, I'll do it all over you

Well, I don't need no money, I just need a day that's sunny
Baby, and my days are gonna come
And I grab me a pint, you know that I'm a giant
When you hear me yellin', "Fee-fi-fo-fum"
Well, you cut me like a jigsaw puzzle
You made me to a walkin' wreck
Then you pushed my heart through my backbone
Then you knocked off my head from my neck
Well, if I'm ever standin' steady
A-doin' what I want to do
Well, I tell you little lover that you better run for cover
'Cause babe, I'll do it all over you

I'm just restin' at your gate so that I won't be late
And, momma, I'm a-just sittin' on the shelf
Look out your window fair and you'll see me squattin' there
Just a-fumblin' and a-mumblin' to myself
Well, after my cigarette's been smoked up
After all my liquor's been drunk
After my dreams are dreamed out
After all my thoughts have been thunk
Well, after I do some of these things
I'm gonna do what I have to do
And I tell you on the side, that you better run and hide
'Cause babe, I'll do it all over you

# John Brown

John Brown went off to war to fight on a foreign shore
His mama sure was proud of him!
He stood straight and tall in his uniform and all
His mama's face broke out all in a grin

"Oh son, you look so fine, I'm glad you're a son of mine
You make me proud to know you hold a gun
Do what the captain says, lots of medals you will get
And we'll put them on the wall when you come home"

As that old train pulled out, John's ma began to shout
Tellin' ev'ryone in the neighborhood:
"That's my son that's about to go, he's a soldier now, you know"
She made well sure her neighbors understood

She got a letter once in a while and her face broke into a smile
As she showed them to the people from next door
And she bragged about her son with his uniform and gun
And these things you called a good old-fashioned war

Oh! Good old-fashioned war!

Then the letters ceased to come, for a long time they did not come
They ceased to come for about ten months or more
Then a letter finally came saying, "Go down and meet the train
Your son's a-coming home from the war"

She smiled and went right down, she looked everywhere around
But she could not see her soldier son in sight
But as all the people passed, she saw her son at last
When she did she could hardly believe her eyes

Oh his face was all shot up and his hand was all blown off
And he wore a metal brace around his waist
He whispered kind of slow, in a voice she did not know
While she couldn't even recognize his face!

Oh! Lord! Not even recognize his face

"Oh tell me, my darling son, pray tell me what they done
How is it you come to be this way?"
He tried his best to talk but his mouth could hardly move
And the mother had to turn her face away

"Don't you remember, Ma, when I went off to war
You thought it was the best thing I could do?
I was on the battleground, you were home . . . acting proud
You wasn't there standing in my shoes"

"Oh, and I thought when I was there, God, what am I doing here?
I'm a-tryin' to kill somebody or die tryin'
But the thing that scared me most was when my enemy came close
And I saw that his face looked just like mine"

Oh! Lord! Just like mine!

"And I couldn't help but think, through the thunder rolling and stink
That I was just a puppet in a play
And through the roar and smoke, this string is finally broke
And a cannonball blew my eyes away"

As he turned away to walk, his Ma was still in shock
At seein' the metal brace that helped him stand
But as he turned to go, he called his mother close
And he dropped his medals down into her hand

# Farewell

Oh it's fare thee well my darlin' true
I'm leavin' in the first hour of the morn
I'm bound off for the bay of Mexico
Or maybe the coast of Californ
So it's fare thee well my own true love
We'll meet another day, another time
It ain't the leavin'
That's a-grievin' me
But my true love who's bound to stay behind

Oh the weather is against me and the wind blows hard
And the rain she's a-turnin' into hail
I still might strike it lucky on a highway goin' west
Though I'm travelin' on a path beaten trail
So it's fare thee well my own true love
We'll meet another day, another time
It ain't the leavin'
That's a-grievin' me
But my true love who's bound to stay behind

I will write you a letter from time to time
As I'm ramblin' you can travel with me too
With my head, my heart and my hands, my love
I will send what I learn back home to you
So it's fare thee well my own true love
We'll meet another day, another time
It ain't the leavin'
That's a-grievin' me
But my true love who's bound to stay behind

I will tell you of the laughter and of troubles
Be them somebody else's or my own
With my hands in my pockets and my coat collar high
I will travel unnoticed and unknown
So it's fare thee well my own true love
We'll meet another day, another time
It ain't the leavin'
That's a-grievin' me
But my true love who's bound to stay behind

I've heard tell of a town where I might as well be bound
It's down around the old Mexican plains
They say that the people are all friendly there
And all they ask of you is your name
So it's fare thee well my own true love
We'll meet another day, another time
It ain't the leavin'
That's a-grievin' me
But my true love who's bound to stay behind

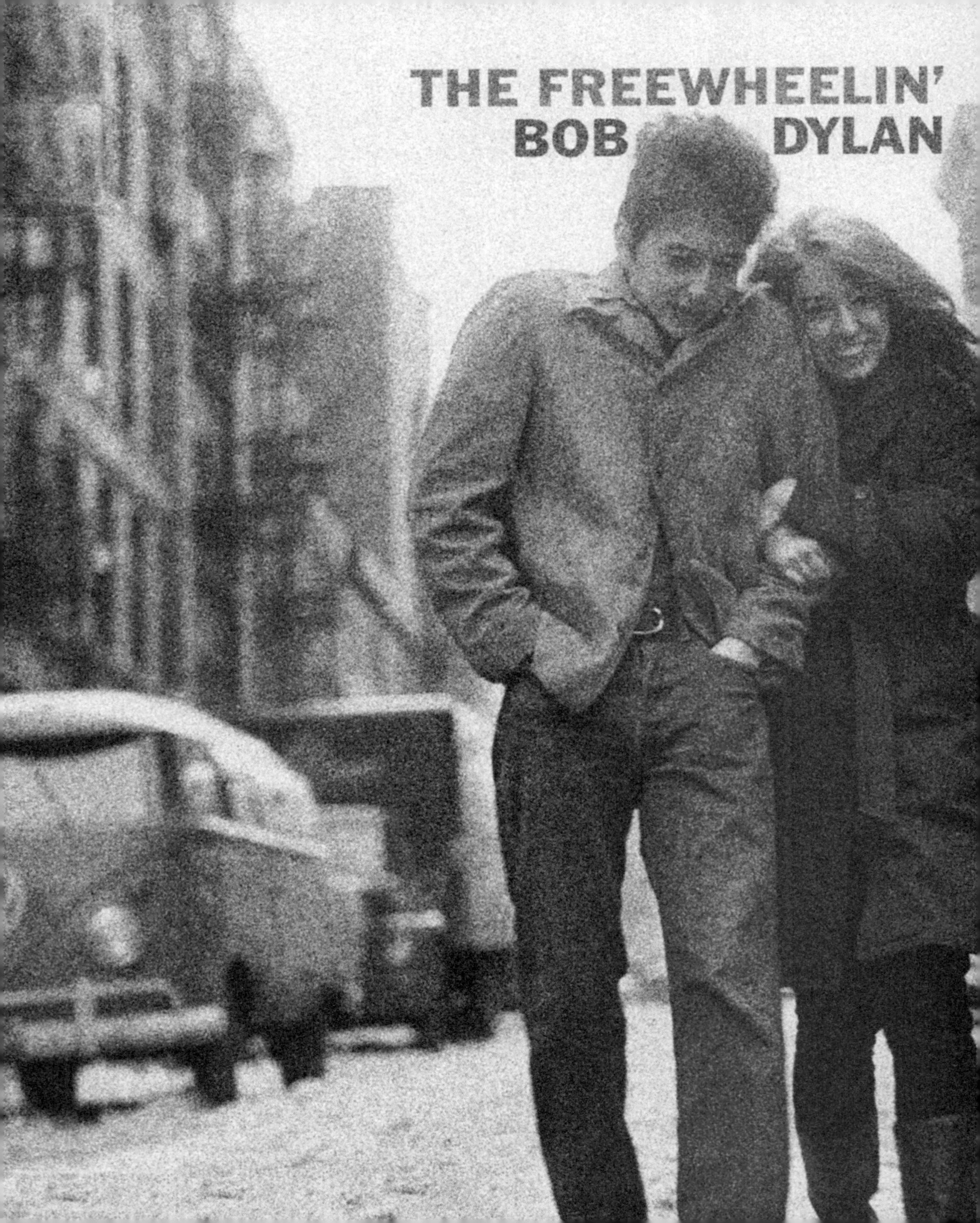
THE FREEWHEELIN'
BOB DYLAN

# The Freewheelin' Bob Dylan

Blowin' in the Wind

Girl of the North Country

Masters of War

Down the Highway

Bob Dylan's Blues

A Hard Rain's A-Gonna Fall

Don't Think Twice, It's All Right

Bob Dylan's Dream

Oxford Town

Talkin' World War III Blues

Corrina, Corrina

Honey, Just Allow Me One More Chance

I Shall Be Free

*additional lyrics*

Whatcha Gonna Do

Walls of Red Wing

Who Killed Davey Moore?

Seven Curses

Dusty Old Fairgrounds

(7) I found a harp job & started to play
Blowing my lungs out for dollar a day
Blowed inside out and blew side down
Boss said he liked my sound
Dollars a days worth

(8) ~~I finally found me a real job~~
~~...~~
~~Yes I got me a job in bigger class~~
~~I struck out for a place to hang~~
~~Yes I played until I hung down~~
~~While~~ After weeks of me hanging around
I got a job in this man's town
In a ~~big little~~ place with ~~... for my pay~~
My name was then posted on the ~~door~~ outside of the place

(9) Now a very great man once said
That some people rob you with a fountain pen
It ~~took~~ didn't take you long to find out
Just what he was talking ~~out~~ about
That — table — fork — knives — cut something

(10) So one morning when the sun was warm
I ~~decided~~ ~~left~~ this here town
I pulled my cap down over my eyes
Headed out for western skies
Goodbye N.Y. Howdy East Orange

# Blowin' in the Wind

How many roads must a man walk down
Before you call him a man?
Yes, 'n' how many seas must a white dove sail
Before she sleeps in the sand?
Yes, 'n' how many times must the cannonballs fly
Before they're forever banned?
The answer, my friend, is blowin' in the wind
The answer is blowin' in the wind

How many years can a mountain exist
Before it's washed to the sea?
Yes, 'n' how many years can some people exist
Before they're allowed to be free?
Yes, 'n' how many times can a man turn his head
Pretending he just doesn't see?
The answer, my friend, is blowin' in the wind
The answer is blowin' in the wind

How many times must a man look up
Before he can see the sky?
Yes, 'n' how many ears must one man have
Before he can hear people cry?
Yes, 'n' how many deaths will it take till he knows
That too many people have died?
The answer, my friend, is blowin' in the wind
The answer is blowin' in the wind

# Girl of the North Country

Well, if you're travelin' in the north country fair
Where the winds hit heavy on the borderline
Remember me to one who lives there
She once was a true love of mine

Well, if you go when the snowflakes storm
When the rivers freeze and summer ends
Please see if she's wearing a coat so warm
To keep her from the howlin' winds

Please see for me if her hair hangs long
If it rolls and flows all down her breast
Please see for me if her hair hangs long
That's the way I remember her best

I'm a-wonderin' if she remembers me at all
Many times I've often prayed
In the darkness of my night
In the brightness of my day

So if you're travelin' in the north country fair
Where the winds hit heavy on the borderline
Remember me to one who lives there
She once was a true love of mine

# Masters of War

Come you masters of war
You that build all the guns
You that build the death planes
You that build the big bombs
You that hide behind walls
You that hide behind desks
I just want you to know
I can see through your masks

You that never done nothin'
But build to destroy
You play with my world
Like it's your little toy
You put a gun in my hand
And you hide from my eyes
And you turn and run farther
When the fast bullets fly

Like Judas of old
You lie and deceive
A world war can be won
You want me to believe
But I see through your eyes
And I see through your brain
Like I see through the water
That runs down my drain

You fasten the triggers
For the others to fire
Then you set back and watch
When the death count gets higher
You hide in your mansion
As young people's blood
Flows out of their bodies
And is buried in the mud

You've thrown the worst fear
That can ever be hurled
Fear to bring children
Into the world
For threatening my baby
Unborn and unnamed
You ain't worth the blood
That runs in your veins

How much do I know
To talk out of turn
You might say that I'm young
You might say I'm unlearned
But there's one thing I know
Though I'm younger than you
Even Jesus would never
Forgive what you do

Let me ask you one question
Is your money that good
Will it buy you forgiveness
Do you think that it could
I think you will find
When your death takes its toll
All the money you made
Will never buy back your soul

And I hope that you die
And your death'll come soon
I will follow your casket
In the pale afternoon
And I'll watch while you're lowered
Down to your deathbed
And I'll stand o'er your grave
'Til I'm sure that you're dead

# Down the Highway

Well, I'm walkin' down the highway
With my suitcase in my hand
Yes, I'm walkin' down the highway
With my suitcase in my hand
Lord, I really miss my baby
She's in some far-off land

Well, your streets are gettin' empty
Lord, your highway's gettin' filled
And your streets are gettin' empty
And your highway's gettin' filled
Well, the way I love that woman
I swear it's bound to get me killed

Well, I been gamblin' so long
Lord, I ain't got much more to lose
Yes, I been gamblin' so long
Lord, I ain't got much more to lose
Right now I'm havin' trouble
Please don't take away my highway shoes

Well, I'm bound to get lucky, baby
Or I'm bound to die tryin'
Yes, I'm a-bound to get lucky, baby
Lord, Lord I'm a-bound to die tryin'
Well, meet me in the middle of the ocean
And we'll leave this ol' highway behind

Well, the ocean took my baby
My baby stole my heart from me
Yes, the ocean took my baby
My baby took my heart from me
She packed it all up in a suitcase
Lord, she took it away to Italy, Italy

So, I'm a-walkin' down your highway
Just as far as my poor eyes can see
Yes, I'm a-walkin' down your highway
Just as far as my eyes can see
From the Golden Gate Bridge
All the way to the Statue of Liberty

# Bob Dylan's Blues

Well, the Lone Ranger and Tonto
They are ridin' down the line
Fixin' ev'rybody's troubles
Ev'rybody's 'cept mine
Somebody musta tol' 'em
That I was doin' fine

Oh you five and ten cent women
With nothin' in your heads
I got a real gal I'm lovin'
And Lord I'll love her till I'm dead
Go away from my door and my window too
Right now

Lord, I ain't goin' down to no race track
See no sports car run
I don't have no sports car
And I don't even care to have one
I can walk anytime around the block

Well, the wind keeps a-blowin' me
Up and down the street
With my hat in my hand
And my boots on my feet
Watch out so you don't step on me

Well, lookit here buddy
You want to be like me
Pull out your six-shooter
And rob every bank you can see
Tell the judge I said it was all right
Yes!

# A Hard Rain's A-Gonna Fall

Oh, where have you been, my blue-eyed son?
Oh, where have you been, my darling young one?
I've stumbled on the side of twelve misty mountains
I've walked and I've crawled on six crooked highways
I've stepped in the middle of seven sad forests
I've been out in front of a dozen dead oceans
I've been ten thousand miles in the mouth of a graveyard
And it's a hard, and it's a hard, it's a hard, and it's a hard
And it's a hard rain's a-gonna fall

Oh, what did you see, my blue-eyed son?
Oh, what did you see, my darling young one?
I saw a newborn baby with wild wolves all around it
I saw a highway of diamonds with nobody on it
I saw a black branch with blood that kept drippin'
I saw a room full of men with their hammers a-bleedin'
I saw a white ladder all covered with water
I saw ten thousand talkers whose tongues were all broken
I saw guns and sharp swords in the hands of young children
And it's a hard, and it's a hard, it's a hard, it's a hard
And it's a hard rain's a-gonna fall

And what did you hear, my blue-eyed son?
And what did you hear, my darling young one?
I heard the sound of a thunder, it roared out a warnin'
Heard the roar of a wave that could drown the whole world
Heard one hundred drummers whose hands were a-blazin'
Heard ten thousand whisperin' and nobody listenin'
Heard one person starve, I heard many people laughin'
Heard the song of a poet who died in the gutter
Heard the sound of a clown who cried in the alley
And it's a hard, and it's a hard, it's a hard, it's a hard
And it's a hard rain's a-gonna fall

Oh, who did you meet, my blue-eyed son?
Who did you meet, my darling young one?
I met a young child beside a dead pony
I met a white man who walked a black dog
I met a young woman whose body was burning
I met a young girl, she gave me a rainbow
I met one man who was wounded in love
I met another man who was wounded with hatred
And it's a hard, it's a hard, it's a hard, it's a hard
It's a hard rain's a-gonna fall

Oh, what'll you do now, my blue-eyed son?
Oh, what'll you do now, my darling young one?
I'm a-goin' back out 'fore the rain starts a-fallin'
I'll walk to the depths of the deepest black forest
Where the people are many and their hands are all empty
Where the pellets of poison are flooding their waters
Where the home in the valley meets the damp dirty prison
Where the executioner's face is always well hidden
Where hunger is ugly, where souls are forgotten
Where black is the color, where none is the number
And I'll tell it and think it and speak it and breathe it
And reflect it from the mountain so all souls can see it
Then I'll stand on the ocean until I start sinkin'
But I'll know my song well before I start singin'
And it's a hard, it's a hard, it's a hard, it's a hard
It's a hard rain's a-gonna fall

# Don't Think Twice, It's All Right

It ain't no use to sit and wonder why, babe
It don't matter, anyhow
An' it ain't no use to sit and wonder why, babe
If you don't know by now
When your rooster crows at the break of dawn
Look out your window and I'll be gone
You're the reason I'm trav'lin' on
Don't think twice, it's all right

It ain't no use in turnin' on your light, babe
That light I never knowed
An' it ain't no use in turnin' on your light, babe
I'm on the dark side of the road
Still I wish there was somethin' you would do or say
To try and make me change my mind and stay
We never did too much talkin' anyway
So don't think twice, it's all right

It ain't no use in callin' out my name, gal
Like you never did before
It ain't no use in callin' out my name, gal
I can't hear you anymore
I'm a-thinkin' and a-wond'rin' all the way down the road
I once loved a woman, a child I'm told
I give her my heart but she wanted my soul
But don't think twice, it's all right

I'm walkin' down that long, lonesome road, babe
Where I'm bound, I can't tell
But goodbye's too good a word, gal
So I'll just say fare thee well
I ain't sayin' you treated me unkind
You could have done better but I don't mind
You just kinda wasted my precious time
But don't think twice, it's all right

# Bob Dylan's Dream

While riding on a train goin' west
I fell asleep for to take my rest
I dreamed a dream that made me sad
Concerning myself and the first few friends I had

With half-damp eyes I stared to the room
Where my friends and I spent many an afternoon
Where we together weathered many a storm
Laughin' and singin' till the early hours of the morn

By the old wooden stove where our hats was hung
Our words were told, our songs were sung
Where we longed for nothin' and were quite satisfied
Talkin' and a-jokin' about the world outside

With haunted hearts through the heat and cold
We never thought we could ever get old
We thought we could sit forever in fun
But our chances really was a million to one

As easy it was to tell black from white
It was all that easy to tell wrong from right
And our choices were few and the thought never hit
That the one road we traveled would ever shatter and split

How many a year has passed and gone
And many a gamble has been lost and won
And many a road taken by many a friend
And each one I've never seen again

I wish, I wish, I wish in vain
That we could sit simply in that room again
Ten thousand dollars at the drop of a hat
I'd give it all gladly if our lives could be like that

# Oxford Town

Oxford Town, Oxford Town
Ev'rybody's got their heads bowed down
The sun don't shine above the ground
Ain't a-goin' down to Oxford Town

He went down to Oxford Town
Guns and clubs followed him down
All because his face was brown
Better get away from Oxford Town

Oxford Town around the bend
He come in to the door, he couldn't get in
All because of the color of his skin
What do you think about that, my frien'?

Me and my gal, my gal's son
We got met with a tear gas bomb
I don't even know why we come
Goin' back where we come from

Oxford Town in the afternoon
Ev'rybody singin' a sorrowful tune
Two men died 'neath the Mississippi moon
Somebody better investigate soon

Oxford Town, Oxford Town
Ev'rybody's got their heads bowed down
The sun don't shine above the ground
Ain't a-goin' down to Oxford Town

# Talkin' World War III Blues

Some time ago a crazy dream came to me
I dreamt I was walkin' into World War Three
I went to the doctor the very next day
To see what kinda words he could say
He said it was a bad dream
I wouldn't worry 'bout it none, though
They were my own dreams and they're only in my head

I said, "Hold it, Doc, a World War passed through my brain"
He said, "Nurse, get your pad, this boy's insane"
He grabbed my arm, I said, "Ouch!"
As I landed on the psychiatric couch
He said, "Tell me about it"

Well, the whole thing started at 3 o'clock fast
It was all over by quarter past
I was down in the sewer with some little lover
When I peeked out from a manhole cover
Wondering who turned the lights on

Well, I got up and walked around
And up and down the lonesome town
I stood a-wondering which way to go
I lit a cigarette on a parking meter and walked on down the road
It was a normal day

Well, I rung the fallout shelter bell
And I leaned my head and I gave a yell
"Give me a string bean, I'm a hungry man"
A shotgun fired and away I ran
I don't blame them too much though, I know I look funny

Down at the corner by a hot-dog stand
I seen a man
I said, "Howdy friend, I guess there's just us two"
He screamed a bit and away he flew
Thought I was a Communist

Well, I spied a girl and before she could leave
"Let's go and play Adam and Eve"
I took her by the hand and my heart it was thumpin'
When she said, "Hey man, you crazy or sumpin'
You see what happened last time they started"

Well, I seen a Cadillac window uptown
And there was nobody aroun'
I got into the driver's seat
And I drove down 42nd Street
In my Cadillac. Good car to drive after a war

Well, I remember seein' some ad
So I turned on my Conelrad
But I didn't pay my Con Ed bill
So the radio didn't work so well
Turned on my record player—
It was Rock-a-day Johnny singin', "Tell Your Ma, Tell Your Pa
Our Love's A-gonna Grow Ooh-wah, Ooh-wah"

I was feelin' kinda lonesome and blue
I needed somebody to talk to
So I called up the operator of time
Just to hear a voice of some kind
"When you hear the beep it will be three o'clock"
She said that for over an hour
And I hung up

Well, the doctor interrupted me just about then
Sayin', "Hey I've been havin' the same old dreams
But mine was a little different you see
I dreamt that the only person left after the war was me
I didn't see you around"

Well, now time passed and now it seems
Everybody's having them dreams
Everybody sees themselves
Walkin' around with no one else
Half of the people can be part right all of the time
Some of the people can be all right part of the time
But all of the people can't be all right all of the time
I think Abraham Lincoln said that
"I'll let you be in my dreams if I can be in yours"
I said that

# Corrina, Corrina

Corrina, Corrina
Gal, where you been so long?
Corrina, Corrina
Gal, where you been so long?
I been worr'in' 'bout you, baby
Baby, please come home

I got a bird that whistles
I got a bird that sings
I got a bird that whistles
I got a bird that sings
But I ain' a-got Corrina
Life don't mean a thing

Corrina, Corrina
Gal, you're on my mind
Corrina, Corrina
Gal, you're on my mind
I'm a-thinkin' 'bout you, baby
I just can't keep from crying

# Honey, Just Allow Me One More Chance

Honey, just allow me one more chance
To get along with you
Honey, just allow me one more chance
Ah'll do anything with you
Well, I'm a-walkin' down the road
With my head in my hand
I'm lookin' for a woman
Needs a worried man
Just-a one kind favor I ask you
'Low me just-a one more chance

Honey, just allow me one more chance
To ride your aeroplane
Honey, just allow me one more chance
To ride your passenger train
Well, I've been lookin' all over
For a gal like you
I can't find nobody
So you'll have to do
Just-a one kind favor I ask you
'Low me just-a one more chance

Honey, just allow me one more chance
To get along with you
Honey, just allow me one more chance
Ah'll do anything with you
Well, lookin' for a woman
That ain't got no man
Is just lookin' for a needle
That is lost in the sand
Just-a one kind favor I ask you
'Low me just-a one more chance

# I Shall Be Free

Well, I took me a woman late last night
I's three-fourths drunk, she looked uptight
She took off her wheel, took off her bell
Took off her wig, said, "How do I smell?"
I hot-footed it . . . bare-naked . . .
Out the window!

Well, sometimes I might get drunk
Walk like a duck and stomp like a skunk
Don't hurt me none, don't hurt my pride
'Cause I got my little lady right by my side
(Right there
Proud as can be)

I's out there paintin' on the old woodshed
When a can a black paint it fell on my head
I went down to scrub and rub
But I had to sit in back of the tub
(Cost a quarter
And I had to get out quick . . .
Someone wanted to come in and take a sauna)

Well, my telephone rang it would not stop
It's President Kennedy callin' me up
He said, "My friend, Bob, what do we need to make the country grow?"
I said, "My friend, John, Brigitte Bardot
Anita Ekberg
Sophia Loren"
(Put 'em all in the same room with Ernest Borgnine!)

Well, I got a woman sleeps on a cot
She yells and hollers and squeals a lot
Licks my face and tickles my ear
Bends me over and buys me beer
(She's a honeymooner
A June crooner
A spoon feeder
And a natural leader)

Oh, there ain't no use in me workin' so heavy
I got a woman who works on the levee
Pumping that water up to her neck
Every week she sends me a monthly check
(She's a humdinger
Folk singer
Dead ringer
For a thing-a-muh jigger)

Late one day in the middle of the week
Eyes were closed I was half asleep
I chased me a woman up the hill
Right in the middle of an air-raid drill
It was Little Bo Peep!
(I jumped a fallout shelter
I jumped a bean stalk
I jumped a Ferris wheel)

Now, the man on the stand he wants my vote
He's a-runnin' for office on the ballot note
He's out there preachin' in front of the steeple
Tellin' me he loves all kinds-a people
(He's eatin' bagels
He's eatin' pizza
He's eatin' chitlins
He's eatin' bullshit!)

Oh, set me down on a television floor
I'll flip the channel to number four
Out of the shower comes a grown-up man
With a bottle of hair oil in his hand
(It's that greasy kid stuff
What I want to know, Mr. Football Man, is
What do you do about Willy Mays and Yul Brynner
Charles de Gaulle
And Robert Louis Stevenson?)

Well, the funniest woman I ever seen
Was the great-granddaughter of Mr. Clean
She takes about fifteen baths a day
Wants me to grow a cigar on my face
(She's a little bit heavy!)

Well, ask me why I'm drunk alla time
It levels my head and eases my mind
I just walk along and stroll and sing
I see better days and I do better things
(I catch dinosaurs
I make love to Elizabeth Taylor . . .
Catch hell from Richard Burton!)

# Whatcha Gonna Do

Tell me what you're gonna do
When the shadow comes under your door
Tell me what you're gonna do
When the shadow comes under your door
Tell me what you're gonna do
When the shadow comes under your door
O Lord, O Lord
What shall you do?

Tell me what you're gonna do
When the devil calls your cards
Tell me what you're gonna do
When the devil calls your cards
Tell me what you're gonna do
When the devil calls your cards
O Lord, O Lord
What shall you do?

Tell me what you're gonna do
When your water turns to wine
Tell me what you're gonna do
When your water turns to wine
Tell me what you're gonna do
When your water turns to wine
O Lord, O Lord
What should you do?

Tell me what you're gonna do
When you can't play God no more
Tell me what you're gonna do
When you can't play God no more
Tell me what you're gonna do
When you can't play God no more
O Lord, O Lord
What shall you do?

Tell me what you're gonna do
When the shadow comes creepin' in your room
Tell me what you're gonna do
When the shadow comes creepin' in your room
Tell me what you're gonna do
When the shadow comes creepin' in your room
O Lord, O Lord
What should you do?

# Walls of Red Wing

Oh, the age of the inmates
I remember quite freely:
No younger than twelve
No older 'n seventeen
Thrown in like bandits
And cast off like criminals
Inside the walls
The walls of Red Wing

From the dirty old mess hall
You march to the brick wall
Too weary to talk
And too tired to sing
Oh, it's all afternoon
You remember your hometown
Inside the walls
The walls of Red Wing

Oh, the gates are cast iron
And the walls are barbed wire
Stay far from the fence
With the 'lectricity sting
And it's keep down your head
And stay in your number
Inside the walls
The walls of Red Wing

Oh, it's fare thee well
To the deep hollow dungeon
Farewell to the boardwalk
That takes you to the screen
And farewell to the minutes
They threaten you with it
Inside the walls
The walls of Red Wing

It's many a guard
That stands around smilin'
Holdin' his club
Like he was a king
Hopin' to get you
Behind a wood pilin'
Inside the walls
The walls of Red Wing

The night aimed shadows
Through the crossbar windows
And the wind punched hard
To make the wall-siding sing
It's many a night
I pretended to be a-sleepin'
Inside the walls
The walls of Red Wing

As the rain rattled heavy
On the bunkhouse shingles
And the sounds in the night
They made my ears ring
'Til the keys of the guards
Clicked the tune of the morning
Inside the walls
The walls of Red Wing

Oh, some of us'll end up
In St. Cloud Prison
And some of us'll wind up
To be lawyers and things
And some of us'll stand up
To meet you on your crossroads
From inside the walls
The walls of Red Wing

# Who Killed Davey Moore?

Who killed Davey Moore
Why an' what's the reason for?

"Not I," says the referee
"Don't point your finger at me
I could've stopped it in the eighth
An' maybe kept him from his fate
But the crowd would've booed, I'm sure
At not gettin' their money's worth
It's too bad he had to go
But there was a pressure on me too, you know
It wasn't me that made him fall
No, you can't blame me at all"

Who killed Davey Moore
Why an' what's the reason for?

"Not us," says the angry crowd
Whose screams filled the arena loud
"It's too bad he died that night
But we just like to see a fight
We didn't mean for him t' meet his death
We just meant to see some sweat
There ain't nothing wrong in that
It wasn't us that made him fall
No, you can't blame us at all"

Who killed Davey Moore
Why an' what's the reason for?

"Not me," says his manager
Puffing on a big cigar
"It's hard to say, it's hard to tell
I always thought that he was well
It's too bad for his wife an' kids he's dead
But if he was sick, he should've said
It wasn't me that made him fall
No, you can't blame me at all"

Who killed Davey Moore
Why an' what's the reason for?

"Not me," says the gambling man
With his ticket stub still in his hand
"It wasn't me that knocked him down
My hands never touched him none
I didn't commit no ugly sin
Anyway, I put money on him to win
It wasn't me that made him fall
No, you can't blame me at all"

Who killed Davey Moore
Why an' what's the reason for?

"Not me," says the boxing writer
Pounding print on his old typewriter
Sayin', "Boxing ain't to blame
There's just as much danger in a football game"
Sayin', "Fistfighting is here to stay
It's just the old American way
It wasn't me that made him fall
No, you can't blame me at all"

Who killed Davey Moore
Why an' what's the reason for?

"Not me," says the man whose fists
Laid him low in a cloud of mist
Who came here from Cuba's door
Where boxing ain't allowed no more
"I hit him, yes, it's true
But that's what I am paid to do
Don't say 'murder,' don't say 'kill'
It was destiny, it was God's will"

Who killed Davey Moore
Why an' what's the reason for?

# Seven Curses

Old Reilly stole a stallion
But they caught him and they brought him back
And they laid him down on the jailhouse ground
With an iron chain around his neck

Old Reilly's daughter got a message
That her father was goin' to hang
She rode by night and came by morning
With gold and silver in her hand

When the judge he saw Reilly's daughter
His old eyes deepened in his head
Sayin', "Gold will never free your father
The price, my dear, is you instead"

"Oh I'm as good as dead," cried Reilly
"It's only you that he does crave
And my skin will surely crawl if he touches you at all
Get on your horse and ride away"

"Oh father you will surely die
If I don't take the chance to try
And pay the price and not take your advice
For that reason I will have to stay"

The gallows shadows shook the evening
In the night a hound dog bayed
In the night the grounds were groanin'
In the night the price was paid

The next mornin' she had awoken
To know that the judge had never spoken
She saw that hangin' branch a-bendin'
She saw her father's body broken

These be seven curses on a judge so cruel:
That one doctor will not save him
That two healers will not heal him
That three eyes will not see him

That four ears will not hear him
That five walls will not hide him
That six diggers will not bury him
And that seven deaths shall never kill him

# Dusty Old Fairgrounds

Well, it's all up from Florida at the start of the spring
The trucks and the trailers will be winding
Like a bullet we'll shoot for the carnival route
We're following them dusty old fairgrounds a-calling

From the Michigan mud past the Wisconsin sun
'Cross that Minnesota border, keep 'em scrambling
Through the clear county lakes and the lumberjack lands
We're following them dusty old fairgrounds a-calling

Hit Fargo on the jump and down to Aberdeen
'Cross them old Black Hills, keep 'em rolling
Through the cow country towns and the sands of old Montana
We're following them fairgrounds a-calling

As the white line on the highway sails under your wheels
I've gazed from the trailer window laughing
Oh, our clothes they was torn but the colors they was bright
Following them dusty old fairgrounds a-calling

It's a-many a friend that follows the bend
The jugglers, the hustlers, the gamblers
Well, I've spent my time with the fortune-telling kind
Following them fairgrounds a-calling

Oh, it's pound down the rails and it's tie down the tents
Get that canvas flag a-flying
Well, let the caterpillars spin, let the Ferris wheel wind
Following them fairgrounds a-calling

Well, it's roll into town straight to the fairgrounds
Just behind the posters that are hanging
And it's fill up every space with a different kind of face
Following them fairgrounds a-calling

Get the dancing girls in front, get the gambling show behind
Hear that old music box a-banging
Hear them kids, faces, smiles, up and down the midway aisles
We're following them fairgrounds a-calling

It's a-drag it on down by the deadline in the town
Hit the old highway by the morning
And it's ride yourself blind for the next town on time
Following them fairgrounds a-calling

As the harmonicas whined in the lonesome nighttime
Drinking red wine as we're rolling
Many a turnin' I turn, many a lesson I learn
From following them fairgrounds a-calling

And it's roll back down to St. Petersburg
Tie down the trailers and camp 'em
And the money that we made will pay for the space
From following them dusty old fairgrounds a-calling

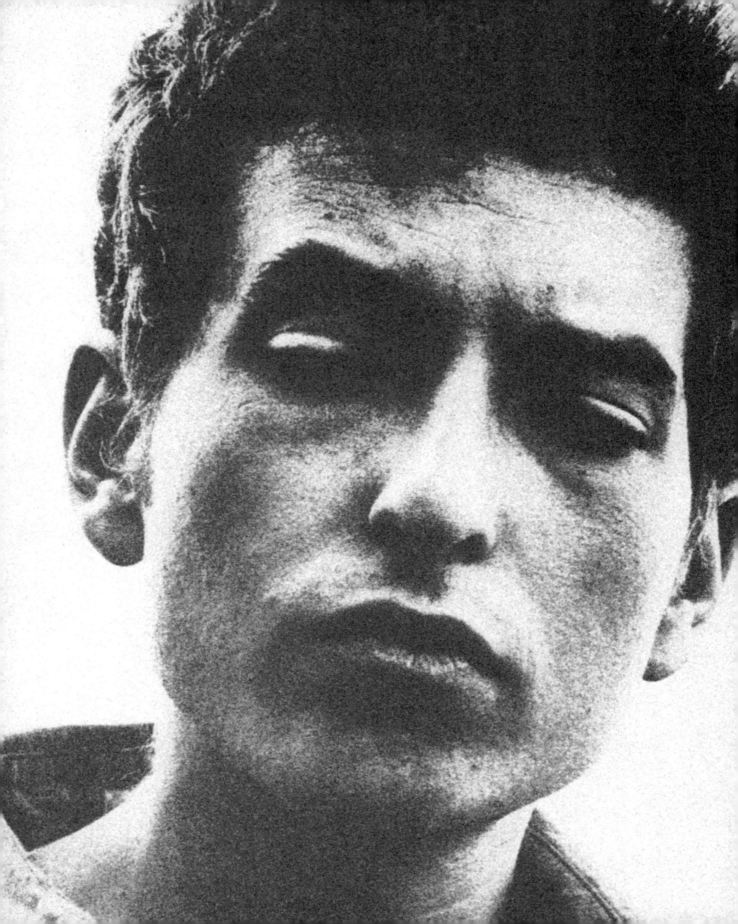

# The Times They Are A-Changin'

1. 〔 Come gather round people wherever yuh roam
   And admit that The waters around yuh have grown

   And accept it that soon you'll be drenched to the bone

   If yer time to you is worth savin'
   And yuh better start swimmin' or you'll sink like a stone
   For the times they are a changin'

# The Times They Are A-Changin'

Come gather 'round people
Wherever you roam
And admit that the waters
Around you have grown
And accept it that soon
You'll be drenched to the bone
If your time to you is worth savin'
Then you better start swimmin' or you'll sink like a stone
For the times they are a-changin'

Come writers and critics
Who prophesize with your pen
And keep your eyes wide
The chance won't come again
And don't speak too soon
For the wheel's still in spin
And there's no tellin' who that it's namin'
For the loser now will be later to win
For the times they are a-changin'

Come senators, congressmen
Please heed the call
Don't stand in the doorway
Don't block up the hall
For he that gets hurt
Will be he who has stalled
There's a battle outside and it is ragin'
It'll soon shake your windows and rattle your walls
For the times they are a-changin'

Come mothers and fathers
Throughout the land
And don't criticize
What you can't understand
Your sons and your daughters
Are beyond your command
Your old road is rapidly agin'
Please get out of the new one if you can't lend your hand
For the times they are a-changin'

The line it is drawn
The curse it is cast
The slow one now
Will later be fast
As the present now
Will later be past
The order is rapidly fadin'
And the first one now will later be last
For the times they are a-changin'

# Ballad of Hollis Brown

Hollis Brown
He lived on the outside of town
Hollis Brown
He lived on the outside of town
With his wife and five children
And his cabin fallin' down

You looked for work and money
And you walked a rugged mile
You looked for work and money
And you walked a rugged mile
Your children are so hungry
That they don't know how to smile

Your baby's eyes look crazy
They're a-tuggin' at your sleeve
Your baby's eyes look crazy
They're a-tuggin' at your sleeve
You walk the floor and wonder why
With every breath you breathe

The rats have got your flour
Bad blood it got your mare
The rats have got your flour
Bad blood it got your mare
If there's anyone that knows
Is there anyone that cares?

You prayed to the Lord above
Oh please send you a friend
You prayed to the Lord above
Oh please send you a friend
Your empty pockets tell yuh
That you ain't a-got no friend

Your babies are crying louder
It's pounding on your brain
Your babies are crying louder now
It's pounding on your brain
Your wife's screams are stabbin' you
Like the dirty drivin' rain

Your grass it is turning black
There's no water in your well
Your grass is turning black
There's no water in your well
You spent your last lone dollar
On seven shotgun shells

Way out in the wilderness
A cold coyote calls
Way out in the wilderness
A cold coyote calls
Your eyes fix on the shotgun
That's hangin' on the wall

Your brain is a-bleedin'
And your legs can't seem to stand
Your brain is a-bleedin'
And your legs can't seem to stand
Your eyes fix on the shotgun
That you're holdin' in your hand

There's seven breezes a-blowin'
All around the cabin door
There's seven breezes a-blowin'
All around the cabin door
Seven shots ring out
Like the ocean's pounding roar

There's seven people dead
On a South Dakota farm
There's seven people dead
On a South Dakota farm
Somewhere in the distance
There's seven new people born

# With God on Our Side

Oh my name it is nothin'
My age it means less
The country I come from
Is called the Midwest
I's taught and brought up there
The laws to abide
And that the land that I live in
Has God on its side

Oh the history books tell it
They tell it so well
The cavalries charged
The Indians fell
The cavalries charged
The Indians died
Oh the country was young
With God on its side

Oh the Spanish-American
War had its day
And the Civil War too
Was soon laid away
And the names of the heroes
I's made to memorize
With guns in their hands
And God on their side

Oh the First World War, boys
It closed out its fate
The reason for fighting
I never got straight
But I learned to accept it
Accept it with pride
For you don't count the dead
When God's on your side

When the Second World War
Came to an end
We forgave the Germans
And we were friends
Though they murdered six million
In the ovens they fried
The Germans now too
Have God on their side

I've learned to hate Russians
All through my whole life
If another war starts
It's them we must fight
To hate them and fear them
To run and to hide
And accept it all bravely
With God on my side

But now we got weapons
Of the chemical dust
If fire them we're forced to
Then fire them we must
One push of the button
And a shot the world wide
And you never ask questions
When God's on your side

Through many dark hour
I've been thinkin' about this
That Jesus Christ
Was betrayed by a kiss
But I can't think for you
You'll have to decide
Whether Judas Iscariot
Had God on his side

So now as I'm leavin'
I'm weary as Hell
The confusion I'm feelin'
Ain't no tongue can tell
The words fill my head
And fall to the floor
If God's on our side
He'll stop the next war

# One Too Many Mornings

Down the street the dogs are barkin'
And the day is a-gettin' dark
As the night comes in a-fallin'
The dogs'll lose their bark
An' the silent night will shatter
From the sounds inside my mind
For I'm one too many mornings
And a thousand miles behind

From the crossroads of my doorstep
My eyes they start to fade
As I turn my head back to the room
Where my love and I have laid
An' I gaze back to the street
The sidewalk and the sign
And I'm one too many mornings
An' a thousand miles behind

It's a restless hungry feeling
That don't mean no one no good
When ev'rything I'm a-sayin'
You can say it just as good
You're right from your side
I'm right from mine
We're both just one too many mornings
An' a thousand miles behind

# North Country Blues

Come gather 'round friends
And I'll tell you a tale
Of when the red iron pits ran plenty
But the cardboard filled windows
And old men on the benches
Tell you now that the whole town is empty

In the north end of town
My own children are grown
But I was raised on the other
In the wee hours of youth
My mother took sick
And I was brought up by my brother

The iron ore poured
As the years passed the door
The drag lines an' the shovels they was a-humming
'Til one day my brother
Failed to come home
The same as my father before him

Well a long winter's wait
From the window I watched
My friends they couldn't have been kinder
And my schooling was cut
As I quit in the spring
To marry John Thomas, a miner

Oh the years passed again
And the givin' was good
With the lunch bucket filled every season
What with three babies born
The work was cut down
To a half a day's shift with no reason

Then the shaft was soon shut
And more work was cut
And the fire in the air, it felt frozen
'Til a man come to speak
And he said in one week
That number eleven was closin'

They complained in the East
They are paying too high
They say that your ore ain't worth digging
That it's much cheaper down
In the South American towns
Where the miners work almost for nothing

So the mining gates locked
And the red iron rotted
And the room smelled heavy from drinking
Where the sad, silent song
Made the hour twice as long
As I waited for the sun to go sinking

I lived by the window
As he talked to himself
This silence of tongues it was building
Then one morning's wake
The bed it was bare
And I's left alone with three children

The summer is gone
The ground's turning cold
The stores one by one they're a-foldin'
My children will go
As soon as they grow
Well, there ain't nothing here now to hold them

# Only a Pawn in Their Game

A bullet from the back of a bush took Medgar Evers' blood
A finger fired the trigger to his name
A handle hid out in the dark
A hand set the spark
Two eyes took the aim
Behind a man's brain
But he can't be blamed
He's only a pawn in their game

A South politician preaches to the poor white man
"You got more than the blacks, don't complain
You're better than them, you been born with white skin," they explain
And the Negro's name
Is used it is plain
For the politician's gain
As he rises to fame
And the poor white remains
On the caboose of the train
But it ain't him to blame
He's only a pawn in their game

The deputy sheriffs, the soldiers, the governors get paid
And the marshals and cops get the same
But the poor white man's used in the hands of them all like a tool
He's taught in his school
From the start by the rule
That the laws are with him
To protect his white skin
To keep up his hate
So he never thinks straight
'Bout the shape that he's in
But it ain't him to blame
He's only a pawn in their game

From the poverty shacks, he looks from the cracks to the tracks
And the hoofbeats pound in his brain
And he's taught how to walk in a pack
Shoot in the back
With his fist in a clinch
To hang and to lynch
To hide 'neath the hood
To kill with no pain
Like a dog on a chain
He ain't got no name
But it ain't him to blame
He's only a pawn in their game

Today, Medgar Evers was buried from the bullet he caught
They lowered him down as a king
But when the shadowy sun sets on the one
That fired the gun
He'll see by his grave
On the stone that remains
Carved next to his name
His epitaph plain:
Only a pawn in their game

# Boots of Spanish Leather

Oh, I'm sailin' away my own true love
I'm sailin' away in the morning
Is there something I can send you from across the sea
From the place that I'll be landing?

No, there's nothin' you can send me, my own true love
There's nothin' I wish to be ownin'
Just carry yourself back to me unspoiled
From across that lonesome ocean

Oh, but I just thought you might want something fine
Made of silver or of golden
Either from the mountains of Madrid
Or from the coast of Barcelona

Oh, but if I had the stars from the darkest night
And the diamonds from the deepest ocean
I'd forsake them all for your sweet kiss
For that's all I'm wishin' to be ownin'

That I might be gone a long time
And it's only that I'm askin'
Is there something I can send you to remember me by
To make your time more easy passin'

Oh, how can, how can you ask me again
It only brings me sorrow
The same thing I want from you today
I would want again tomorrow

I got a letter on a lonesome day
It was from her ship a-sailin'
Saying I don't know when I'll be comin' back again
It depends on how I'm a-feelin'

Well, if you, my love, must think that-a-way
I'm sure your mind is roamin'
I'm sure your heart is not with me
But with the country to where you're goin'

So take heed, take heed of the western wind
Take heed of the stormy weather
And yes, there's something you can send back to me
Spanish boots of Spanish leather

# When the Ship Comes In

Oh the time will come up
When the winds will stop
And the breeze will cease to be breathin'
Like the stillness in the wind
'Fore the hurricane begins
The hour when the ship comes in

Oh the seas will split
And the ship will hit
And the sands on the shoreline will be shaking
Then the tide will sound
And the wind will pound
And the morning will be breaking

Oh the fishes will laugh
As they swim out of the path
And the seagulls they'll be smiling
And the rocks on the sand
Will proudly stand
The hour that the ship comes in

And the words that are used
For to get the ship confused
Will not be understood as they're spoken
For the chains of the sea
Will have busted in the night
And will be buried at the bottom of the ocean

A song will lift
As the mainsail shifts
And the boat drifts on to the shoreline
And the sun will respect
Every face on the deck
The hour that the ship comes in

Then the sands will roll
Out a carpet of gold
For your weary toes to be a-touchin'
And the ship's wise men
Will remind you once again
That the whole wide world is watchin'

Oh the foes will rise
With the sleep still in their eyes
And they'll jerk from their beds and think they're dreamin'
But they'll pinch themselves and squeal
And know that it's for real
The hour when the ship comes in

Then they'll raise their hands
Sayin' we'll meet all your demands
But we'll shout from the bow your days are numbered
And like Pharoah's tribe
They'll be drownded in the tide
And like Goliath, they'll be conquered

# The Lonesome Death of Hattie Carroll

William Zanzinger killed poor Hattie Carroll
With a cane that he twirled around his diamond ring finger
At a Baltimore hotel society gath'rin'
And the cops were called in and his weapon took from him
As they rode him in custody down to the station
And booked William Zanzinger for first-degree murder
But you who philosophize disgrace and criticize all fears
Take the rag away from your face
Now ain't the time for your tears

William Zanzinger, who at twenty-four years
Owns a tobacco farm of six hundred acres
With rich wealthy parents who provide and protect him
And high office relations in the politics of Maryland
Reacted to his deed with a shrug of his shoulders
And swear words and sneering, and his tongue it was snarling
In a matter of minutes on bail was out walking
But you who philosophize disgrace and criticize all fears
Take the rag away from your face
Now ain't the time for your tears

Hattie Carroll was a maid of the kitchen
She was fifty-one years old and gave birth to ten children
Who carried the dishes and took out the garbage
And never sat once at the head of the table
And didn't even talk to the people at the table
Who just cleaned up all the food from the table
And emptied the ashtrays on a whole other level
Got killed by a blow, lay slain by a cane
That sailed through the air and came down through the room
Doomed and determined to destroy all the gentle
And she never done nothing to William Zanzinger
But you who philosophize disgrace and criticize all fears
Take the rag away from your face
Now ain't the time for your tears

In the courtroom of honor, the judge pounded his gavel
To show that all's equal and that the courts are on the level
And that the strings in the books ain't pulled and persuaded
And that even the nobles get properly handled
Once that the cops have chased after and caught 'em
And that the ladder of law has no top and no bottom
Stared at the person who killed for no reason
Who just happened to be feelin' that way without warnin'
And he spoke through his cloak, most deep and distinguished
And handed out strongly, for penalty and repentance
William Zanzinger with a six-month sentence
Oh, but you who philosophize disgrace and criticize all fears
Bury the rag deep in your face
For now's the time for your tears

# Restless Farewell

Oh all the money that in my whole life I did spend
Be it mine right or wrongfully
I let it slip gladly past the hands of my friends
To tie up the time most forcefully
But the bottles are done
We've killed each one
And the table's full and overflowed
And the corner sign
Says it's closing time
So I'll bid farewell and be down the road

Oh ev'ry girl that ever I've touched
I did not do it harmfully
And ev'ry girl that ever I've hurt
I did not do it knowin'ly
But to remain as friends
And make amends
You need the time and stay behind
And since my feet are now fast
And point away from the past
I'll bid farewell and be down the line

Oh ev'ry foe that ever I faced
The cause was there before we came
And ev'ry cause that ever I fought
I fought it full without regret or shame
But the dark does die
As the curtain is drawn and somebody's eyes
Must meet the dawn
And if I see the day
I'd only have to stay
So I'll bid farewell in the night and be gone

Oh, ev'ry thought that's strung a knot in my mind
I might go insane if it couldn't be sprung
But it's not to stand naked under unknowin' eyes
It's for myself and my friends my stories are sung
But the time ain't tall, yet on time you depend
And no word is possessed by no special friend
And though the line is cut
It ain't quite the end
I'll just bid farewell till we meet again

Oh a false clock tries to tick out my time
To disgrace, distract, and bother me
And the dirt of gossip blows into my face
And the dust of rumors covers me
But if the arrow is straight
And the point is slick
It can pierce through dust no matter how thick
So I'll make my stand
And remain as I am
And bid farewell and not give a damn

# Eternal Circle

I sang the song slowly
As she stood in the shadows
She stepped to the light
As my silver strings spun
She called with her eyes
To the tune I's a-playin'
But the song it was long
And I'd only begun

Through a bullet of light
Her face was reflectin'
The fast fading words
That rolled from my tongue
With a long-distance look
Her eyes was on fire
But the song it was long
And there was more to be sung

My eyes danced a circle
Across her clear outline
With her head tilted sideways
She called me again
As the tune drifted out
She breathed hard through the echo
But the song it was long
And it was far to the end

I glanced at my guitar
And played it pretendin'
That of all the eyes out there
I could see none
As her thoughts pounded hard
Like the pierce of an arrow
But the song it was long
And it had to get done

As the tune finally folded
I laid down the guitar
Then looked for the girl
Who'd stayed for so long
But her shadow was missin'
For all of my searchin'
So I picked up my guitar
And began the next song

# Paths of Victory

Trails of troubles
Roads of battles
Paths of victory
I shall walk

The trail is dusty
And my road it might be rough
But the better roads are waiting
And boys it ain't far off

Trails of troubles
Roads of battles
Paths of victory
We shall walk

I walked down by the river
I turned my head up high
I saw that silver linin'
That was hangin' in the sky

Trails of troubles
Roads of battles
Paths of victory
We shall walk

The evenin' dusk was rollin'
I was walking down the track
There was a one-way wind a-blowin'
And it was blowin' at my back

Trails of troubles
Roads of battles
Paths of victory
We shall walk

The gravel road is bumpy
It's a hard road to ride
But there's a clearer road a-waitin'
With the cinders on the side

Trails of troubles
Roads of battles
Paths of victory
We shall walk

That evening train was rollin'
The hummin' of its wheels
My eyes they saw a better day
As I looked across the fields

Trails of troubles
Roads of battles
Paths of victory
We shall walk

The trail is dusty
The road it might be rough
But the good road is a-waitin'
And boys it ain't far off

Trails of troubles
Roads of battles
Paths of victory
We shall walk

# Only a Hobo

As I was out walking on a corner one day
I spied an old hobo, in a doorway he lay
His face was all grounded in the cold sidewalk floor
And I guess he'd been there for the whole night or more

Only a hobo, but one more is gone
Leavin' nobody to sing his sad song
Leavin' nobody to carry him home
Only a hobo, but one more is gone

A blanket of newspaper covered his head
As the curb was his pillow, the street was his bed
One look at his face showed the hard road he'd come
And a fistful of coins showed the money he bummed

Only a hobo, but one more is gone
Leavin' nobody to sing his sad song
Leavin' nobody to carry him home
Only a hobo, but one more is gone

Does it take much of a man to see his whole life go down
To look up on the world from a hole in the ground
To wait for your future like a horse that's gone lame
To lie in the gutter and die with no name?

Only a hobo, but one more is gone
Leavin' nobody to sing his sad song
Leavin' nobody to carry him home
Only a hobo, but one more is gone

# Lay Down Your Weary Tune

Lay down your weary tune, lay down
Lay down the song you strum
And rest yourself 'neath the strength of strings
No voice can hope to hum

Struck by the sounds before the sun
I knew the night had gone
The morning breeze like a bugle blew
Against the drums of dawn

Lay down your weary tune, lay down
Lay down the song you strum
And rest yourself 'neath the strength of strings
No voice can hope to hum

The ocean wild like an organ played
The seaweed's wove its strands
The crashin' waves like cymbals clashed
Against the rocks and sands

Lay down your weary tune, lay down
Lay down the song you strum
And rest yourself 'neath the strength of strings
No voice can hope to hum

I stood unwound beneath the skies
And clouds unbound by laws
The cryin' rain like a trumpet sang
And asked for no applause

Lay down your weary tune, lay down
Lay down the song you strum
And rest yourself 'neath the strength of strings
No voice can hope to hum

The last of leaves fell from the trees
And clung to a new love's breast
The branches bare like a banjo played
To the winds that listened best

I gazed down in the river's mirror
And watched its winding strum
The water smooth ran like a hymn
And like a harp did hum

Lay down your weary tune, lay down
Lay down the song you strum
And rest yourself 'neath the strength of strings
No voice can hope to hum

# Percy's Song

Bad news, bad news
Come to me where I sleep
Turn, turn, turn again
Sayin' one of your friends
Is in trouble deep
Turn, turn to the rain
And the wind

Tell me the trouble
Tell once to my ear
Turn, turn, turn again
Joliet prison
And ninety-nine years
Turn, turn to the rain
And the wind

Oh what's the charge
Of how this came to be
Turn, turn, turn again
Manslaughter
In the highest of degree
Turn, turn to the rain
And the wind

I sat down and wrote
The best words I could write
Turn, turn, turn again
Explaining to the judge
I'd be there on Wednesday night
Turn, turn to the rain
And the wind

Without a reply
I left by the moon
Turn, turn, turn again
And was in his chambers
By the next afternoon
Turn, turn to the rain
And the wind

Could ya tell me the facts?
I said without fear
Turn, turn, turn again
That a friend of mine
Would get ninety-nine years
Turn, turn to the rain
And the wind

A crash on the highway
Flew the car to a field
Turn, turn, turn again
There was four persons killed
And he was at the wheel
Turn, turn to the rain
And the wind

But I knew him as good
As I'm knowin' myself
Turn, turn, turn again
And he wouldn't harm a life
That belonged to someone else
Turn, turn to the rain
And the wind

The judge spoke
Out of the side of his mouth
Turn, turn, turn again
Sayin', "The witness who saw
He left little doubt"
Turn, turn to the rain
And the wind

That may be true
He's got a sentence to serve
Turn, turn, turn again
But ninety-nine years
He just don't deserve
Turn, turn to the rain
And the wind

Too late, too late
For his case it is sealed
Turn, turn, turn again
His sentence is passed
And it cannot be repealed
Turn, turn to the rain
And the wind

But he ain't no criminal
And his crime it is none
Turn, turn, turn again
What happened to him
Could happen to anyone
Turn, turn to the rain
And the wind

And at that the judge jerked forward
And his face it did freeze
Turn, turn, turn again
Sayin', "Could you kindly leave
My office now, please"
Turn, turn to the rain
And the wind

Well his eyes looked funny
And I stood up so slow
Turn, turn, turn again
With no other choice
Except for to go
Turn, turn to the rain
And the wind

I walked down the hallway
And I heard his door slam
Turn, turn, turn again
I walked down the courthouse stairs
And I did not understand
Turn, turn to the rain
And the wind

And I played my guitar
Through the night to the day
Turn, turn, turn again
And the only tune
My guitar could play
Was, "Oh the Cruel Rain
And the Wind"

# Guess I'm Doin' Fine

Well, I ain't got my childhood
Or friends I once did know
No, I ain't got my childhood
Or friends I once did know
But I still got my voice left
I can take it anywhere I go
Hey, hey, so I guess I'm doin' fine

And I've never had much money
But I'm still around somehow
No, I've never had much money
But I'm still around somehow
Many times I've bended
But I ain't never yet bowed
Hey, hey, so I guess I'm doin' fine

Trouble, oh trouble
I've trouble on my mind
Trouble, oh trouble
Trouble on my mind
But the trouble in the world, Lord
Is much more bigger than mine
Hey, hey, so I guess I'm doin' fine

And I never had no armies
To jump at my command
No, I ain't got no armies
To jump at my command
But I don't need no armies
I got me one good friend
Hey, hey, so I guess I'm doin' fine

I been kicked and whipped and trampled on
I been shot at just like you
I been kicked and whipped and trampled on
I been shot at just like you.
But as long as the world keeps a-turnin'
I just keep a-turnin' too
Hey, hey, so I guess I'm doin' fine

Well, my road might be rocky
The stones might cut my face
My road it might be rocky
The stones might cut my face
But as some folks ain't got no road at all
They gotta stand in the same old place
Hey, hey, so I guess I'm doin' fine

# Another Side of Bob Dylan

All I Really Want to Do

Black Crow Blues

Spanish Harlem Incident

Chimes of Freedom

I Shall Be Free No. 10

To Ramona

Motorpsycho Nightmare

My Back Pages

I Don't Believe You
   (She Acts Like We Never Have Met)

Ballad in Plain D

It Ain't Me, Babe

*additional lyrics*
Denise
If You Gotta Go, Go Now (Or Else You Got to Stay All Night)
Mama, You Been on My Mind
Playboys and Playgirls

# Some other kinds of songs...

Poems by Bob Dylan

baby black's
been had
aint bad
smokestacked
chicken shacked
dressed in black
silver monkey
on her back
mammy ma
juiced pa
janitored
between the law
brothers ten
rat-faced
gravestoned
ditch dug
firescaped an substracked
choked
baby black
hits back
robs. pawns
lives by trade
sits an waits on fire plug
digs the heat
eyes meet
picket line
across the street
head rings
of bed springs
freedom's holler
you ask of order
she'd hock
the world
for a dollar an a quarter
baby black
dressed in black
gunny sack
about t crack
been gone
carry on
i'm givin you
myself t pawn

* * *

for françoise hardy
at the seine's edge
a giant shadow
of notre dame
seeks t grab my foot
sorbonne students
whirl by on thin bicycles
swirlin' lifelike colors of leather spin
tho breeze yawns food
far from the bellies
of erhardt meetin johnson
piles of lovers
fishing
kissing
lay themselves on their books. boats.
old men
clothed in curly mustaches
float on the benches
blankets of tourists
in bright red nylon shirts
with straw hats of ambassadors
(cannot hear nixon's
dawg bark now)
will sail away
as the sun goes down
the doors of the river are open
i must remember that

"what d you mean?"
"i mean i lose all the time"
his jaw tightened an he took
a deep breath
"hummm. now i gotta beat you"

straight away an into the ring
juno takes twenty pills an
paints all day. life he says
is a head kinda thing. outside
of chicago. private come down
junkie nurse home heals countless
common housewives strung out
fully on drugstore dope. legally
sold t help clean the kitchen.
lenny bruce shows his seventh
avenue hand made movies. while a
bunch of women sneak little white
tablets into shoes. stockings. hats
an other hidin places. newspapers
an writes me that there. they
hate nazis much more n we over here
do. eichmann dies yes. an west
germany sends eighty year old
renata tell me that i might wear
i wanna go. back here, literate
rebel flag above
home sweet
vote for goldwater. "talks too
much. i should keep his mouth sh
i walk between back yards an see
little boy with feather in his hair
lyin dead on the grass. he gets
up an hands feather t another
little boy who immediately falls
down. "it's my turn t be the good
guy . . . take that, redskin" bang bang.
henry miller stands on other side
"did you ask
someone t drink" i say
an look at the pool. my worst
enemies i'nt even put me down
in such a way. a foreign
college student trails me with
a microphone an tape machine
what d you a
party? what communist party?
he rattles off names an numbers.
he cant answer my questions "you
have t answer my questions
gets all squishy. i say
there's worlds to
anyhow there's an
my thoughts get lost too
i caught him
turns red above his cups an
i'm monstrously against the house
unamerican activities committee
an also the cia an i beg her please
not t ask me why for it would take
too long t tell she asks me about
humanity an i say i'm not sure
what that word means. she wants me
t say what she wants me t say. she
wants me t say what she
can understand. a loose tempered fat
man in borrowed stomach slams wife
in the face an rushes off t civil
rights meeting. while some strange
girl chases me up smoky mountain
tryin t find out what sign i am.

between pillars of chips
springs on their like samson
thumps thumps
strikes
is on the prowl
you'll only lose
shouldnt stay
jack o' diamonds
is a hard t play

jack o' diamonds
wrecked my hand
left me here t stand
little tin men play
their drums now
upside my head
in the midst of cheers
flowers
four queens
with pawed out hearts
make make believe
they're too good
but should drop
for
an dean martin should apologize
t the rolling stones
hum
weird mistakes
young babies horseback ride
their fathers' necks
two dudes in hopped ford
for
its your turn
cut the deck
if you're goin under
stayed too long
chinese gong
down the way
says jack o' diamonds
(a high card)
jack o' diamonds
(but ain't high enough)

jack o' diamonds
a hard card t play
jack o' diamonds used t laugh at me
used t be ashamed of me
now wants t walk long side of me
jack o' diamonds
wears but a single glove
as he shoves
the moon's too bright
as he's fixed mirrors
round the room at nite
there's probably someone
in my drink
inside the sink
give no gain
jug a stain
jack o' diamonds
an all his crap
needs some acid
in his lap
what hour now
it feels late somehow
my hounddog bays
need more ashtrays
i cant even remember
the early days
please dont stay
gather your bells an go
jack o' diamonds
(can open for riches)

jack o' diamonds
(a king's death)
jack o' diamonds
(at the ace's breath
jack o' diamonds
is a hard card t play

* * *

run go get out of h
quick
leave joshua
split
go fit your battle
do your thing
i lost my glasses
cant see jerico
the wind is tyin kn
in my hair
nothin seems
t be straight
out there
so i shant go with y
i cant go with you

on the brooklyn br
he was cockeyed
an stood on the ed
there was a priest
i was shiftin mysel
so i could see from
in an out of stretch
an things
cops held people
the lady in back of
burst into my groin
'sick sick some a
like a circus trape
"oh i hope he don
he was on the oth
both eyes fiery wi
wet with sweat
the mouth of a sha
rolled up soiled sh
his arms were thic
an he wore a silve
i could tell at a gla
he was uselessly l
i couldnt stay an l
i couldnt stay an l
because i sudden
deep in my heart
i really wanted
t see him jump

(a mob. each mem
that they all know
they have the sam
can stare at each
they do not have t
about havin nothin
soaked by the ten
of 'that their searc
for findin a way t c
giant cop out. all
an i was in it an ca

an i walked away
i wanted t see him
that i had t walk a
uptown uptown
orchard street
thru all those peop
orchard street
pants' legs in my f
"comere! comere
i don't need no cl
an cross the stree
skull caps climb
by themselves out
an shoeboxes ride
the cracks of the
fishermen—

# All I Really Want to Do

I ain't lookin' to compete with you
Beat or cheat or mistreat you
Simplify you, classify you
Deny, defy or crucify you
All I really want to do
Is, baby, be friends with you

No, and I ain't lookin' to fight with you
Frighten you or tighten you
Drag you down or drain you down
Chain you down or bring you down
All I really want to do
Is, baby, be friends with you

I ain't lookin' to block you up
Shock or knock or lock you up
Analyze you, categorize you
Finalize you or advertise you
All I really want to do
Is, baby, be friends with you

I don't want to straight-face you
Race or chase you, track or trace you
Or disgrace you or displace you
Or define you or confine you
All I really want to do
Is, baby, be friends with you

I don't want to meet your kin
Make you spin or do you in
Or select you or dissect you
Or inspect you or reject you
All I really want to do
Is, baby, be friends with you

I don't want to fake you out
Take or shake or forsake you out
I ain't lookin' for you to feel like me
See like me or be like me
All I really want to do
Is, baby, be friends with you

# Black Crow Blues

I woke in the mornin', wand'rin'
Wasted and worn out
I woke in the mornin', wand'rin'
Wasted and worn out
Wishin' my long-lost lover
Will walk to me, talk to me
Tell me what it's all about

I was standin' at the side road
Listenin' to the billboard knock
Standin' at the side road
Listenin' to the billboard knock
Well, my wrist was empty
But my nerves were kickin'
Tickin' like a clock

If I got anything you need, babe
Let me tell you in front
If I got anything you need, babe
Let me tell you in front
You can come to me sometime
Night time, day time
Any time you want

Sometimes I'm thinkin' I'm
Too high to fall
Sometimes I'm thinkin' I'm
Too high to fall
Other times I'm thinkin' I'm
So low I don't know
If I can come up at all

Black crows in the meadow
Across a broad highway
Black crows in the meadow
Across a broad highway
Though it's funny, honey
I just don't feel much like a
Scarecrow today

# Spanish Harlem Incident

Gypsy gal, the hands of Harlem
Cannot hold you to its heat
Your temperature's too hot for taming
Your flaming feet burn up the street
I am homeless, come and take me
Into reach of your rattling drums
Let me know, babe, about my fortune
Down along my restless palms

Gypsy gal, you got me swallowed
I have fallen far beneath
Your pearly eyes, so fast an' slashing
An' your flashing diamond teeth
The night is pitch black, come an' make my
Pale face fit into place, ah, please!
Let me know, babe, I'm nearly drowning
If it's you my lifelines trace

I been wond'rin' all about me
Ever since I seen you there
On the cliffs of your wildcat charms I'm riding
I know I'm 'round you but I don't know where
You have slayed me, you have made me
I got to laugh halfways off my heels
I got to know, babe, will you surround me?
So I can tell if I'm really real

# Chimes of Freedom

Far between sundown's finish an' midnight's broken toll
We ducked inside the doorway, thunder crashing
As majestic bells of bolts struck shadows in the sounds
Seeming to be the chimes of freedom flashing
Flashing for the warriors whose strength is not to fight
Flashing for the refugees on the unarmed road of flight
An' for each an' ev'ry underdog soldier in the night
An' we gazed upon the chimes of freedom flashing

In the city's melted furnace, unexpectedly we watched
With faces hidden while the walls were tightening
As the echo of the wedding bells before the blowin' rain
Dissolved into the bells of the lightning
Tolling for the rebel, tolling for the rake
Tolling for the luckless, the abandoned an' forsaked
Tolling for the outcast, burnin' constantly at stake
An' we gazed upon the chimes of freedom flashing

Through the mad mystic hammering of the wild ripping hail
The sky cracked its poems in naked wonder
That the clinging of the church bells blew far into the breeze
Leaving only bells of lightning and its thunder
Striking for the gentle, striking for the kind
Striking for the guardians and protectors of the mind
An' the unpawned painter behind beyond his rightful time
An' we gazed upon the chimes of freedom flashing

Through the wild cathedral evening the rain unraveled tales
For the disrobed faceless forms of no position
Tolling for the tongues with no place to bring their thoughts
All down in taken-for-granted situations
Tolling for the deaf an' blind, tolling for the mute
Tolling for the mistreated, mateless mother, the mistitled prostitute
For the misdemeanor outlaw, chased an' cheated by pursuit
An' we gazed upon the chimes of freedom flashing

Even though a cloud's white curtain in a far-off corner flashed
An' the hypnotic splattered mist was slowly lifting
Electric light still struck like arrows, fired but for the ones
Condemned to drift or else be kept from drifting
Tolling for the searching ones, on their speechless, seeking trail
For the lonesome-hearted lovers with too personal a tale
An' for each unharmful, gentle soul misplaced inside a jail
An' we gazed upon the chimes of freedom flashing

Starry-eyed an' laughing as I recall when we were caught
Trapped by no track of hours for they hanged suspended
As we listened one last time an' we watched with one last look
Spellbound an' swallowed 'til the tolling ended
Tolling for the aching ones whose wounds cannot be nursed
For the countless confused, accused, misused, strung-out ones an' worse
An' for every hung-up person in the whole wide universe
An' we gazed upon the chimes of freedom flashing

# I Shall Be Free No. 10

I'm just average, common too
I'm just like him, the same as you
I'm everybody's brother and son
I ain't different from anyone
It ain't no use a-talking to me
It's just the same as talking to you

I was shadow-boxing earlier in the day
I figured I was ready for Cassius Clay
I said "Fee, fie, fo, fum, Cassius Clay, here I come
26, 27, 28, 29, I'm gonna make your face look just like mine
Five, four, three, two, one, Cassius Clay you'd better run
99, 100, 101, 102, your ma won't even recognize you
14, 15, 16, 17, 18, 19, gonna knock him clean right out of his spleen"

Well, I don't know, but I've been told
The streets in heaven are lined with gold
I ask you how things could get much worse
If the Russians happen to get up there first
Wowee! pretty scary!

Now, I'm liberal, but to a degree
I want ev'rybody to be free
But if you think that I'll let Barry Goldwater
Move in next door and marry my daughter
You must think I'm crazy!
I wouldn't let him do it for all the farms in Cuba

Well, I set my monkey on the log
And ordered him to do the Dog
He wagged his tail and shook his head
And he went and did the Cat instead
He's a weird monkey, very funky

I sat with my high-heeled sneakers on
Waiting to play tennis in the noonday sun
I had my white shorts rolled up past my waist
And my wig-hat was falling in my face
But they wouldn't let me on the tennis court

I got a woman, she's so mean
She sticks my boots in the washing machine
Sticks me with buckshot when I'm nude
Puts bubblegum in my food
She's funny, wants my money, calls me "honey"

Now I got a friend who spends his life
Stabbing my picture with a bowie knife
Dreams of strangling me with a scarf
When my name comes up he pretends to barf
I've got a million friends!

Now they asked me to read a poem
At the sorority sisters' home
I got knocked down and my head was swimmin'
I wound up with the Dean of Women
Yippee! I'm a poet, and I know it
Hope I don't blow it

I'm gonna grow my hair down to my feet so strange
So I look like a walking mountain range
And I'm gonna ride into Omaha on a horse
Out to the country club and the golf course
Carry *The New York Times,* shoot a few holes, blow their minds

Now you're probably wondering by now
Just what this song is all about
What's probably got you baffled more
Is what this thing here is for
It's nothing
It's something I learned over in England

# To Ramona

Ramona
Come closer
Shut softly your watery eyes
The pangs of your sadness
Shall pass as your senses will rise
The flowers of the city
Though breathlike
Get deathlike at times
And there's no use in tryin'
T' deal with the dyin'
Though I cannot explain that in lines

Your cracked country lips
I still wish to kiss
As to be under the strength of your skin
Your magnetic movements
Still capture the minutes I'm in
But it grieves my heart, love
To see you tryin' to be a part of
A world that just don't exist
It's all just a dream, babe
A vacuum, a scheme, babe
That sucks you into feelin' like this

I can see that your head
Has been twisted and fed
By worthless foam from the mouth
I can tell you are torn
Between stayin' and returnin'
On back to the South
You've been fooled into thinking
That the finishin' end is at hand
Yet there's no one to beat you
No one t' defeat you
'Cept the thoughts of yourself feeling bad

I've heard you say many times
That you're better 'n no one
And no one is better 'n you
If you really believe that
You know you got
Nothing to win and nothing to lose
From fixtures and forces and friends
Your sorrow does stem
That hype you and type you
Making you feel
That you must be exactly like them

I'd forever talk to you
But soon my words
They would turn into a meaningless ring
For deep in my heart
I know there is no help I can bring
Everything passes
Everything changes
Just do what you think you should do
And someday maybe
Who knows, baby
I'll come and be cryin' to you

# Motorpsycho Nightmare

I pounded on a farmhouse
Lookin' for a place to stay
I was mighty, mighty tired
I had come a long, long way
I said, "Hey, hey, in there
Is there anybody home?"
I was standin' on the steps
Feelin' most alone
Well, out comes a farmer
He must have thought that I was nuts
He immediately looked at me
And stuck a gun into my guts

I fell down
To my bended knees
Saying, "I dig farmers
Don't shoot me, please!"
He cocked his rifle
And began to shout
"You're that travelin' salesman
That I have heard about"
I said, "No! No! No!
I'm a doctor and it's true
I'm a clean-cut kid
And I been to college, too"

Then in comes his daughter
Whose name was Rita
She looked like she stepped out of
*La Dolce Vita*
I immediately tried to cool it
With her dad
And told him what a
Nice, pretty farm he had
He said, "What do doctors
Know about farms, pray tell?"
I said, "I was born
At the bottom of a wishing well"

Well, by the dirt 'neath my nails
I guess he knew I wouldn't lie
"I guess you're tired"
He said, kinda sly
I said, "Yes, ten thousand miles
Today I drove"
He said, "I got a bed for you
Underneath the stove
Just one condition
And you go to sleep right now
That you don't touch my daughter
And in the morning, milk the cow"

I was sleepin' like a rat
When I heard something jerkin'
There stood Rita
Lookin' just like Tony Perkins
She said, "Would you like to take a shower?
I'll show you up to the door"
I said, "Oh, no! no!
I've been through this before"
I knew I had to split
But I didn't know how
When she said
"Would you like to take that shower, now?"

Well, I couldn't leave
Unless the old man chased me out
'Cause I'd already promised
That I'd milk his cows
I had to say something
To strike him very weird
So I yelled out
"I like Fidel Castro and his beard"
Rita looked offended
But she got out of the way
As he came charging down the stairs
Sayin', "What's that I heard you say?"

I said, "I like Fidel Castro
I think you heard me right"
And ducked as he swung
At me with all his might
Rita mumbled something
'Bout her mother on the hill
As his fist hit the icebox
He said he's going to kill me
If I don't get out the door
In two seconds flat
"You unpatriotic
Rotten doctor Commie rat"

Well, he threw a *Reader's Digest*
At my head and I did run
I did a somersault
As I seen him get his gun
And crashed through the window
At a hundred miles an hour
And landed fully blast
In his garden flowers
Rita said, "Come back!"
As he started to load
The sun was comin' up
And I was runnin' down the road

Well, I don't figure I'll be back
There for a spell
Even though Rita moved away
And got a job in a motel
He still waits for me
Constant, on the sly
He wants to turn me in
To the F.B.I.
Me, I romp and stomp
Thankful as I romp
Without freedom of speech
I might be in the swamp

# My Back Pages

Crimson flames tied through my ears
Rollin' high and mighty traps
Pounced with fire on flaming roads
Using ideas as my maps
"We'll meet on edges, soon," said I
Proud 'neath heated brow
Ah, but I was so much older then
I'm younger than that now

Half-wracked prejudice leaped forth
"Rip down all hate," I screamed
Lies that life is black and white
Spoke from my skull. I dreamed
Romantic facts of musketeers
Foundationed deep, somehow
Ah, but I was so much older then
I'm younger than that now

Girls' faces formed the forward path
From phony jealousy
To memorizing politics
Of ancient history
Flung down by corpse evangelists
Unthought of, though, somehow
Ah, but I was so much older then
I'm younger than that now

A self-ordained professor's tongue
Too serious to fool
Spouted out that liberty
Is just equality in school
"Equality," I spoke the word
As if a wedding vow
Ah, but I was so much older then
I'm younger than that now

In a soldier's stance, I aimed my hand
At the mongrel dogs who teach
Fearing not that I'd become my enemy
In the instant that I preach
My pathway led by confusion boats
Mutiny from stern to bow
Ah, but I was so much older then
I'm younger than that now

Yes, my guard stood hard when abstract threats
Too noble to neglect
Deceived me into thinking
I had something to protect
Good and bad, I define these terms
Quite clear, no doubt, somehow
Ah, but I was so much older then
I'm younger than that now

# Don't Believe You
# (She Acts Like We Never Have Met)

I can't understand
She let go of my hand
An' left me here facing the wall
I'd sure like t' know
Why she did go
But I can't get close t' her at all
Though we kissed through the wild blazing nighttime
She said she would never forget
But now mornin's clear
It's like I ain't here
She just acts like we never have met

It's all new t' me
Like some mystery
It could even be like a myth
Yet it's hard t' think on
That she's the same one
That last night I was with
From darkness, dreams're deserted
Am I still dreamin' yet?
I wish she'd unlock
Her voice once an' talk
'Stead of acting like we never have met

If she ain't feelin' well
Then why don't she tell
'Stead of turnin' her back t' my face?
Without any doubt
She seems too far out
For me t' return t' her chase
Though the night ran swirling an' whirling
I remember her whispering yet
But evidently she don't
An' evidently she won't
She just acts like we never have met

If I didn't have t' guess
I'd gladly confess
T' anything I might've tried
If I was with 'er too long
Or have done something wrong
I wish she'd tell me what it is, I'll run an' hide
Though her skirt it swayed as a guitar played
Her mouth was watery and wet
But now something has changed
For she ain't the same
She just acts like we never have met

I'm leavin' today
I'll be on my way
Of this I can't say very much
But if you want me to
I can be just like you
An' pretend that we never have touched
An' if anybody asks me
"Is it easy to forget?"
I'll say, "It's easily done
You just pick anyone
An' pretend that you never have met!"

# Ballad in Plain D

I once loved a girl, her skin it was bronze
With the innocence of a lamb, she was gentle like a fawn
I courted her proudly but now she is gone
Gone as the season she's taken

Through young summer's breeze, I stole her away
From her mother and sister, though close did they stay
Each one of them suffering from the failures of their day
With strings of guilt they tried hard to guide us

Of the two sisters, I loved the young
With sensitive instincts, she was the creative one
The constant scapegoat, she was easily undone
By the jealousy of others around her

For her parasite sister, I had no respect
Bound by her boredom, her pride to protect
Countless visions of the other she'd reflect
As a crutch for her scenes and her society

Myself, for what I did, I cannot be excused
The changes I was going through can't even be used
For the lies that I told her in hopes not to lose
The could-be dream-lover of my lifetime

With unknown consciousness, I possessed in my grip
A magnificent mantelpiece, though its heart being chipped
Noticing not that I'd already slipped
To a sin of love's false security

From silhouetted anger to manufactured peace
Answers of emptiness, voice vacancies
Till the tombstones of damage read me no questions but, "Please
What's wrong and what's exactly the matter?"

And so it did happen like it could have been foreseen
The timeless explosion of fantasy's dream
At the peak of the night, the king and the queen
Tumbled all down into pieces

"The tragic figure!" her sister did shout
"Leave her alone, God damn you, get out!"
And I in my armor, turning about
And nailing her to the ruins of her pettiness

Beneath a bare lightbulb the plaster did pound
Her sister and I in a screaming battleground
And she in between, the victim of sound
Soon shattered as a child 'neath her shadows

All is gone, all is gone, admit it, take flight
I gagged twice, doubled, tears blinding my sight
My mind it was mangled, I ran into the night
Leaving all of love's ashes behind me

The wind knocks my window, the room it is wet
The words to say I'm sorry, I haven't found yet
I think of her often and hope whoever she's met
Will be fully aware of how precious she is

Ah, my friends from the prison, they ask unto me
"How good, how good does it feel to be free?"
And I answer them most mysteriously
"Are birds free from the chains of the skyway?"

# It Ain't Me, Babe

Go 'way from my window
Leave at your own chosen speed
I'm not the one you want, babe
I'm not the one you need
You say you're lookin' for someone
Never weak but always strong
To protect you an' defend you
Whether you are right or wrong
Someone to open each and every door
But it ain't me, babe
No, no, no, it ain't me, babe
It ain't me you're lookin' for, babe

Go lightly from the ledge, babe
Go lightly on the ground
I'm not the one you want, babe
I will only let you down
You say you're lookin' for someone
Who will promise never to part
Someone to close his eyes for you
Someone to close his heart
Someone who will die for you an' more
But it ain't me, babe
No, no, no, it ain't me, babe
It ain't me you're lookin' for, babe

Go melt back into the night, babe
Everything inside is made of stone
There's nothing in here moving
An' anyway I'm not alone
You say you're looking for someone
Who'll pick you up each time you fall
To gather flowers constantly
An' to come each time you call
A lover for your life an' nothing more
But it ain't me, babe
No, no, no, it ain't me, babe
It ain't me you're lookin' for, babe

# Denise

Denise, Denise
Gal, what's on your mind?
Denise, Denise
Gal, what's on your mind?
You got your eyes closed
Heaven knows that you ain't blind

Well, I can see you smiling
But oh your mouth is inside out
I can see you smiling
But you're smiling inside out
Well, I know you're laughin'
But what are you laughin' about

Well, if you're tryin' to throw me
Babe, I've already been tossed
If you're tryin' to throw me
Babe, I've already been tossed
Babe, you're tryin' to lose me
Babe, I'm already lost

Well, what are you doing
Are you flying or have you flipped?
Oh, what are you doing
Are you flying or have you flipped?
Well, you call my name
And then say your tongue just slipped

Denise, Denise
You're concealed here on the shelf
Denise, Denise
You're concealed here on the shelf
I'm looking deep in your eyes, babe
And all I can see is myself

# If You Gotta Go, Go Now (Or Else You Got to Stay All Night)

Listen to me, baby
There's something you must see
I want to be with you, gal
If you want to be with me

But if you got to go
It's all right
But if you got to go, go now
Or else you gotta stay all night

It ain't that I'm questionin' you
To take part in any quiz
It's just that I ain't got no watch
An' you keep askin' me what time it is

But if you got to go
It's all right
But if you got to go, go now
Or else you gotta stay all night

I am just a poor boy, baby
Lookin' to connect
But I certainly don't want you thinkin'
That I ain't got any respect

But if you got to go
It's all right
But if you got to go, go now
Or else you gotta stay all night

You know I'd have nightmares
And a guilty conscience, too
If I kept you from anything
That you really wanted to do

But if you got to go
It's all right
But if you got to go, go now
Or else you gotta stay all night

It ain't that I'm wantin'
Anything you never gave before
It's just that I'll be sleepin' soon
It'll be too dark for you to find the door

But if you got to go
It's all right
But if you got to go, go now
Or else you gotta stay all night

# Mama, You Been on My Mind

Perhaps it's the color of the sun cut flat
An' cov'rin' the crossroads I'm standing at
Or maybe it's the weather or something like that
But mama, you been on my mind

I don't mean trouble, please don't put me down or get upset
I am not pleadin' or sayin', "I can't forget"
I do not walk the floor bowed down an' bent, but yet
Mama, you been on my mind

Even though my mind is hazy an' my thoughts they might be narrow
Where you been don't bother me nor bring me down in sorrow
It don't even matter to me where you're wakin' up tomorrow
But mama, you're just on my mind

I am not askin' you to say words like "yes" or "no"
Please understand me, I got no place for you t' go
I'm just breathin' to myself, pretendin' not that I don't know
Mama, you been on my mind

When you wake up in the mornin', baby, look inside your mirror
You know I won't be next to you, you know I won't be near
I'd just be curious to know if you can see yourself as clear
As someone who has had you on his mind

# Playboys and Playgirls

Oh, ye playboys and playgirls
Ain't a-gonna run my world
Ain't a-gonna run my world
Ain't a-gonna run my world
Ye playboys and playgirls
Ain't a-gonna run my world
Not now or no other time

You fallout shelter sellers
Can't get in my door
Can't get in my door
Can't get in my door
You fallout shelter sellers
Can't get in my door
Not now or no other time

Your Jim Crow ground
Can't turn me around
Can't turn me around
Can't turn me around
Your Jim Crow ground
Can't turn me around
Not now or no other time

The laughter in the lynch mob
Ain't a-gonna do no more
Ain't a-gonna do no more
Ain't a-gonna do no more
The laughter in the lynch mob
Ain't a-gonna do no more
Not now or no other time

You insane tongues of war talk
Ain't a-gonna guide my road
Ain't a-gonna guide my road
Ain't a-gonna guide my road
You insane tongues of war talk
Ain't a-gonna guide my road
Not now or no other time

You red baiters and race haters
Ain't a-gonna hang around here
Ain't a-gonna hang around here
Ain't a-gonna hang around here
You red baiters and race haters
Ain't a-gonna hang around here
Not now or no other time

Ye playboys and playgirls
Ain't a-gonna own my world
Ain't a-gonna own my world
Ain't a-gonna own my world
Ye playboys and playgirls
Ain't a-gonna own my world
Not now or no other time

# Bringing It All Back Home

Subterranean Homesick Blues

She Belongs to Me

Maggie's Farm

Love Minus Zero/No Limit

Outlaw Blues

On the Road Again

Bob Dylan's 115th Dream

Mr. Tambourine Man

Gates of Eden

It's Alright, Ma (I'm Only Bleeding)

It's All Over Now, Baby Blue

*additional lyrics*

California (Early version of "Outlaw Blues")

Farewell Angelina

Love Is Just a Four Letter Word

xxxxxxx I'd talk all nite to you but soon my words would turn into a
meaningless ring
for deep in my heart I know there's no help I can bring
everything  passes. everything changes just do what you think you should do
for someday baby who know maybe I'll come an be cryin t you.

just t add
talk t their time

# Subterranean Homesick Blues

Johnny's in the basement
Mixing up the medicine
I'm on the pavement
Thinking about the government
The man in the trench coat
Badge out, laid off
Says he's got a bad cough
Wants to get it paid off
Look out kid
It's somethin' you did
God knows when
But you're doin' it again
You better duck down the alley way
Lookin' for a new friend
The man in the coon-skin cap
In the big pen
Wants eleven dollar bills
You only got ten

Maggie comes fleet foot
Face full of black soot
Talkin' that the heat put
Plants in the bed but
The phone's tapped anyway
Maggie says that many say
They must bust in early May
Orders from the D.A.
Look out kid
Don't matter what you did
Walk on your tiptoes
Don't try "No-Doz"
Better stay away from those
That carry around a fire hose
Keep a clean nose
Watch the plain clothes
You don't need a weatherman
To know which way the wind blows

Get sick, get well
Hang around a ink well
Ring bell, hard to tell
If anything is goin' to sell
Try hard, get barred
Get back, write braille
Get jailed, jump bail
Join the army, if you fail
Look out kid
You're gonna get hit
But users, cheaters
Six-time losers
Hang around the theaters
Girl by the whirlpool
Lookin' for a new fool
Don't follow leaders
Watch the parkin' meters

Ah get born, keep warm
Short pants, romance, learn to dance
Get dressed, get blessed
Try to be a success
Please her, please him, buy gifts
Don't steal, don't lift
Twenty years of schoolin'
And they put you on the day shift
Look out kid
They keep it all hid
Better jump down a manhole
Light yourself a candle
Don't wear sandals
Try to avoid the scandals
Don't wanna be a bum
You better chew gum
The pump don't work
'Cause the vandals took the handles

# She Belongs to Me

She's got everything she needs
She's an artist, she don't look back
She's got everything she needs
She's an artist, she don't look back
She can take the dark out of the nighttime
And paint the daytime black

You will start out standing
Proud to steal her anything she sees
You will start out standing
Proud to steal her anything she sees
But you will wind up peeking through her keyhole
Down upon your knees

She never stumbles
She's got no place to fall
She never stumbles
She's got no place to fall
She's nobody's child
The Law can't touch her at all

She wears an Egyptian ring
That sparkles before she speaks
She wears an Egyptian ring
That sparkles before she speaks
She's a hypnotist collector
You are a walking antique

Bow down to her on Sunday
Salute her when her birthday comes
Bow down to her on Sunday
Salute her when her birthday comes
For Halloween give her a trumpet
And for Christmas, buy her a drum

# Maggie's Farm

I ain't gonna work on Maggie's farm no more
No, I ain't gonna work on Maggie's farm no more
Well, I wake in the morning
Fold my hands and pray for rain
I got a head full of ideas
That are drivin' me insane
It's a shame the way she makes me scrub the floor
I ain't gonna work on Maggie's farm no more

I ain't gonna work for Maggie's brother no more
No, I ain't gonna work for Maggie's brother no more
Well, he hands you a nickel
He hands you a dime
He asks you with a grin
If you're havin' a good time
Then he fines you every time you slam the door
I ain't gonna work for Maggie's brother no more

I ain't gonna work for Maggie's pa no more
No, I ain't gonna work for Maggie's pa no more
Well, he puts his cigar
Out in your face just for kicks
His bedroom window
It is made out of bricks
The National Guard stands around his door
Ah, I ain't gonna work for Maggie's pa no more

I ain't gonna work for Maggie's ma no more
No, I ain't gonna work for Maggie's ma no more
Well, she talks to all the servants
About man and God and law
Everybody says
She's the brains behind pa
She's sixty-eight, but she says she's twenty-four
I ain't gonna work for Maggie's ma no more

I ain't gonna work on Maggie's farm no more
No, I ain't gonna work on Maggie's farm no more
Well, I try my best
To be just like I am
But everybody wants you
To be just like them
They sing while you slave and I just get bored
I ain't gonna work on Maggie's farm no more

# Love Minus Zero/No Limit

My love she speaks like silence
Without ideals or violence
She doesn't have to say she's faithful
Yet she's true, like ice, like fire
People carry roses
Make promises by the hours
My love she laughs like the flowers
Valentines can't buy her

In the dime stores and bus stations
People talk of situations
Read books, repeat quotations
Draw conclusions on the wall
Some speak of the future
My love she speaks softly
She knows there's no success like failure
And that failure's no success at all

The cloak and dagger dangles
Madams light the candles
In ceremonies of the horsemen
Even the pawn must hold a grudge
Statues made of matchsticks
Crumble into one another
My love winks, she does not bother
She knows too much to argue or to judge

The bridge at midnight trembles
The country doctor rambles
Bankers' nieces seek perfection
Expecting all the gifts that wise men bring
The wind howls like a hammer
The night blows cold and rainy
My love she's like some raven
At my window with a broken wing

# Outlaw Blues

Ain't it hard to stumble
And land in some funny lagoon?
Ain't it hard to stumble
And land in some muddy lagoon?
Especially when it's nine below zero
And three o'clock in the afternoon

Ain't gonna hang no picture
Ain't gonna hang no picture frame
Ain't gonna hang no picture
Ain't gonna hang no picture frame
Well, I might look like Robert Ford
But I feel just like a Jesse James

Well, I wish I was on some
Australian mountain range
Oh, I wish I was on some
Australian mountain range
I got no reason to be there, but I
Imagine it would be some kind of change

I got my dark sunglasses
I got for good luck my black tooth
I got my dark sunglasses
I'm carryin' for good luck my black tooth
Don't ask me nothin' about nothin'
I just might tell you the truth

I got a woman in Jackson
I ain't gonna say her name
I got a woman in Jackson
I ain't gonna say her name
She's a brown-skin woman, but I
Love her just the same

# On the Road Again

Well, I woke up in the morning
There's frogs inside my socks
Your mama, she's a-hidin'
Inside the icebox
Your daddy walks in wearin'
A Napoleon Bonaparte mask
Then you ask why I don't live here
Honey, do you have to ask?

Well, I go to pet your monkey
I get a face full of claws
I ask who's in the fireplace
And you tell me Santa Claus
The milkman comes in
He's wearing a derby hat
Then you ask why I don't live here
Honey, how come you have to ask me that?

Well, I asked for something to eat
I'm hungry as a hog
So I get brown rice, seaweed
And a dirty hot dog
I've got a hole
Where my stomach disappeared
Then you ask why I don't live here
Honey, I gotta think you're really weird

Your grandpa's cane
It turns into a sword
Your grandma prays to pictures
That are pasted on a board
Everything inside my pockets
Your uncle steals
Then you ask why I don't live here
Honey, I can't believe that you're for real

Well, there's fistfights in the kitchen
They're enough to make me cry
The mailman comes in
Even he's gotta take a side
Even the butler
He's got something to prove
Then you ask why I don't live here
Honey, how come you don't move?

# Bob Dylan's 115th Dream

I was riding on the Mayflower
When I thought I spied some land
I yelled for Captain Arab
I have yuh understand
Who came running to the deck
Said, "Boys, forget the whale
Look on over yonder
Cut the engines
Change the sail
Haul on the bowline"
We sang that melody
Like all tough sailors do
When they are far away at sea

"I think I'll call it America"
I said as we hit land
I took a deep breath
I fell down, I could not stand
Captain Arab he started
Writing up some deeds
He said, "Let's set up a fort
And start buying the place with beads"
Just then this cop comes down the street
Crazy as a loon
He throw us all in jail
For carryin' harpoons

Ah me I busted out
Don't even ask me how
I went to get some help
I walked by a Guernsey cow
Who directed me down
To the Bowery slums
Where people carried signs around
Saying, "Ban the bums"
I jumped right into line
Sayin', "I hope that I'm not late"
When I realized I hadn't eaten
For five days straight

I went into a restaurant
Lookin' for the cook
I told them I was the editor
Of a famous etiquette book
The waitress he was handsome
He wore a powder blue cape
I ordered some suzette, I said
"Could you please make that crepe"
Just then the whole kitchen exploded
From boilin' fat
Food was flying everywhere
And I left without my hat

Now, I didn't mean to be nosy
But I went into a bank
To get some bail for Arab
And all the boys back in the tank
They asked me for some collateral
And I pulled down my pants
They threw me in the alley
When up comes this girl from France
Who invited me to her house
I went, but she had a friend
Who knocked me out
And robbed my boots
And I was on the street again

Well, I rapped upon a house
With the U.S. flag upon display
I said, "Could you help me out
I got some friends down the way"
The man says, "Get out of here
I'll tear you limb from limb"
I said, "You know they refused Jesus, too"
He said, "You're not Him
Get out of here before I break your bones
I ain't your pop"
I decided to have him arrested
And I went looking for a cop

I ran right outside
And I hopped inside a cab
I went out the other door
This Englishman said, "Fab"
As he saw me leap a hot dog stand
And a chariot that stood
Parked across from a building
Advertising brotherhood
I ran right through the front door
Like a hobo sailor does
But it was just a funeral parlor
And the man asked me who I was

I repeated that my friends
Were all in jail, with a sigh
He gave me his card
He said, "Call me if they die"
I shook his hand and said goodbye
Ran out to the street
When a bowling ball came down the road
And knocked me off my feet
A pay phone was ringing
It just about blew my mind
When I picked it up and said hello
This foot came through the line

Well, by this time I was fed up
At tryin' to make a stab
At bringin' back any help
For my friends and Captain Arab
I decided to flip a coin
Like either heads or tails
Would let me know if I should go
Back to ship or back to jail
So I hocked my sailor suit
And I got a coin to flip
It came up tails
It rhymed with sails
So I made it back to the ship

Well, I got back and took
The parkin' ticket off the mast
I was ripping it to shreds
When this coastguard boat went past
They asked me my name
And I said, "Captain Kidd"
They believed me but
They wanted to know
What exactly that I did
I said for the Pope of Eruke
I was employed
They let me go right away
They were very paranoid

Well, the last I heard of Arab
He was stuck on a whale
That was married to the deputy
Sheriff of the jail
But the funniest thing was
When I was leavin' the bay
I saw three ships a-sailin'
They were all heading my way
I asked the captain what his name was
And how come he didn't drive a truck
He said his name was Columbus
I just said, "Good luck"

# Mr. Tambourine Man

Hey! Mr. Tambourine Man, play a song for me
I'm not sleepy and there is no place I'm going to
Hey! Mr. Tambourine Man, play a song for me
In the jingle jangle morning I'll come followin' you

Though I know that evenin's empire has returned into sand
Vanished from my hand
Left me blindly here to stand but still not sleeping
My weariness amazes me, I'm branded on my feet
I have no one to meet
And the ancient empty street's too dead for dreaming

Hey! Mr. Tambourine Man, play a song for me
I'm not sleepy and there is no place I'm going to
Hey! Mr. Tambourine Man, play a song for me
In the jingle jangle morning I'll come followin' you

Take me on a trip upon your magic swirlin' ship
My senses have been stripped, my hands can't feel to grip
My toes too numb to step
Wait only for my boot heels to be wanderin'
I'm ready to go anywhere, I'm ready for to fade
Into my own parade, cast your dancing spell my way
I promise to go under it

Hey! Mr. Tambourine Man, play a song for me
I'm not sleepy and there is no place I'm going to
Hey! Mr. Tambourine Man, play a song for me
In the jingle jangle morning I'll come followin' you

Though you might hear laughin', spinnin', swingin' madly across the sun
It's not aimed at anyone, it's just escapin' on the run
And but for the sky there are no fences facin'
And if you hear vague traces of skippin' reels of rhyme
To your tambourine in time, it's just a ragged clown behind
I wouldn't pay it any mind
It's just a shadow you're seein' that he's chasing

Hey! Mr. Tambourine Man, play a song for me
I'm not sleepy and there is no place I'm going to
Hey! Mr. Tambourine Man, play a song for me
In the jingle jangle morning I'll come followin' you

Then take me disappearin' through the smoke rings of my mind
Down the foggy ruins of time, far past the frozen leaves
The haunted, frightened trees, out to the windy beach
Far from the twisted reach of crazy sorrow
Yes, to dance beneath the diamond sky with one hand waving free
Silhouetted by the sea, circled by the circus sands
With all memory and fate driven deep beneath the waves
Let me forget about today until tomorrow

Hey! Mr. Tambourine Man, play a song for me
I'm not sleepy and there is no place I'm going to
Hey! Mr. Tambourine Man, play a song for me
In the jingle jangle morning I'll come followin' you

# Gates of Eden

Of war and peace the truth just twists
Its curfew gull just glides
Upon four-legged forest clouds
The cowboy angel rides
With his candle lit into the sun
Though its glow is waxed in black
All except when 'neath the trees of Eden

The lamppost stands with folded arms
Its iron claws attached
To curbs 'neath holes where babies wail
Though it shadows metal badge
All and all can only fall
With a crashing but meaningless blow
No sound ever comes from the Gates of Eden

The savage soldier sticks his head in sand
And then complains
Unto the shoeless hunter who's gone deaf
But still remains
Upon the beach where hound dogs bay
At ships with tattooed sails
Heading for the Gates of Eden

With a time-rusted compass blade
Aladdin and his lamp
Sits with Utopian hermit monks
Sidesaddle on the Golden Calf
And on their promises of paradise
You will not hear a laugh
All except inside the Gates of Eden

Relationships of ownership
They whisper in the wings
To those condemned to act accordingly
And wait for succeeding kings
And I try to harmonize with songs
The lonesome sparrow sings
There are no kings inside the Gates of Eden

The motorcycle black madonna
Two-wheeled gypsy queen
And her silver-studded phantom cause
The gray flannel dwarf to scream
As he weeps to wicked birds of prey
Who pick up on his bread crumb sins
And there are no sins inside the Gates of Eden

The kingdoms of Experience
In the precious wind they rot
While paupers change possessions
Each one wishing for what the other has got
And the princess and the prince
Discuss what's real and what is not
It doesn't matter inside the Gates of Eden

The foreign sun, it squints upon
A bed that is never mine
As friends and other strangers
From their fates try to resign
Leaving men wholly, totally free
To do anything they wish to do but die
And there are no trials inside the Gates of Eden

At dawn my lover comes to me
And tells me of her dreams
With no attempts to shovel the glimpse
Into the ditch of what each one means
At times I think there are no words
But these to tell what's true
And there are no truths outside the Gates of Eden

# It's Alright, Ma (I'm Only Bleeding)

Darkness at the break of noon
Shadows even the silver spoon
The handmade blade, the child's balloon
Eclipses both the sun and moon
To understand you know too soon
There is no sense in trying

Pointed threats, they bluff with scorn
Suicide remarks are torn
From the fool's gold mouthpiece the hollow horn
Plays wasted words, proves to warn
That he not busy being born is busy dying

Temptation's page flies out the door
You follow, find yourself at war
Watch waterfalls of pity roar
You feel to moan but unlike before
You discover that you'd just be one more
Person crying

So don't fear if you hear
A foreign sound to your ear
It's alright, Ma, I'm only sighing

As some warn victory, some downfall
Private reasons great or small
Can be seen in the eyes of those that call
To make all that should be killed to crawl
While others say don't hate nothing at all
Except hatred

Disillusioned words like bullets bark
As human gods aim for their mark
Make everything from toy guns that spark
To flesh-colored Christs that glow in the dark
It's easy to see without looking too far
That not much is really sacred

While preachers preach of evil fates
Teachers teach that knowledge waits
Can lead to hundred-dollar plates
Goodness hides behind its gates
But even the president of the United States
Sometimes must have to stand naked

An' though the rules of the road have been lodged
It's only people's games that you got to dodge
And it's alright, Ma, I can make it

Advertising signs they con
You into thinking you're the one
That can do what's never been done
That can win what's never been won
Meantime life outside goes on
All around you

You lose yourself, you reappear
You suddenly find you got nothing to fear
Alone you stand with nobody near
When a trembling distant voice, unclear
Startles your sleeping ears to hear
That somebody thinks they really found you

A question in your nerves is lit
Yet you know there is no answer fit
To satisfy, insure you not to quit
To keep it in your mind and not forget
That it is not he or she or them or it
That you belong to

Although the masters make the rules
For the wise men and the fools
I got nothing, Ma, to live up to

For them that must obey authority
That they do not respect in any degree
Who despise their jobs, their destinies
Speak jealously of them that are free
Cultivate their flowers to be
Nothing more than something they invest in

While some on principles baptized
To strict party platform ties
Social clubs in drag disguise
Outsiders they can freely criticize
Tell nothing except who to idolize
And then say God bless him

While one who sings with his tongue on fire
Gargles in the rat race choir
Bent out of shape from society's pliers
Cares not to come up any higher
But rather get you down in the hole
That he's in

But I mean no harm nor put fault
On anyone that lives in a vault
But it's alright, Ma, if I can't please him

Old lady judges watch people in pairs
Limited in sex, they dare
To push fake morals, insult and stare
While money doesn't talk, it swears
Obscenity, who really cares
Propaganda, all is phony

While them that defend what they cannot see
With a killer's pride, security
It blows the minds most bitterly
For them that think death's honesty
Won't fall upon them naturally
Life sometimes must get lonely

My eyes collide head-on with stuffed
Graveyards, false gods, I scuff
At pettiness which plays so rough
Walk upside-down inside handcuffs
Kick my legs to crash it off
Say okay, I have had enough
What else can you show me?

And if my thought-dreams could be seen
They'd probably put my head in a guillotine
But it's alright, Ma, it's life, and life only

# It's All Over Now, Baby Blue

You must leave now, take what you need, you think will last
But whatever you wish to keep, you better grab it fast
Yonder stands your orphan with his gun
Crying like a fire in the sun
Look out the saints are comin' through
And it's all over now, Baby Blue

The highway is for gamblers, better use your sense
Take what you have gathered from coincidence
The empty-handed painter from your streets
Is drawing crazy patterns on your sheets
This sky, too, is folding under you
And it's all over now, Baby Blue

All your seasick sailors, they are rowing home
All your reindeer armies, are all going home
The lover who just walked out your door
Has taken all his blankets from the floor
The carpet, too, is moving under you
And it's all over now, Baby Blue

Leave your stepping stones behind, something calls for you
Forget the dead you've left, they will not follow you
The vagabond who's rapping at your door
Is standing in the clothes that you once wore
Strike another match, go start anew
And it's all over now, Baby Blue

# California

(Early version of "Outlaw Blues")

I'm goin' down south
'Neath the borderline
I'm goin' down south
'Neath the borderline
Some fat momma
Kissed my mouth one time

Well, I needed it this morning
Without a shadow of doubt
My suitcase is packed
My clothes are hangin' out

San Francisco's fine
You sure get lots of sun
San Francisco is fine
You sure get lots of sun
But I'm used to four seasons
California's got but one

Well, I got my dark sunglasses
I got for good luck my black tooth
I got my dark sunglasses
And for good luck I got my black tooth
Don't ask me nothin' about nothin'
I just might tell you the truth

# Farewell Angelina

Farewell Angelina
The bells of the crown
Are being stolen by bandits
I must follow the sound
The triangle tingles
And the trumpets play slow
Farewell Angelina
The sky is on fire
And I must go

There's no need for anger
There's no need for blame
There's nothing to prove
Ev'rything's still the same
Just a table standing empty
By the edge of the sea
Farewell Angelina
The sky is trembling
And I must leave

The jacks and the queens
Have forsaken the courtyard
Fifty-two gypsies
Now file past the guards
In the space where the deuce
And the ace once ran wild
Farewell Angelina
The sky is folding
I'll see you in a while

See the cross-eyed pirates sitting
Perched in the sun
Shooting tin cans
With a sawed-off shotgun
And the neighbors they clap
And they cheer with each blast
Farewell Angelina
The sky's changing color
And I must leave fast

King Kong, little elves
On the rooftops they dance
Valentino-type tangos
While the makeup man's hands
Shut the eyes of the dead
Not to embarrass anyone
Farewell Angelina
The sky is embarrassed
And I must be gone

The machine guns are roaring
The puppets heave rocks
The fiends nail time bombs
To the hands of the clocks
Call me any name you like
I will never deny it
Farewell Angelina
The sky is erupting
I must go where it's quiet

# Love Is Just a Four Letter Word

Seems like only yesterday
I left my mind behind
Down in the Gypsy Café
With a friend of a friend of mine
She sat with a baby heavy on her knee
Yet spoke of life most free from slavery
With eyes that showed no trace of misery
A phrase in connection first with she I heard
That love is just a four letter word

Outside a rambling storefront window
Cats meowed to the break of day
Me, I kept my mouth shut, too
To you I had no words to say
My experience was limited and underfed
You were talking while I hid
To the one who was the father of your kid
You probably didn't think I did, but I heard
You say that love is just a four letter word

I said goodbye unnoticed
Pushed towards things in my own games
Drifting in and out of lifetimes
Unmentionable by name
Searching for my double, looking for
Complete evaporation to the core
Though I tried and failed at finding any door
I must have thought that there was nothing more
Absurd than that love is just a four letter word

Though I never knew just what you meant
When you were speaking to your man
I can only think in terms of me
And now I understand
After waking enough times to think I see
The Holy Kiss that's supposed to last eternity
Blow up in smoke, its destiny
Falls on strangers, travels free
Yes, I know now, traps are only set by me
And I do not really need to be
Assured that love is just a four letter word

# Highway 61 Revisited

1. Of war an peace/ the truth does twist/ it's curfew gull jist glides/
upon the fungus forest cloud, ~~the~~ cowboy angel rides
         he lights his candle in the sun
An tho ~~his candle burns the day~~, it's glow is waxed in black
All ecpt when neath the trees of eden ——

                                        it's ~~turns~~ upon ^ claws
2. The lampport stands with folded arms/ ~~pretends to be~~ ^ attached
+ the curbs neath wailing babys — tho it's shadow's metal badge/
All in all, can only fall, with a crashing but meaningless blow
No sound comes from the depths of EDEN ——

3. The SAVAGE SOLDIER sticks his head in sand An then complains
unto the shoeless hunter/who's grown deaf but still remains
upon the beach where hound dogs bay At ships with TATTOED SAILS
heading for the gates of eden ——

4. With his time rusted compass blade, ALLADIN An his LAMP
sits with utopian hermit monks   SIDE SADDLE ON THE GOLDEN CALF
An on their promises of PARADICE, you will not hear a laugh
excpt inside the gates of eden ——

5. The motorcycle black MADONNA/ two wheeled GYPSY queen
An her silver studded phantom cause the grey flannel dwarf t scream
As he weeps + wicked birds of prey, who pick up his bread crumb sins
there are no sins once in the gates of eden ——

                                    (smile)
6. relationships of ~~ownership~~ ownership wait outside the wings
of those ~~that~~ condemned fact accordingly ~~to~~ waiting for ~~each~~ succeeding kings
An I try + harmonize ~~the~~ with songs/ the lonesome sparrow sings
~~For~~ all men are kings inside the gates of eden ——

7. the kingdoms of experience /in the precious wind they rot
while paupers change possessions/each wishing for what the other's got
An the princess ~~in~~ the ~~princess~~ desires what is real An what is not
It doesn't matter inside the gates of eden ——

8. the foreign sun/it rises/on a house that is not MINE
As friends an other strangers from their fates try to resign
Leaving men wholly total free t do anything they wish but die
There's no where + hide inside the gates of eden

9. At dawn my lover comes t me an tells me of her dreams

   At times i ~~think~~ /there are no words, but these + tell
                                    no truths,

# Like a Rolling Stone

Once upon a time you dressed so fine
You threw the bums a dime in your prime, didn't you?
People'd call, say, "Beware doll, you're bound to fall"
You thought they were all kiddin' you
You used to laugh about
Everybody that was hangin' out
Now you don't talk so loud
Now you don't seem so proud
About having to be scrounging for your next meal

How does it feel
How does it feel
To be without a home
Like a complete unknown
Like a rolling stone?

You've gone to the finest school all right, Miss Lonely
But you know you only used to get juiced in it
And nobody has ever taught you how to live on the street
And now you find out you're gonna have to get used to it
You said you'd never compromise
With the mystery tramp, but now you realize
He's not selling any alibis
As you stare into the vacuum of his eyes
And ask him do you want to make a deal?

How does it feel
How does it feel
To be on your own
With no direction home
Like a complete unknown
Like a rolling stone?

You never turned around to see the frowns on the jugglers and the clowns
When they all come down and did tricks for you
You never understood that it ain't no good
You shouldn't let other people get your kicks for you
You used to ride on the chrome horse with your diplomat
Who carried on his shoulder a Siamese cat
Ain't it hard when you discover that
He really wasn't where it's at
After he took from you everything he could steal

How does it feel
How does it feel
To be on your own
With no direction home
Like a complete unknown
Like a rolling stone?

Princess on the steeple and all the pretty people
They're drinkin', thinkin' that they got it made
Exchanging all kinds of precious gifts and things
But you'd better lift your diamond ring, you'd better pawn it babe
You used to be so amused
At Napoleon in rags and the language that he used
Go to him now, he calls you, you can't refuse
When you got nothing, you got nothing to lose
You're invisible now, you got no secrets to conceal

How does it feel
How does it feel
To be on your own
With no direction home
Like a complete unknown
Like a rolling stone?

# Tombstone Blues

The sweet pretty things are in bed now of course
The city fathers they're trying to endorse
The reincarnation of Paul Revere's horse
But the town has no need to be nervous

The ghost of Belle Starr she hands down her wits
To Jezebel the nun she violently knits
A bald wig for Jack the Ripper who sits
At the head of the chamber of commerce

Mama's in the fact'ry
She ain't got no shoes
Daddy's in the alley
He's lookin' for the fuse
I'm in the streets
With the tombstone blues

The hysterical bride in the penny arcade
Screaming she moans, "I've just been made"
Then sends out for the doctor who pulls down the shade
Says, "My advice is to not let the boys in"

Now the medicine man comes and he shuffles inside
He walks with a swagger and he says to the bride
"Stop all this weeping, swallow your pride
You will not die, it's not poison"

Mama's in the fact'ry
She ain't got no shoes
Daddy's in the alley
He's lookin' for the fuse
I'm in the streets
With the tombstone blues

Well, John the Baptist after torturing a thief
Looks up at his hero the Commander-in-Chief
Saying, "Tell me great hero, but please make it brief
Is there a hole for me to get sick in?"

The Commander-in-Chief answers him while chasing a fly
Saying, "Death to all those who would whimper and cry"
And dropping a barbell he points to the sky
Saying, "The sun's not yellow it's chicken"

Mama's in the fact'ry
She ain't got no shoes
Daddy's in the alley
He's lookin' for the fuse
I'm in the streets
With the tombstone blues

The king of the Philistines his soldiers to save
Puts jawbones on their tombstones and flatters their graves
Puts the pied pipers in prison and fattens the slaves
Then sends them out to the jungle

Gypsy Davey with a blowtorch he burns out their camps
With his faithful slave Pedro behind him he tramps
With a fantastic collection of stamps
To win friends and influence his uncle

Mama's in the fact'ry
She ain't got no shoes
Daddy's in the alley
He's lookin' for the fuse
I'm in the streets
With the tombstone blues

The geometry of innocence flesh on the bone
Causes Galileo's math book to get thrown
At Delilah who sits worthlessly alone
But the tears on her cheeks are from laughter

Now I wish I could give Brother Bill his great thrill
I would set him in chains at the top of the hill
Then send out for some pillars and Cecil B. DeMille
He could die happily ever after

Mama's in the fact'ry
She ain't got no shoes
Daddy's in the alley
He's lookin' for the fuse
I'm in the streets
With the tombstone blues

Where Ma Rainey and Beethoven once unwrapped their bedroll
Tuba players now rehearse around the flagpole
And the National Bank at a profit sells road maps for the soul
To the old folks home and the college

Now I wish I could write you a melody so plain
That could hold you dear lady from going insane
That could ease you and cool you and cease the pain
Of your useless and pointless knowledge

Mama's in the fact'ry
She ain't got no shoes
Daddy's in the alley
He's lookin' for the fuse
I'm in the streets
With the tombstone blues

# It Takes a Lot to Laugh, It Takes a Train to Cry

Well, I ride on a mailtrain, baby
Can't buy a thrill
Well, I've been up all night, baby
Leanin' on the windowsill
Well, if I die
On top of the hill
And if I don't make it
You know my baby will

Don't the moon look good, mama
Shinin' through the trees?
Don't the brakeman look good, mama
Flagging down the "Double E"?
Don't the sun look good
Goin' down over the sea?
Don't my gal look fine
When she's comin' after me?

Now the wintertime is coming
The windows are filled with frost
I went to tell everybody
But I could not get across
Well, I wanna be your lover, baby
I don't wanna be your boss
Don't say I never warned you
When your train gets lost

# From a Buick 6

I got this graveyard woman, you know she keeps my kid
But my soulful mama, you know she keeps me hid
She's a junkyard angel and she always gives me bread
Well, if I go down dyin', you know she bound to put a blanket on my bed

Well, when the pipeline gets broken and I'm lost on the river bridge
I'm cracked up on the highway and on the water's edge
She comes down the thruway ready to sew me up with thread
Well, if I go down dyin', you know she bound to put a blanket on my bed

Well, she don't make me nervous, she don't talk too much
She walks like Bo Diddley and she don't need no crutch
She keeps this four-ten all loaded with lead
Well, if I go down dyin', you know she bound to put a blanket on my bed

Well, you know I need a steam shovel mama to keep away the dead
I need a dump truck mama to unload my head
She brings me everything and more, and just like I said
Well, if I go down dyin', you know she bound to put a blanket on my bed

# Ballad of a Thin Man

You walk into the room
With your pencil in your hand
You see somebody naked
And you say, "Who is that man?"
You try so hard
But you don't understand
Just what you'll say
When you get home

Because something is happening here
But you don't know what it is
Do you, Mister Jones?

You raise up your head
And you ask, "Is this where it is?"
And somebody points to you and says
"It's his"
And you say, "What's mine?"
And somebody else says, "Where what is?"
And you say, "Oh my God
Am I here all alone?"

Because something is happening here
But you don't know what it is
Do you, Mister Jones?

You hand in your ticket
And you go watch the geek
Who immediately walks up to you
When he hears you speak
And says, "How does it feel
To be such a freak?"
And you say, "Impossible"
As he hands you a bone

Because something is happening here
But you don't know what it is
Do you, Mister Jones?

You have many contacts
Among the lumberjacks
To get you facts
When someone attacks your imagination
But nobody has any respect
Anyway they already expect you
To just give a check
To tax-deductible charity organizations

You've been with the professors
And they've all liked your looks
With great lawyers you have
Discussed lepers and crooks
You've been through all of
F. Scott Fitzgerald's books
You're very well read
It's well known

Because something is happening here
But you don't know what it is
Do you, Mister Jones?

Well, the sword swallower, he comes up to you
And then he kneels
He crosses himself
And then he clicks his high heels
And without further notice
He asks you how it feels
And he says, "Here is your throat back
Thanks for the loan"

Because something is happening here
But you don't know what it is
Do you, Mister Jones?

Now you see this one-eyed midget
Shouting the word "NOW"
And you say, "For what reason?"
And he says, "How?"
And you say, "What does this mean?"
And he screams back, "You're a cow
Give me some milk
Or else go home"

Because something is happening here
But you don't know what it is
Do you, Mister Jones?

Well, you walk into the room
Like a camel and then you frown
You put your eyes in your pocket
And your nose on the ground
There ought to be a law
Against you comin' around
You should be made
To wear earphones

Because something is happening here
But you don't know what it is
Do you, Mister Jones?

# Queen Jane Approximately

When your mother sends back all your invitations
And your father to your sister he explains
That you're tired of yourself and all of your creations
Won't you come see me, Queen Jane?
Won't you come see me, Queen Jane?

Now when all of the flower ladies want back what they have lent you
And the smell of their roses does not remain
And all of your children start to resent you
Won't you come see me, Queen Jane?
Won't you come see me, Queen Jane?

Now when all the clowns that you have commissioned
Have died in battle or in vain
And you're sick of all this repetition
Won't you come see me, Queen Jane?
Won't you come see me, Queen Jane?

When all of your advisers heave their plastic
At your feet to convince you of your pain
Trying to prove that your conclusions should be more drastic
Won't you come see me, Queen Jane?
Won't you come see me, Queen Jane?

Now when all the bandits that you turned your other cheek to
All lay down their bandanas and complain
And you want somebody you don't have to speak to
Won't you come see me, Queen Jane?
Won't you come see me, Queen Jane?

# Highway 61 Revisited

Oh God said to Abraham, "Kill me a son"
Abe says, "Man, you must be puttin' me on"
God say, "No." Abe say, "What?"
God say, "You can do what you want Abe, but
The next time you see me comin' you better run"
Well Abe says, "Where do you want this killin' done?"
God says, "Out on Highway 61"

Well Georgia Sam he had a bloody nose
Welfare Department they wouldn't give him no clothes
He asked poor Howard where can I go
Howard said there's only one place I know
Sam said tell me quick man I got to run
Ol' Howard just pointed with his gun
And said that way down on Highway 61

Well Mack the Finger said to Louie the King
I got forty red white and blue shoestrings
And a thousand telephones that don't ring
Do you know where I can get rid of these things
And Louie the King said let me think for a minute son
And he said yes I think it can be easily done
Just take everything down to Highway 61

Now the fifth daughter on the twelfth night
Told the first father that things weren't right
My complexion she said is much too white
He said come here and step into the light he says hmm you're right
Let me tell the second mother this has been done
But the second mother was with the seventh son
And they were both out on Highway 61

Now the rovin' gambler he was very bored
He was tryin' to create a next world war
He found a promoter who nearly fell off the floor
He said I never engaged in this kind of thing before
But yes I think it can be very easily done
We'll just put some bleachers out in the sun
And have it on Highway 61

# Just Like Tom Thumb's Blues

When you're lost in the rain in Juarez
And it's Eastertime too
And your gravity fails
And negativity don't pull you through
Don't put on any airs
When you're down on Rue Morgue Avenue
They got some hungry women there
And they really make a mess outa you

Now if you see Saint Annie
Please tell her thanks a lot
I cannot move
My fingers are all in a knot
I don't have the strength
To get up and take another shot
And my best friend, my doctor
Won't even say what it is I've got

Sweet Melinda
The peasants call her the goddess of gloom
She speaks good English
And she invites you up into her room
And you're so kind
And careful not to go to her too soon
And she takes your voice
And leaves you howling at the moon

Up on Housing Project Hill
It's either fortune or fame
You must pick up one or the other
Though neither of them are to be what they claim
If you're lookin' to get silly
You better go back to from where you came
Because the cops don't need you
And man they expect the same

Now all the authorities
They just stand around and boast
How they blackmailed the sergeant-at-arms
Into leaving his post
And picking up Angel who
Just arrived here from the coast
Who looked so fine at first
But left looking just like a ghost

I started out on burgundy
But soon hit the harder stuff
Everybody said they'd stand behind me
When the game got rough
But the joke was on me
There was nobody even there to call my bluff
I'm going back to New York City
I do believe I've had enough

# Desolation Row

They're selling postcards of the hanging
They're painting the passports brown
The beauty parlor is filled with sailors
The circus is in town
Here comes the blind commissioner
They've got him in a trance
One hand is tied to the tight-rope walker
The other is in his pants
And the riot squad they're restless
They need somewhere to go
As Lady and I look out tonight
From Desolation Row

Cinderella, she seems so easy
"It takes one to know one," she smiles
And puts her hands in her back pockets
Bette Davis style
And in comes Romeo, he's moaning
"You Belong to Me I Believe"
And someone says, "You're in the wrong place my friend
You better leave"
And the only sound that's left
After the ambulances go
Is Cinderella sweeping up
On Desolation Row

Now the moon is almost hidden
The stars are beginning to hide
The fortune-telling lady
Has even taken all her things inside
All except for Cain and Abel
And the hunchback of Notre Dame
Everybody is making love
Or else expecting rain
And the Good Samaritan, he's dressing
He's getting ready for the show
He's going to the carnival tonight
On Desolation Row

Now Ophelia, she's 'neath the window
For her I feel so afraid
On her twenty-second birthday
She already is an old maid
To her, death is quite romantic
She wears an iron vest
Her profession's her religion
Her sin is her lifelessness
And though her eyes are fixed upon
Noah's great rainbow
She spends her time peeking
Into Desolation Row

Einstein, disguised as Robin Hood
With his memories in a trunk
Passed this way an hour ago
With his friend, a jealous monk
He looked so immaculately frightful
As he bummed a cigarette
Then he went off sniffing drainpipes
And reciting the alphabet
Now you would not think to look at him
But he was famous long ago
For playing the electric violin
On Desolation Row

Dr. Filth, he keeps his world
Inside of a leather cup
But all his sexless patients
They're trying to blow it up
Now his nurse, some local loser
She's in charge of the cyanide hole
And she also keeps the cards that read
"Have Mercy on His Soul"
They all play on pennywhistles
You can hear them blow
If you lean your head out far enough
From Desolation Row

Across the street they've nailed the curtains
They're getting ready for the feast
The Phantom of the Opera
A perfect image of a priest
They're spoonfeeding Casanova
To get him to feel more assured
Then they'll kill him with self-confidence
After poisoning him with words
And the Phantom's shouting to skinny girls
"Get Outa Here If You Don't Know
Casanova is just being punished for going
To Desolation Row"

Now at midnight all the agents
And the superhuman crew
Come out and round up everyone
That knows more than they do
Then they bring them to the factory
Where the heart-attack machine
Is strapped across their shoulders
And then the kerosene
Is brought down from the castles
By insurance men who go
Check to see that nobody is escaping
To Desolation Row

Praise be to Nero's Neptune
The Titanic sails at dawn
And everybody's shouting
"Which Side Are You On?"
And Ezra Pound and T. S. Eliot
Fighting in the captain's tower
While calypso singers laugh at them
And fishermen hold flowers
Between the windows of the sea
Where lovely mermaids flow
And nobody has to think too much
About Desolation Row

Yes, I received your letter yesterday
(About the time the doorknob broke)
When you asked how I was doing
Was that some kind of joke?
All these people that you mention
Yes, I know them, they're quite lame
I had to rearrange their faces
And give them all another name
Right now I can't read too good
Don't send me no more letters no
Not unless you mail them
From Desolation Row

# Positively 4th Street

You got a lotta nerve
To say you are my friend
When I was down
You just stood there grinning

You got a lotta nerve
To say you got a helping hand to lend
You just want to be on
The side that's winning

You say I let you down
You know it's not like that
If you're so hurt
Why then don't you show it

You say you lost your faith
But that's not where it's at
You had no faith to lose
And you know it

I know the reason
That you talk behind my back
I used to be among the crowd
You're in with

Do you take me for such a fool
To think I'd make contact
With the one who tries to hide
What he don't know to begin with

You see me on the street
You always act surprised
You say, "How are you?" "Good luck"
But you don't mean it

When you know as well as me
You'd rather see me paralyzed
Why don't you just come out once
And scream it

No, I do not feel that good
When I see the heartbreaks you embrace
If I was a master thief
Perhaps I'd rob them

And now I know you're dissatisfied
With your position and your place
Don't you understand
It's not my problem

I wish that for just one time
You could stand inside my shoes
And just for that one moment
I could be you

Yes, I wish that for just one time
You could stand inside my shoes
You'd know what a drag it is
To see you

# Can You Please Crawl Out Your Window?

He sits in your room, his tomb, with a fist full of tacks
Preoccupied with his vengeance
Cursing the dead that can't answer him back
I'm sure that he has no intentions
Of looking your way, unless it's to say
That he needs you to test his inventions

Can you please crawl out your window?
Use your arms and legs it won't ruin you
How can you say he will haunt you?
You can go back to him any time you want to

He looks so truthful, is this how he feels
Trying to peel the moon and expose it
With his businesslike anger and his bloodhounds that kneel
If he needs a third eye he just grows it
He just needs you to talk or to hand him his chalk
Or pick it up after he throws it

Can you please crawl out your window?
Use your arms and legs it won't ruin you
How can you say he will haunt you?
You can go back to him any time you want to

Why does he look so righteous while your face is so changed
Are you frightened of the box you keep him in
While his genocide fools and his friends rearrange
Their religion of the little tin women
That backs up their views but your face is so bruised
Come on out the dark is beginning

Can you please crawl out your window?
Use your arms and legs it won't ruin you
How can you say he will haunt you?
You can go back to him any time you want to

# Sitting on a Barbed-Wire Fence

I paid fifteen million dollars, twelve hundred and seventy-two cents
I paid one thousand two hundred twenty-seven dollars and fifty-five cents
See my hound dog bite a rabbit
And my football's sittin' on a barbed-wire fence

Well, my temperature rises and my feet don't walk so fast
Yes, my temperature rises and my feet don't walk so fast
Well, this Arabian doctor came in, gave me a shot
But wouldn't tell me if what I had would last

Well, this woman I've got, she's filling me with her drive
Yes, this woman I've got, she's thrillin' me with her hive
She's calling me Stan
Or else she calls me Mister Clive

Of course, you're gonna think this song is a riff
I know you're gonna think this song is a cliff
Unless you've been inside a tunnel
And fell down 69, 70 feet over a barbed-wire fence

All night!

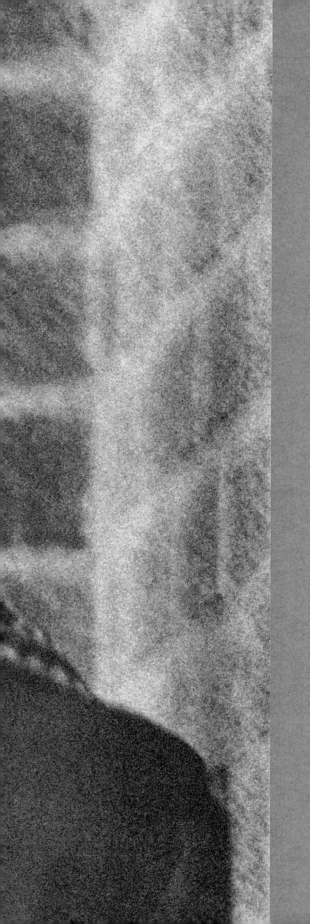

# Blonde on Blonde

Rainy Day Women #12 & 35

Pledging My Time

Visions of Johanna

One of Us Must Know
 (Sooner or Later)

I Want You

Stuck Inside of Mobile
 with the Memphis Blues Again

Leopard-Skin Pill-Box Hat

Just Like a Woman

Most Likely You Go Your Way
 (and I'll Go Mine)

Temporary Like Achilles

Absolutely Sweet Marie

Fourth Time Around

Obviously Five Believers

Sad-Eyed Lady of the Lowlands

*additional lyrics*

I'll Keep It with Mine

I Wanna Be Your Lover

Tell Me, Momma

She's Your Lover Now

2. i got 14 fevers/ i got 5 believers...dressed up like men
tell your mama not to worry/

2. (a) tell your mama & your pappa i'm trying to keep from dying to

3. tell your mama & your pappa that there's nothing wrong with my jugler vein
tell your mama i love her & tell your sister Alice the same

*Lonely Lonely miss*

4. (comes from) (ing) when you sleep on windows & you stay up all nite swallowing rocks

*!making love to / making love to*

5. i shoulda sent her to Hong Kong stead of leaving

# Rainy Day Women #12 & 35

Well, they'll stone ya when you're trying to be so good
They'll stone ya just a-like they said they would
They'll stone ya when you're tryin' to go home
Then they'll stone ya when you're there all alone
But I would not feel so all alone
Everybody must get stoned

Well, they'll stone ya when you're walkin' 'long the street
They'll stone ya when you're tryin' to keep your seat
They'll stone ya when you're walkin' on the floor
They'll stone ya when you're walkin' to the door
But I would not feel so all alone
Everybody must get stoned

They'll stone ya when you're at the breakfast table
They'll stone ya when you are young and able
They'll stone ya when you're tryin' to make a buck
They'll stone ya and then they'll say, "good luck"
Tell ya what, I would not feel so all alone
Everybody must get stoned

Well, they'll stone you and say that it's the end
Then they'll stone you and then they'll come back again
They'll stone you when you're riding in your car
They'll stone you when you're playing your guitar
Yes, but I would not feel so all alone
Everybody must get stoned

Well, they'll stone you when you walk all alone
They'll stone you when you are walking home
They'll stone you and then say you are brave
They'll stone you when you are set down in your grave
But I would not feel so all alone
Everybody must get stoned

# Pledging My Time

Well, early in the mornin'
'Til late at night
I got a poison headache
But I feel all right
I'm pledging my time to you
Hopin' you'll come through, too

Well, the hobo jumped up
He came down natur'lly
After he stole my baby
Then he wanted to steal me
But I'm pledging my time to you
Hopin' you'll come through, too

Won't you come with me, baby?
I'll take you where you wanna go
And if it don't work out
You'll be the first to know
I'm pledging my time to you
Hopin' you'll come through, too

Well, the room is so stuffy
I can hardly breathe
Ev'rybody's gone but me and you
And I can't be the last to leave
I'm pledging my time to you
Hopin' you'll come through, too

Well, they sent for the ambulance
And one was sent
Somebody got lucky
But it was an accident
Now I'm pledging my time to you
Hopin' you'll come through, too

# Visions of Johanna

Ain't it just like the night to play tricks when you're trying to be so quiet?
We sit here stranded, though we're all doin' our best to deny it
And Louise holds a handful of rain, temptin' you to defy it
Lights flicker from the opposite loft
In this room the heat pipes just cough
The country music station plays soft
But there's nothing, really nothing to turn off
Just Louise and her lover so entwined
And these visions of Johanna that conquer my mind

In the empty lot where the ladies play blindman's bluff with the key chain
And the all-night girls they whisper of escapades out on the "D" train
We can hear the night watchman click his flashlight
Ask himself if it's him or them that's really insane
Louise, she's all right, she's just near
She's delicate and seems like the mirror
But she just makes it all too concise and too clear
That Johanna's not here
The ghost of 'lectricity howls in the bones of her face
Where these visions of Johanna have now taken my place

Now, little boy lost, he takes himself so seriously
He brags of his misery, he likes to live dangerously
And when bringing her name up
He speaks of a farewell kiss to me
He's sure got a lotta gall to be so useless and all
Muttering small talk at the wall while I'm in the hall
How can I explain?
Oh, it's so hard to get on
And these visions of Johanna, they kept me up past the dawn

Inside the museums, Infinity goes up on trial
Voices echo this is what salvation must be like after a while
But Mona Lisa musta had the highway blues
You can tell by the way she smiles
See the primitive wallflower freeze
When the jelly-faced women all sneeze
Hear the one with the mustache say, "Jeeze
I can't find my knees"
Oh, jewels and binoculars hang from the head of the mule
But these visions of Johanna, they make it all seem so cruel

---

The peddler now speaks to the countess who's pretending to care for him
Sayin', "Name me someone that's not a parasite and I'll go out and say a prayer for him"
But like Louise always says
"Ya can't look at much, can ya man?"
As she, herself, prepares for him
And Madonna, she still has not showed
We see this empty cage now corrode
Where her cape of the stage once had flowed
The fiddler, he now steps to the road
He writes ev'rything's been returned which was owed
On the back of the fish truck that loads
While my conscience explodes
The harmonicas play the skeleton keys and the rain
And these visions of Johanna are now all that remain

# One of Us Must Know (Sooner or Later)

I didn't mean to treat you so bad
You shouldn't take it so personal
I didn't mean to make you so sad
You just happened to be there, that's all
When I saw you say "goodbye" to your friend and smile
I thought that it was well understood
That you'd be comin' back in a little while
I didn't know that you were sayin' "goodbye" for good

But, sooner or later, one of us must know
You just did what you're supposed to do
Sooner or later, one of us must know
That I really did try to get close to you

I couldn't see what you could show me
Your scarf had kept your mouth well hid
I couldn't see how you could know me
But you said you knew me and I believed you did
When you whispered in my ear
And asked me if I was leavin' with you or her
I didn't realize just what I did hear
I didn't realize how young you were

But, sooner or later, one of us must know
You just did what you're supposed to do
Sooner or later, one of us must know
That I really did try to get close to you

I couldn't see when it started snowin'
Your voice was all that I heard
I couldn't see where we were goin'
But you said you knew an' I took your word
And then you told me later, as I apologized
That you were just kiddin' me, you weren't really from the farm
An' I told you, as you clawed out my eyes
That I never really meant to do you any harm

But, sooner or later, one of us must know
You just did what you're supposed to do
Sooner or later, one of us must know
That I really did try to get close to you

# I Want You

The guilty undertaker sighs
The lonesome organ grinder cries
The silver saxophones say I should refuse you
The cracked bells and washed-out horns
Blow into my face with scorn
But it's not that way
I wasn't born to lose you

I want you, I want you
I want you so bad
Honey, I want you

The drunken politician leaps
Upon the street where mothers weep
And the saviors who are fast asleep, they wait for you
And I wait for them to interrupt
Me drinkin' from my broken cup
And ask me to
Open up the gate for you

I want you, I want you
I want you so bad
Honey, I want you

How all my fathers, they've gone down
True love they've been without it
But all their daughters put me down
'Cause I don't think about it

Well, I return to the Queen of Spades
And talk with my chambermaid
She knows that I'm not afraid to look at her
She is good to me
And there's nothing she doesn't see
She knows where I'd like to be
But it doesn't matter

I want you, I want you
I want you so bad
Honey, I want you

Now your dancing child with his Chinese suit
He spoke to me, I took his flute
No, I wasn't very cute to him, was I?
But I did it, though, because he lied
Because he took you for a ride
And because time was on his side
And because I . . .

I want you, I want you
I want you so bad
Honey, I want you

# Stuck Inside of Mobile with the Memphis Blues Again

Oh, the ragman draws circles
Up and down the block
I'd ask him what the matter was
But I know that he don't talk
And the ladies treat me kindly
And furnish me with tape
But deep inside my heart
I know I can't escape
Oh, Mama, can this really be the end
To be stuck inside of Mobile
With the Memphis blues again

Well, Shakespeare, he's in the alley
With his pointed shoes and his bells
Speaking to some French girl
Who says she knows me well
And I would send a message
To find out if she's talked
But the post office has been stolen
And the mailbox is locked
Oh, Mama, can this really be the end
To be stuck inside of Mobile
With the Memphis blues again

Mona tried to tell me
To stay away from the train line
She said that all the railroad men
Just drink up your blood like wine
An' I said, "Oh, I didn't know that
But then again, there's only one I've met
An' he just smoked my eyelids
An' punched my cigarette"
Oh, Mama, can this really be the end
To be stuck inside of Mobile
With the Memphis blues again

Grandpa died last week
And now he's buried in the rocks
But everybody still talks about
How badly they were shocked
But me, I expected it to happen
I knew he'd lost control
When he built a fire on Main Street
And shot it full of holes
Oh, Mama, can this really be the end
To be stuck inside of Mobile
With the Memphis blues again

Now the senator came down here
Showing ev'ryone his gun
Handing out free tickets
To the wedding of his son
An' me, I nearly got busted
An' wouldn't it be my luck
To get caught without a ticket
And be discovered beneath a truck
Oh, Mama, can this really be the end
To be stuck inside of Mobile
With the Memphis blues again

Now the preacher looked so baffled
When I asked him why he dressed
With twenty pounds of headlines
Stapled to his chest
But he cursed me when I proved it to him
Then I whispered, "Not even you can hide
You see, you're just like me
I hope you're satisfied"
Oh, Mama, can this really be the end
To be stuck inside of Mobile
With the Memphis blues again

Now the rainman gave me two cures
Then he said, "Jump right in"
The one was Texas medicine
The other was just railroad gin
An' like a fool I mixed them
An' it strangled up my mind
An' now people just get uglier
An' I have no sense of time
Oh, Mama, can this really be the end
To be stuck inside of Mobile
With the Memphis blues again

When Ruthie says come see her
In her honky-tonk lagoon
Where I can watch her waltz for free
'Neath her Panamanian moon
An' I say, "Aw come on now
You must know about my debutante"
An' she says, "Your debutante just knows what you need
But I know what you want"
Oh, Mama, can this really be the end
To be stuck inside of Mobile
With the Memphis blues again

Now the bricks lay on Grand Street
Where the neon madmen climb
They all fall there so perfectly
It all seems so well timed
An' here I sit so patiently
Waiting to find out what price
You have to pay to get out of
Going through all these things twice
Oh, Mama, can this really be the end
To be stuck inside of Mobile
With the Memphis blues again

# Leopard-Skin Pill-Box Hat

Well, I see you got your brand new leopard-skin pill-box hat
Yes, I see you got your brand new leopard-skin pill-box hat
Well, you must tell me, baby
How your head feels under somethin' like that
Under your brand new leopard-skin pill-box hat

Well, you look so pretty in it
Honey, can I jump on it sometime?
Yes, I just wanna see
If it's really that expensive kind
You know it balances on your head
Just like a mattress balances
On a bottle of wine
Your brand new leopard-skin pill-box hat

Well, if you wanna see the sun rise
Honey, I know where
We'll go out and see it sometime
We'll both just sit there and stare
Me with my belt
Wrapped around my head
And you just sittin' there
In your brand new leopard-skin pill-box hat

Well, I asked the doctor if I could see you
It's bad for your health, he said
Yes, I disobeyed his orders
I came to see you
But I found him there instead
You know, I don't mind him cheatin' on me
But I sure wish he'd take that off his head
Your brand new leopard-skin pill-box hat

Well, I see you got a new boyfriend
You know, I never seen him before
Well, I saw him
Makin' love to you
You forgot to close the garage door
You might think he loves you for your money
But I know what he really loves you for
It's your brand new leopard-skin pill-box hat

# Just Like a Woman

Nobody feels any pain
Tonight as I stand inside the rain
Ev'rybody knows
That Baby's got new clothes
But lately I see her ribbons and her bows
Have fallen from her curls
She takes just like a woman, yes, she does
She makes love just like a woman, yes, she does
And she aches just like a woman
But she breaks just like a little girl

Queen Mary, she's my friend
Yes, I believe I'll go see her again
Nobody has to guess
That Baby can't be blessed
Till she sees finally that she's like all the rest
With her fog, her amphetamine and her pearls
She takes just like a woman, yes, she does
She makes love just like a woman, yes, she does
And she aches just like a woman
But she breaks just like a little girl

It was raining from the first
And I was dying there of thirst
So I came in here
And your long-time curse hurts
But what's worse
Is this pain in here
I can't stay in here
Ain't it clear that—

I just can't fit
Yes, I believe it's time for us to quit
When we meet again
Introduced as friends
Please don't let on that you knew me when
I was hungry and it was your world
Ah, you fake just like a woman, yes, you do
You make love just like a woman, yes, you do
Then you ache just like a woman
But you break just like a little girl

# Most Likely You Go Your Way (and I'll Go Mine)

You say you love me
And you're thinkin' of me
But you know you could be wrong
You say you told me
That you wanna hold me
But you know you're not that strong
I just can't do what I done before
I just can't beg you anymore
I'm gonna let you pass
And I'll go last
Then time will tell just who fell
And who's been left behind
When you go your way and I go mine

You say you disturb me
And you don't deserve me
But you know sometimes you lie
You say you're shakin'
And you're always achin'
But you know how hard you try
Sometimes it gets so hard to care
It can't be this way ev'rywhere
And I'm gonna let you pass
Yes, and I'll go last
Then time will tell just who fell
And who's been left behind
When you go your way and I go mine

The judge, he holds a grudge
He's gonna call on you
But he's badly built
And he walks on stilts
Watch out he don't fall on you

You say you're sorry
For tellin' stories
That you know I believe are true
You say ya got some
Other kinda lover
And yes, I believe you do
You say my kisses are not like his
But this time I'm not gonna tell you why that is
I'm just gonna let you pass
Yes, and I'll go last
Then time will tell who fell
And who's been left behind
When you go your way and I go mine

# Temporary Like Achilles

Standing on your window, honey
Yes, I've been here before
Feeling so harmless
I'm looking at your second door
How come you don't send me no regards?
You know I want your lovin'
Honey, why are you so hard?

Kneeling 'neath your ceiling
Yes, I guess I'll be here for a while
I'm tryin' to read your portrait, but
I'm helpless, like a rich man's child
How come you send someone out to have me barred?
You know I want your lovin'
Honey, why are you so hard?

Like a poor fool in his prime
Yes, I know you can hear me walk
But is your heart made out of stone, or is it lime
Or is it just solid rock?

Well, I rush into your hallway
Lean against your velvet door
I watch upon your scorpion
Who crawls across your circus floor
Just what do you think you have to guard?
You know I want your lovin'
Honey, but you're so hard

Achilles is in your alleyway
He don't want me here, he does brag
He's pointing to the sky
And he's hungry, like a man in drag
How come you get someone like him to be your guard?
You know I want your lovin'
Honey, but you're so hard

# Absolutely Sweet Marie

Well, your railroad gate, you know I just can't jump it
Sometimes it gets so hard, you see
I'm just sitting here beating on my trumpet
With all these promises you left for me
But where are you tonight, sweet Marie?

Well, I waited for you when I was half sick
Yes, I waited for you when you hated me
Well, I waited for you inside of the frozen traffic
When you knew I had some other place to be
Now, where are you tonight, sweet Marie?

Well, anybody can be just like me, obviously
But then, now again, not too many can be like you, fortunately

Well, six white horses that you did promise
Were fin'lly delivered down to the penitentiary
But to live outside the law, you must be honest
I know you always say that you agree
But where are you tonight, sweet Marie?

Well, I don't know how it happened
But the riverboat captain, he knows my fate
But ev'rybody else, even yourself
They're just gonna have to wait

Well, I got the fever down in my pockets
The Persian drunkard, he follows me
Yes, I can take him to your house but I can't unlock it
You see, you forgot to leave me with the key
Oh, where are you tonight, sweet Marie?

Now, I been in jail when all my mail showed
That a man can't give his address out to bad company
And now I stand here lookin' at your yellow railroad
In the ruins of your balcony
Wond'ring where you are tonight, sweet Marie

# Fourth Time Around

When she said
"Don't waste your words, they're just lies"
I cried she was deaf
And she worked on my face until breaking my eyes
Then said, "What else you got left?"
It was then that I got up to leave
But she said, "Don't forget
Everybody must give something back
For something they get"

I stood there and hummed
I tapped on her drum and asked her how come
And she buttoned her boot
And straightened her suit
Then she said, "Don't get cute"
So I forced my hands in my pockets
And felt with my thumbs
And gallantly handed her
My very last piece of gum

She threw me outside
I stood in the dirt where ev'ryone walked
And after finding I'd
Forgotten my shirt
I went back and knocked
I waited in the hallway, she went to get it
And I tried to make sense
Out of that picture of you in your wheelchair
That leaned up against . . .

Her Jamaican rum
And when she did come, I asked her for some
She said, "No, dear"
I said, "Your words aren't clear
You'd better spit out your gum"
She screamed till her face got so red
Then she fell on the floor
And I covered her up and then
Thought I'd go look through her drawer

And when I was through
I filled up my shoe
And brought it to you
And you, you took me in
You loved me then
You didn't waste time
And I, I never took much
I never asked for your crutch
Now don't ask for mine

# Obviously Five Believers

Early in the mornin'
Early in the mornin'
I'm callin' you to
I'm callin' you to
Please come home
Yes, I guess I could make it without you
If I just didn't feel so all alone

Don't let me down
Don't let me down
I won't let you down
I won't let you down
No I won't
You know I can if you can, honey
But, honey, please don't

I got my black dog barkin'
Black dog barkin'
Yes it is now
Yes it is now
Outside my yard
Yes, I could tell you what he means
If I just didn't have to try so hard

Your mama's workin'
Your mama's moanin'
She's cryin' you know
She's tryin' you know
You better go now
Well, I'd tell you what she wants
But I just don't know how

Fifteen jugglers
Fifteen jugglers
Five believers
Five believers
All dressed like men
Tell yo' mama not to worry because
They're just my friends

Early in the mornin'
Early in the mornin'
I'm callin' you to
I'm callin' you to
Please come home
Yes, I could make it without you
If I just did not feel so all alone

# Sad-Eyed Lady of the Lowlands

With your mercury mouth in the missionary times
And your eyes like smoke and your prayers like rhymes
And your silver cross, and your voice like chimes
Oh, who among them do they think could bury you?
With your pockets well protected at last
And your streetcar visions which you place on the grass
And your flesh like silk, and your face like glass
Who among them do they think could carry you?
Sad-eyed lady of the lowlands
Where the sad-eyed prophet says that no man comes
My warehouse eyes, my Arabian drums
Should I leave them by your gate
Or, sad-eyed lady, should I wait?

With your sheets like metal and your belt like lace
And your deck of cards missing the jack and the ace
And your basement clothes and your hollow face
Who among them can think he could outguess you?
With your silhouette when the sunlight dims
Into your eyes where the moonlight swims
And your matchbook songs and your gypsy hymns
Who among them would try to impress you?
Sad-eyed lady of the lowlands
Where the sad-eyed prophet says that no man comes
My warehouse eyes, my Arabian drums
Should I leave them by your gate
Or, sad-eyed lady, should I wait?

The kings of Tyrus with their convict list
Are waiting in line for their geranium kiss
And you wouldn't know it would happen like this
But who among them really wants just to kiss you?
With your childhood flames on your midnight rug
And your Spanish manners and your mother's drugs
And your cowboy mouth and your curfew plugs
Who among them do you think could resist you?
Sad-eyed lady of the lowlands
Where the sad-eyed prophet says that no man comes
My warehouse eyes, my Arabian drums
Should I leave them by your gate
Or, sad-eyed lady, should I wait?

Oh, the farmers and the businessmen, they all did decide
To show you the dead angels that they used to hide
But why did they pick you to sympathize with their side?
Oh, how could they ever mistake you?
They wished you'd accepted the blame for the farm
But with the sea at your feet and the phony false alarm
And with the child of a hoodlum wrapped up in your arms
How could they ever, ever persuade you?
Sad-eyed lady of the lowlands
Where the sad-eyed prophet says that no man comes
My warehouse eyes, my Arabian drums
Should I leave them by your gate
Or, sad-eyed lady, should I wait?

With your sheet-metal memory of Cannery Row
And your magazine-husband who one day just had to go
And your gentleness now, which you just can't help but show
Who among them do you think would employ you?
Now you stand with your thief, you're on his parole
With your holy medallion which your fingertips fold
And your saintlike face and your ghostlike soul
Oh, who among them do you think could destroy you?
Sad-eyed lady of the lowlands
Where the sad-eyed prophet says that no man comes
My warehouse eyes, my Arabian drums
Should I leave them by your gate
Or, sad-eyed lady, should I wait?

# I'll Keep It with Mine

You will search, babe
At any cost
But how long, babe
Can you search for what's not lost?
Everybody will help you
Some people are very kind
But if I can save you any time
Come on, give it to me
I'll keep it with mine

I can't help it
If you might think I'm odd
If I say I'm not loving you for what you are
But for what you're not
Everybody will help you
Discover what you set out to find
But if I can save you any time
Come on, give it to me
I'll keep it with mine

The train leaves
At half past ten
But it'll be back tomorrow
Same time again
The conductor he's weary
He's still stuck on the line
But if I can save you any time
Come on, give it to me
I'll keep it with mine

# I Wanna Be Your Lover

Well, the rainman comes with his magic wand
And the judge says, "Mona can't have no bond"
And the walls collide, Mona cries
And the rainman leaves in the wolfman's disguise

I wanna be your lover, baby, I wanna be your man
I wanna be your lover, baby
I don't wanna be hers, I wanna be yours

Well, the undertaker in his midnight suit
Says to the masked man, "Ain't you cute!"
Well, the mask man he gets up on the shelf
And he says, "You ain't so bad yourself"

I wanna be your lover, baby, I wanna be your man
I wanna be your lover, baby
I don't wanna be hers, I wanna be yours

Well, jumpin' Judy can't go no higher
She had bullets in her eyes, and they fire
Rasputin he's so dignified
He touched the back of her head an' he died

I wanna be your lover, baby, I wanna be your man
I wanna be your lover, baby
I don't wanna be hers, I wanna be yours

Well, Phaedra with her looking glass
Stretchin' out upon the grass
She gets all messed up and she faints—
That's 'cause she's so obvious and you ain't

I wanna be your lover, baby, I wanna be your man
I wanna be your lover, baby
I don't wanna be hers, I wanna be yours

# Tell Me, Momma

Ol' black Bascom, don't break no mirrors
Cold black water dog, make no tears
You say you love me with what may be love
Don't you remember makin' baby love?
Got your steam drill built and you're lookin' for some kid
To get it to work for you like your nine-pound hammer did
But I know that you know that I know that you show
Something is tearing up your mind

Tell me, momma
Tell me, momma
Tell me, momma, what is it?
What's wrong with you this time?

Hey, John, come and get me some candy goods
Shucks, it sure feels like it's in the woods
Spend some time on your January trips
You got tombstone moose up and your grave-yard whips
If you're anxious to find out when your friendship's gonna end
Come on, baby, I'm your friend!
And I know that you know that I know that you show
Something is tearing up your mind

Tell me, momma
Tell me, momma
Tell me, momma, what is it?
What's wrong with you this time?

Ohh, we bone the editor, can't get read
But his painted sled, instead it's a bed
Yes, I see you on your window ledge
But I can't tell just how far away you are from the edge
And, anyway, you're just gonna make people jump and roar
Watcha wanna go and do that for?
For I know that you know that I know that you know
Something is tearing up your mind

Ah, tell me, momma
Tell me, momma
Tell me, momma, what is it?
What's wrong with you this time?

# She's Your Lover Now

The pawnbroker roared
Also, so, so did the landlord
The scene was so crazy, wasn't it?
Both were so glad
To watch me destroy what I had
Pain sure brings out the best in people, doesn't it?
Why didn't you just leave me if you didn't want to stay?
Why'd you have to treat me so bad?
Did it have to be that way?
Now you stand here expectin' me to remember somethin' you forgot to say
Yes, and you, I see you're still with her, well
That's fine 'cause she's comin' on so strange, can't you tell?
Somebody had better explain
She's got her iron chain
I'd do it, but I, I just can't remember how
You talk to her
She's your lover now

I already assumed
That we're in the felony room
But I ain't a judge, you don't have to be nice to me
But please tell that
To your friend in the cowboy hat
You know he keeps on sayin' ev'rythin' twice to me
You know I was straight with you
You know I've never tried to change you in any way
You know if you didn't want to be with me
That you could . . . didn't have to stay
Now you stand here sayin' you forgive and forget. Honey, what can I say?
Yes, you, you just sit around and ask for ashtrays, can't you reach?
I see you kiss her on the cheek ev'rytime she gives a speech
With her picture books of the pyramid
And her postcards of Billy the Kid (why must everybody bow?)
You better talk to her 'bout it
You're her lover now

Oh, ev'rybody that cares
Is goin' up the castle stairs
But I'm not up in your castle, honey
It's true, I just can't recall
San Francisco at all
I can't even remember El Paso, uh, honey
You never had to be faithful
I didn't want you to grieve
Oh, why was it so hard for you
If you didn't want to be with me, just to leave?
Now you stand here while your finger's goin' up my sleeve
An' you, just what do you do anyway? Ain't there nothin' you can say?
She'll be standin' on the bar soon
With a fish head an' a harpoon
An' a fake beard plastered on her brow
You'd better do somethin' quick
She's your lover now

# John Wesley Harding

John Wesley Harding
As I Went Out One Morning
I Dreamed I Saw St. Augustine
All Along the Watchtower
The Ballad of Frankie Lee
    and Judas Priest
Drifter's Escape
Dear Landlord
I Am a Lonesome Hobo
I Pity the Poor Immigrant
The Wicked Messenger
Down Along the Cove
I'll Be Your Baby Tonight

now all my fathers theyve gone down  hugging one another
& all their daughters put me down cause i say i aint their brother

now all my fathers/ theyve gone down/ true love, they been without it
& all their sons & daughters put me down cause i dont think about it

~~here i stand~~ i stand here
~~hoping~~ hoping, that these frozen ships
~~that are dance~~ madly up & down my lips
wont fall on you

# John Wesley Harding

John Wesley Harding
Was a friend to the poor
He trav'led with a gun in ev'ry hand
All along this countryside
He opened many a door
But he was never known
To hurt an honest man

'Twas down in Chaynee County
A time they talk about
With his lady by his side
He took a stand
And soon the situation there
Was all but straightened out
For he was always known
To lend a helping hand

All across the telegraph
His name it did resound
But no charge held against him
Could they prove
And there was no man around
Who could track or chain him down
He was never known
To make a foolish move

# As I Went Out One Morning

As I went out one morning
To breathe the air around Tom Paine's
I spied the fairest damsel
That ever did walk in chains
I offer'd her my hand
She took me by the arm
I knew that very instant
She meant to do me harm

"Depart from me this moment"
I told her with my voice
Said she, "But I don't wish to"
Said I, "But you have no choice"
"I beg you, sir," she pleaded
From the corners of her mouth
"I will secretly accept you
And together we'll fly south"

Just then Tom Paine, himself
Came running from across the field
Shouting at this lovely girl
And commanding her to yield
And as she was letting go her grip
Up Tom Paine did run
"I'm sorry, sir," he said to me
"I'm sorry for what she's done"

# I Dreamed I Saw St. Augustine

I dreamed I saw St. Augustine
Alive as you or me
Tearing through these quarters
In the utmost misery
With a blanket underneath his arm
And a coat of solid gold
Searching for the very souls
Whom already have been sold

"Arise, arise," he cried so loud
In a voice without restraint
"Come out, ye gifted kings and queens
And hear my sad complaint
No martyr is among ye now
Whom you can call your own
So go on your way accordingly
But know you're not alone"

I dreamed I saw St. Augustine
Alive with fiery breath
And I dreamed I was amongst the ones
That put him out to death
Oh, I awoke in anger
So alone and terrified
I put my fingers against the glass
And bowed my head and cried

# All Along the Watchtower

"There must be some way out of here," said the joker to the thief
"There's too much confusion, I can't get no relief
Businessmen, they drink my wine, plowmen dig my earth
None of them along the line know what any of it is worth"

"No reason to get excited," the thief, he kindly spoke
"There are many here among us who feel that life is but a joke
But you and I, we've been through that, and this is not our fate
So let us not talk falsely now, the hour is getting late"

All along the watchtower, princes kept the view
While all the women came and went, barefoot servants, too

Outside in the distance a wildcat did growl
Two riders were approaching, the wind began to howl

# The Ballad of Frankie Lee and Judas Priest

Well, Frankie Lee and Judas Priest
They were the best of friends
So when Frankie Lee needed money one day
Judas quickly pulled out a roll of tens
And placed them on a footstool
Just above the plotted plain
Sayin', "Take your pick, Frankie Boy
My loss will be your gain"

Well, Frankie Lee, he sat right down
And put his fingers to his chin
But with the cold eyes of Judas on him
His head began to spin
"Would ya please not stare at me like that," he said
"It's just my foolish pride
But sometimes a man must be alone
And this is no place to hide"

Well, Judas, he just winked and said
"All right, I'll leave you here
But you'd better hurry up and choose which of those bills you want
Before they all disappear"
"I'm gonna start my pickin' right now
Just tell me where you'll be"
Judas pointed down the road
And said, "Eternity!"

"Eternity?" said Frankie Lee
With a voice as cold as ice
"That's right," said Judas Priest, "Eternity
Though you might call it 'Paradise'"
"I don't call it anything"
Said Frankie Lee with a smile
"All right," said Judas Priest
"I'll see you after a while"

Well, Frankie Lee, he sat back down
Feelin' low and mean
When just then a passing stranger
Burst upon the scene
Saying, "Are you Frankie Lee, the gambler
Whose father is deceased?
Well, if you are, there's a fellow callin' you down the road
And they say his name is Priest"

"Oh, yes, he is my friend"
Said Frankie Lee in fright
"I do recall him very well
In fact, he just left my sight"
"Yes, that's the one," said the stranger
As quiet as a mouse
"Well, my message is, he's down the road
Stranded in a house"

Well, Frankie Lee, he panicked
He dropped ev'rything and ran
Until he came up to the spot
Where Judas Priest did stand
"What kind of house is this," he said
"Where I have come to roam?"
"It's not a house," said Judas Priest
"It's not a house . . . it's a home"

Well, Frankie Lee, he trembled
He soon lost all control
Over ev'rything which he had made
While the mission bells did toll
He just stood there staring
At that big house as bright as any sun
With four and twenty windows
And a woman's face in ev'ry one

Well, up the stairs ran Frankie Lee
With a soulful, bounding leap
And, foaming at the mouth
He began to make his midnight creep
For sixteen nights and days he raved
But on the seventeenth he burst
Into the arms of Judas Priest
Which is where he died of thirst

No one tried to say a thing
When they took him out in jest
Except, of course, the little neighbor boy
Who carried him to rest
And he just walked along, alone
With his guilt so well concealed
And muttered underneath his breath
"Nothing is revealed"

Well, the moral of the story
The moral of this song
Is simply that one should never be
Where one does not belong
So when you see your neighbor carryin' somethin'
Help him with his load
And don't go mistaking Paradise
For that home across the road

# Drifter's Escape

"Oh, help me in my weakness"
I heard the drifter say
As they carried him from the courtroom
And were taking him away
"My trip hasn't been a pleasant one
And my time it isn't long
And I still do not know
What it was that I've done wrong"

Well, the judge, he cast his robe aside
A tear came to his eye
"You fail to understand," he said
"Why must you even try?"
Outside, the crowd was stirring
You could hear it from the door
Inside, the judge was stepping down
While the jury cried for more

"Oh, stop that cursed jury"
Cried the attendant and the nurse
"The trial was bad enough
But this is ten times worse"
Just then a bolt of lightning
Struck the courthouse out of shape
And while ev'rybody knelt to pray
The drifter did escape

# Dear Landlord

Dear landlord
Please don't put a price on my soul
My burden is heavy
My dreams are beyond control
When that steamboat whistle blows
I'm gonna give you all I got to give
And I do hope you receive it well
Dependin' on the way you feel that you live

Dear landlord
Please heed these words that I speak
I know you've suffered much
But in this you are not so unique
All of us, at times, we might work too hard
To have it too fast and too much
And anyone can fill his life up
With things he can see but he just cannot touch

Dear landlord
Please don't dismiss my case
I'm not about to argue
I'm not about to move to no other place
Now, each of us has his own special gift
And you know this was meant to be true
And if you don't underestimate me
I won't underestimate you

# I Am a Lonesome Hobo

I am a lonesome hobo
Without family or friends
Where another man's life might begin
That's exactly where mine ends
I have tried my hand at bribery
Blackmail and deceit
And I've served time for ev'rything
'Cept beggin' on the street

Well, once I was rather prosperous
There was nothing I did lack
I had fourteen-karat gold in my mouth
And silk upon my back
But I did not trust my brother
I carried him to blame
Which led me to my fatal doom
To wander off in shame

Kind ladies and kind gentlemen
Soon I will be gone
But let me just warn you all
Before I do pass on
Stay free from petty jealousies
Live by no man's code
And hold your judgment for yourself
Lest you wind up on this road

# I Pity the Poor Immigrant

I pity the poor immigrant
Who wishes he would've stayed home
Who uses all his power to do evil
But in the end is always left so alone
That man whom with his fingers cheats
And who lies with ev'ry breath
Who passionately hates his life
And likewise, fears his death

I pity the poor immigrant
Whose strength is spent in vain
Whose heaven is like Ironsides
Whose tears are like rain
Who eats but is not satisfied
Who hears but does not see
Who falls in love with wealth itself
And turns his back on me

I pity the poor immigrant
Who tramples through the mud
Who fills his mouth with laughing
And who builds his town with blood
Whose visions in the final end
Must shatter like the glass
I pity the poor immigrant
When his gladness comes to pass

# The Wicked Messenger

There was a wicked messenger
From Eli he did come
With a mind that multiplied the smallest matter
When questioned who had sent for him
He answered with his thumb
For his tongue it could not speak, but only flatter

He stayed behind the assembly hall
It was there he made his bed
Oftentimes he could be seen returning
Until one day he just appeared
With a note in his hand which read
"The soles of my feet, I swear they're burning"

Oh, the leaves began to fallin'
And the seas began to part
And the people that confronted him were many
And he was told but these few words
Which opened up his heart
"If ye cannot bring good news, then don't bring any"

# Down Along the Cove

Down along the cove
I spied my true love comin' my way
Down along the cove
I spied my true love comin' my way
I say, "Lord, have mercy, mama
It sure is good to see you comin' today"

Down along the cove
I spied my little bundle of joy
Down along the cove
I spied my little bundle of joy
She said, "Lord, have mercy, honey
I'm so glad you're my boy!"

Down along the cove
We walked together hand in hand
Down along the cove
We walked together hand in hand
Ev'rybody watchin' us go by
Knows we're in love, yes, and they understand

# Down Along the Cove

(Alternate Version)

Down along the cove I spied my little bundle of joy
Down along the cove I spied my little bundle of joy
I said, "Lord have mercy, baby
You make me feel just like a baby boy"

Down along the cove a bunch of people are milling around
Down along the cove a bunch of people are milling around
I said, "Lord have mercy, baby, they're gonna knock you when you're up
They're gonna kick you when you're down"

Down along the cove I feel as high as a bird
Down along the cove I feel as high as a bird
I said, "Lord have mercy, baby
How come you never say more than a word?"

Down along the cove I seen the Jacks and the River Queen
Down along the cove I seen the Jacks and the River Queen
I said, "Lord have mercy, baby
Ain't that the biggest boat you ever seen?"

Down along the cove, you can lay all your money down
Down along the cove, you can lay all your money down
I said, "Lord have mercy, baby
Ain't it a shame how they shove you and they push you around?"

Down along the cove, I got my suitcase in my hand
Down along the cove, I got my suitcase in my hand
I said, "Lord have mercy, baby
Ain't you glad that I'm your man?"

# I'll Be Your Baby Tonight

Close your eyes, close the door
You don't have to worry anymore
I'll be your baby tonight

Shut the light, shut the shade
You don't have to be afraid
I'll be your baby tonight

Well, that mockingbird's gonna sail away
We're gonna forget it
That big, fat moon is gonna shine like a spoon
But we're gonna let it
You won't regret it

Kick your shoes off, do not fear
Bring that bottle over here
I'll be your baby tonight

# Nashville Skyline

To Be Alone with You

I Threw It All Away

Peggy Day

Lay, Lady, Lay

One More Night

Tell Me That It Isn't True

Country Pie

Tonight I'll Be Staying Here with You

*additional lyrics*

Wanted Man

1. Throw my ticket out the window
Throw my suitcase out there too
Throw my troubles out The door -
I don't need them anymore
Cause tonight I'm staying here with you

# To Be Alone with You

To be alone with you
Just you and me
Now won't you tell me true
Ain't that the way it oughta be?
To hold each other tight
The whole night through
Ev'rything is always right
When I'm alone with you

To be alone with you
At the close of the day
With only you in view
While evening slips away
It only goes to show
That while life's pleasures be few
The only one I know
Is when I'm alone with you

They say that nighttime is the right time
To be with the one you love
Too many thoughts get in the way in the day
But you're always what I'm thinkin' of
I wish the night were here
Bringin' me all of your charms
When only you are near
To hold me in your arms

I'll always thank the Lord
When my working day's through
I get my sweet reward
To be alone with you

# I Threw It All Away

I once held her in my arms
She said she would always stay
But I was cruel
I treated her like a fool
I threw it all away

Once I had mountains in the palm of my hand
And rivers that ran through ev'ry day
I must have been mad
I never knew what I had
Until I threw it all away

Love is all there is, it makes the world go 'round
Love and only love, it can't be denied
No matter what you think about it
You just won't be able to do without it
Take a tip from one who's tried

So if you find someone that gives you all of her love
Take it to your heart, don't let it stray
For one thing that's certain
You will surely be a-hurtin'
If you throw it all away

# Peggy Day

Peggy Day stole my poor heart away
By golly, what more can I say
Love to spend the night with Peggy Day

Peggy night makes my future look so bright
Man, that girl is out of sight
Love to spend the day with Peggy night

Well, you know that even before I learned her name
You know I loved her just the same
An' I tell 'em all, wherever I may go
Just so they'll know, that she's my little lady
And I love her so

Peggy Day stole my poor heart away
Turned my skies to blue from gray
Love to spend the night with Peggy Day

Peggy Day stole my poor heart away
By golly, what more can I say
Love to spend the night with Peggy Day
Love to spend the night with Peggy Day

# Lay, Lady, Lay

Lay, lady, lay, lay across my big brass bed
Lay, lady, lay, lay across my big brass bed
Whatever colors you have in your mind
I'll show them to you and you'll see them shine

Lay, lady, lay, lay across my big brass bed
Stay, lady, stay, stay with your man awhile
Until the break of day, let me see you make him smile
His clothes are dirty but his hands are clean
And you're the best thing that he's ever seen

Stay, lady, stay, stay with your man awhile
Why wait any longer for the world to begin
You can have your cake and eat it too
Why wait any longer for the one you love
When he's standing in front of you

Lay, lady, lay, lay across my big brass bed
Stay, lady, stay, stay while the night is still ahead
I long to see you in the morning light
I long to reach for you in the night
Stay, lady, stay, stay while the night is still ahead

# One More Night

One more night, the stars are in sight
But tonight I'm as lonesome as can be
Oh, the moon is shinin' bright
Lighting ev'rything in sight
But tonight no light will shine on me

Oh, it's shameful and it's sad I lost the only pal I had
I just could not be what she wanted me to be
I will turn my head up high
To that dark and rolling sky
For tonight no light will shine on me

I was so mistaken when I thought that she'd be true
I had no idea what a woman in love would do!

One more night, I will wait for the light
While the wind blows high above the tree
Oh, I miss my darling so
I didn't mean to see her go
But tonight no light will shine on me

One more night, the moon is shinin' bright
And the wind blows high above the tree
Oh, I miss that woman so
I didn't mean to see her go
But tonight no light will shine on me

# Tell Me That It Isn't True

I have heard rumors all over town
They say that you're planning to put me down
All I would like you to do
Is tell me that it isn't true

They say that you've been seen with some other man
That he's tall, dark and handsome, and you're holding his hand
Darlin', I'm a-countin' on you
Tell me that it isn't true

To know that some other man is holdin' you tight
It hurts me all over, it doesn't seem right

All of those awful things that I have heard
I don't want to believe them, all I want is your word
So darlin', you better come through
Tell me that it isn't true

All of those awful things that I have heard
I don't want to believe them, all I want is your word
So darlin', I'm countin' on you
Tell me that it isn't true

# Country Pie

Just like old Saxophone Joe
When he's got the hogshead up on his toe
Oh me, oh my
Love that country pie

Listen to the fiddler play
When he's playin' 'til the break of day
Oh me, oh my
Love that country pie

Raspberry, strawberry, lemon and lime
What do I care?
Blueberry, apple, cherry, pumpkin and plum
Call me for dinner, honey, I'll be there

Saddle me up my big white goose
Tie me on 'er and turn her loose
Oh me, oh my
Love that country pie

I don't need much and that ain't no lie
Ain't runnin' any race
Give to me my country pie
I won't throw it up in anybody's face

Shake me up that old peach tree
Little Jack Horner's got nothin' on me
Oh me, oh my
Love that country pie

# Tonight I'll Be Staying Here with You

Throw my ticket out the window
Throw my suitcase out there, too
Throw my troubles out the door
I don't need them anymore
'Cause tonight I'll be staying here with you

I should have left this town this morning
But it was more than I could do
Oh, your love comes on so strong
And I've waited all day long
For tonight when I'll be staying here with you

Is it really any wonder
The love that a stranger might receive
You cast your spell and I went under
I find it so difficult to leave

I can hear that whistle blowin'
I see that stationmaster, too
If there's a poor boy on the street
Then let him have my seat
'Cause tonight I'll be staying here with you

Throw my ticket out the window
Throw my suitcase out there, too
Throw my troubles out the door
I don't need them anymore
'Cause tonight I'll be staying here with you

# Wanted Man

Wanted man in California, wanted man in Buffalo
Wanted man in Kansas City, wanted man in Ohio
Wanted man in Mississippi, wanted man in old Cheyenne
Wherever you might look tonight, you might see this wanted man

I might be in Colorado or Georgia by the sea
Working for some man who may not know at all who I might be
If you ever see me comin' and if you know who I am
Don't you breathe it to nobody 'cause you know I'm on the lam

Wanted man by Lucy Watson, wanted man by Jeannie Brown
Wanted man by Nellie Johnson, wanted man in this next town
But I've had all that I've wanted of a lot of things I had
And a lot more than I needed of some things that turned out bad

I got sidetracked in El Paso, stopped to get myself a map
Went the wrong way into Juarez with Juanita on my lap
Then I went to sleep in Shreveport, woke up in Abilene
Wonderin' why the hell I'm wanted at some town halfway between

Wanted man in Albuquerque, wanted man in Syracuse
Wanted man in Tallahassee, wanted man in Baton Rouge
There's somebody set to grab me anywhere that I might be
And wherever you might look tonight, you might get a glimpse of me

Wanted man in California, wanted man in Buffalo
Wanted man in Kansas City, wanted man in Ohio
Wanted man in Mississippi, wanted man in old Cheyenne
Wherever you might look tonight, you might see this wanted man

# Self Portrait

Living the Blues
Minstrel Boy

Now

there + I am waiting / to find out the price
you got to pay to get out of ~~going~~ going thru everything twice

Asking some little french girl with his pointed shoes + bell
if she knows me very well

Oh Mama / this could be the end
(John) in Mobile with —
stuck in

# Living the Blues

Since you've been gone
I've been walking around
With my head bowed down to my shoes
I've been living the blues
Ev'ry night without you

I don't have to go far
To know where you are
Strangers all give me the news
I've been living the blues
Ev'ry night without you

I think that it's best
I soon get some rest
And forget my pride
But I can't deny
This feeling that I
Carry for you deep down inside

If you see me this way
You'd come back and you'd stay
Oh, how could you refuse
I've been living the blues
Ev'ry night without you

# Minstrel Boy

Who's gonna throw that minstrel boy a coin?
Who's gonna let it roll?
Who's gonna throw that minstrel boy a coin?
Who's gonna let it down easy to save his soul?

Oh, Lucky's been drivin' a long, long time
And now he's stuck on top of the hill
With twelve forward gears, it's been a long hard climb
And with all of them ladies, though, he's lonely still

Who's gonna throw that minstrel boy a coin?
Who's gonna let it roll?
Who's gonna throw that minstrel boy a coin?
Who's gonna let it down easy to save his soul?

Well, he deep in number and heavy in toil
Mighty Mockingbird, he still has such a heavy load
Beneath his bound'ries, what more can I tell
With all of his trav'lin', but I'm still on that road

Who's gonna throw that minstrel boy a coin?
Who's gonna let it roll?
Who's gonna throw that minstrel boy a coin?
Who's gonna let it down easy to save his soul?

# New Morning

BIRD ON THE HORIZON, SITTING ON A FENCE
He's singing his song for me at his own expence
And I'm just like that Bird
oh singing just for you
I hope that you can hear
HEAR ME singing thru these tears

# If Not for You

If not for you
Babe, I couldn't find the door
Couldn't even see the floor
I'd be sad and blue
If not for you

If not for you
Babe, I'd lay awake all night
Wait for the mornin' light
To shine in through
But it would not be new
If not for you

If not for you
My sky would fall
Rain would gather too
Without your love I'd be nowhere at all
I'd be lost if not for you
And you know it's true

If not for you
My sky would fall
Rain would gather too
Without your love I'd be nowhere at all
Oh! what would I do
If not for you

If not for you
Winter would have no spring
Couldn't hear the robin sing
I just wouldn't have a clue
Anyway it wouldn't ring true
If not for you

# Day of the Locusts

Oh, the benches were stained with tears and perspiration
The birdies were flying from tree to tree
There was little to say, there was no conversation
As I stepped to the stage to pick up my degree
And the locusts sang off in the distance
Yeah, the locusts sang such a sweet melody
Oh, the locusts sang off in the distance
Yeah, the locusts sang and they were singing for me

I glanced into the chamber where the judges were talking
Darkness was everywhere, it smelled like a tomb
I was ready to leave, I was already walkin'
But the next time I looked there was light in the room
And the locusts sang, yeah, it give me a chill
Oh, the locusts sang such a sweet melody
Oh, the locusts sang their high whining trill
Yeah, the locusts sang and they were singing for me

Outside of the gates the trucks were unloadin'
The weather was hot, a-nearly 90 degrees
The man standin' next to me, his head was exploding
Well, I was prayin' the pieces wouldn't fall on me
Yeah, the locusts sang off in the distance
Yeah, the locusts sang such a sweet melody
Oh, the locusts sang off in the distance
And the locusts sang and they were singing for me

I put down my robe, picked up my diploma
Took hold of my sweetheart and away we did drive
Straight for the hills, the black hills of Dakota
Sure was glad to get out of there alive
And the locusts sang, well, it give me a chill
Yeah, the locusts sang such a sweet melody
And the locusts sang with a high whinin' trill
Yeah, the locusts sang and they was singing for me
Singing for me, well, singing for me

# Time Passes Slowly

Time passes slowly up here in the mountains
We sit beside bridges and walk beside fountains
Catch the wild fishes that float through the stream
Time passes slowly when you're lost in a dream

Once I had a sweetheart, she was fine and good-lookin'
We sat in her kitchen while her mama was cookin'
Stared out the window to the stars high above
Time passes slowly when you're searchin' for love

Ain't no reason to go in a wagon to town
Ain't no reason to go to the fair
Ain't no reason to go up, ain't no reason to go down
Ain't no reason to go anywhere

Time passes slowly up here in the daylight
We stare straight ahead and try so hard to stay right
Like the red rose of summer that blooms in the day
Time passes slowly and fades away

# Went to See the Gypsy

Went to see the gypsy
Stayin' in a big hotel
He smiled when he saw me coming
And he said, "Well, well, well"
His room was dark and crowded
Lights were low and dim
"How are you?" he said to me
I said it back to him

I went down to the lobby
To make a small call out
A pretty dancing girl was there
And she began to shout
"Go on back to see the gypsy
He can move you from the rear
Drive you from your fear
Bring you through the mirror
He did it in Las Vegas
And he can do it here"

Outside the lights were shining
On the river of tears
I watched them from the distance
With music in my ears

I went back to see the gypsy
It was nearly early dawn
The gypsy's door was open wide
But the gypsy was gone
And that pretty dancing girl
She could not be found
So I watched that sun come rising
From that little Minnesota town

# Winterlude

Winterlude, Winterlude, oh darlin'
Winterlude by the road tonight
Tonight there will be no quarrelin'
Ev'rything is gonna be all right
Oh, I see by the angel beside me
That love has a reason to shine
You're the one I adore, come over here and give me more
Then Winterlude, this dude thinks you're fine

Winterlude, Winterlude, my little apple
Winterlude by the corn in the field
Winterlude, let's go down to the chapel
Then come back and cook up a meal
Well, come out when the skating rink glistens
By the sun, near the old crossroads sign
The snow is so cold, but our love can be bold
Winterlude, don't be rude, please be mine

Winterlude, Winterlude, my little daisy
Winterlude by the telephone wire
Winterlude, it's makin' me lazy
Come on, sit by the logs in the fire
The moonlight reflects from the window
Where the snowflakes, they cover the sand
Come out tonight, ev'rything will be tight
Winterlude, this dude thinks you're grand

# If Dogs Run Free

If dogs run free, then why not we
Across the swooping plain?
My ears hear a symphony
Of two mules, trains and rain
The best is always yet to come
That's what they explain to me
Just do your thing, you'll be king
If dogs run free

If dogs run free, why not me
Across the swamp of time?
My mind weaves a symphony
And tapestry of rhyme
Oh, winds which rush my tale to thee
So it may flow and be
To each his own, it's all unknown
If dogs run free

If dogs run free, then what must be
Must be, and that is all
True love can make a blade of grass
Stand up straight and tall
In harmony with the cosmic sea
True love needs no company
It can cure the soul, it can make it whole
If dogs run free

# New Morning

Can't you hear that rooster crowin'?
Rabbit runnin' down across the road
Underneath the bridge where the water flowed through
So happy just to see you smile
Underneath the sky of blue
On this new morning, new morning
On this new morning with you

Can't you hear that motor turnin'?
Automobile comin' into style
Comin' down the road for a country mile or two
So happy just to see you smile
Underneath the sky of blue
On this new morning, new morning
On this new morning with you

The night passed away so quickly
It always does when you're with me

Can't you feel that sun a-shinin'?
Groundhog runnin' by the country stream
This must be the day that all of my dreams come true
So happy just to be alive
Underneath the sky of blue
On this new morning, new morning
On this new morning with you

So happy just to be alive
Underneath the sky of blue
On this new morning, new morning
On this new morning with you
New morning . . .

# Sign on the Window

Sign on the window says "Lonely"
Sign on the door said "No Company Allowed"
Sign on the street says "Y' Don't Own Me"
Sign on the porch says "Three's A Crowd"
Sign on the porch says "Three's A Crowd"

Her and her boyfriend went to California
Her and her boyfriend done changed their tune
My best friend said, "Now didn' I warn ya
Brighton girls are like the moon
Brighton girls are like the moon"

Looks like a-nothing but rain . . .
Sure gonna be wet tonight on Main Street . . .
Hope that it don't sleet

Build me a cabin in Utah
Marry me a wife, catch rainbow trout
Have a bunch of kids who call me "Pa"
That must be what it's all about
That must be what it's all about

# One More Weekend

Slippin' and slidin' like a weasel on the run
I'm lookin' good to see you, yeah, and we can have some fun
One more weekend, one more weekend with you
One more weekend, one more weekend'll do

Come on down to my ship, honey, ride on deck
We'll fly over the ocean just like you suspect
One more weekend, one more weekend with you
One more weekend, one more weekend'll do

We'll fly the night away
Hang out the whole next day
Things will be okay
You wait and see
We'll go someplace unknown
Leave all the children home
Honey, why not go alone
Just you and me

Comin' and goin' like a rabbit in the wood
I'm happy just to see you, yeah, lookin' so good
One more weekend, one more weekend with you
One more weekend, one more weekend'll do (yes, you will!)

Like a needle in a haystack, I'm gonna find you yet
You're the sweetest gone mama that this boy's ever gonna get
One more weekend, one more weekend with you
One more weekend, one more weekend'll do

# The Man in Me

The man in me will do nearly any task
And as for compensation, there's little he would ask
Take a woman like you
To get through to the man in me

Storm clouds are raging all around my door
I think to myself I might not take it anymore
Take a woman like your kind
To find the man in me

But, oh, what a wonderful feeling
Just to know that you are near
Sets my heart a-reeling
From my toes up to my ears

The man in me will hide sometimes to keep from bein' seen
But that's just because he doesn't want to turn into some machine
Took a woman like you
To get through to the man in me

# Three Angels

Three angels up above the street
Each one playing a horn
Dressed in green robes with wings that stick out
They've been there since Christmas morn
The wildest cat from Montana passes by in a flash
Then a lady in a bright orange dress
One U-Haul trailer, a truck with no wheels
The Tenth Avenue bus going west
The dogs and pigeons fly up and they flutter around
A man with a badge skips by
Three fellas crawlin' on their way back to work
Nobody stops to ask why
The bakery truck stops outside of that fence
Where the angels stand high on their poles
The driver peeks out, trying to find one face
In this concrete world full of souls
The angels play on their horns all day
The whole earth in progression seems to pass by
But does anyone hear the music they play
Does anyone even try?

# Father of Night

Father of night, Father of day
Father, who taketh the darkness away
Father, who teacheth the bird to fly
Builder of rainbows up in the sky
Father of loneliness and pain
Father of love and Father of rain

Father of day, Father of night
Father of black, Father of white
Father, who build the mountain so high
Who shapeth the cloud up in the sky
Father of time, Father of dreams
Father, who turneth the rivers and streams

Father of grain, Father of wheat
Father of cold and Father of heat
Father of air and Father of trees
Who dwells in our hearts and our memories
Father of minutes, Father of days
Father of whom we most solemnly praise

# I'd Have You Any Time

(with George Harrison)

Let me in here, I know I've been here
Let me into your heart
Let me know you, let me show you
Let me roll it to you
All I have is yours
All you see is mine
And I'm glad to have you in my arms
I'd have you any time

Let me say it, let me play it
Let me lay it on you
Let me know you, let me show you
Let me grow it on you
All I have is yours
All you see is mine
And I'm glad to have you in my arms
I'd have you any time

Let me in here, I know I've been here
Let me into your heart
Let me know you, let me show you
Let me roll it to you
All I have is yours
All you see is mine
And I'm glad to have you in my arms
I'd have you any time

# Watching the River Flow

What's the matter with me
I don't have much to say
Daylight sneakin' through the window
And I'm still in this all-night café
Walkin' to and fro beneath the moon
Out to where the trucks are rollin' slow
To sit down on this bank of sand
And watch the river flow

Wish I was back in the city
Instead of this old bank of sand
With the sun beating down over the chimney tops
And the one I love so close at hand
If I had wings and I could fly
I know where I would go
But right now I'll just sit here so contentedly
And watch the river flow

People disagreeing on all just about everything, yeah
Makes you stop and all wonder why
Why only yesterday I saw somebody on the street
Who just couldn't help but cry
Oh, this ol' river keeps on rollin', though
No matter what gets in the way and which way the wind does blow
And as long as it does I'll just sit here
And watch the river flow

People disagreeing everywhere you look
Makes you wanna stop and read a book
Why only yesterday I saw somebody on the street
That was really shook
But this ol' river keeps on rollin', though
No matter what gets in the way and which way the wind does blow
And as long as it does I'll just sit here
And watch the river flow

Watch the river flow
Watchin' the river flow
Watchin' the river flow
But I'll sit down on this bank of sand
And watch the river flow

# When I Paint My Masterpiece

Oh, the streets of Rome are filled with rubble
Ancient footprints are everywhere
You can almost think that you're seein' double
On a cold, dark night on the Spanish Stairs
Got to hurry on back to my hotel room
Where I've got me a date with Botticelli's niece
She promised that she'd be right there with me
When I paint my masterpiece

Oh, the hours I've spent inside the Coliseum
Dodging lions and wastin' time
Oh, those mighty kings of the jungle, I could hardly stand to see 'em
Yes, it sure has been a long, hard climb
Train wheels runnin' through the back of my memory
When I ran on the hilltop following a pack of wild geese
Someday, everything is gonna be smooth like a rhapsody
When I paint my masterpiece

Sailin' round the world in a dirty gondola
Oh, to be back in the land of Coca-Cola!

I left Rome and landed in Brussels
On a plane ride so bumpy that I almost cried
Clergymen in uniform and young girls pullin' muscles
Everyone was there to greet me when I stepped inside
Newspapermen eating candy
Had to be held down by big police
Someday, everything is gonna be diff'rent
When I paint my masterpiece

# Wallflower

Wallflower, wallflower
Won't you dance with me?
I'm sad and lonely too
Wallflower, wallflower
Won't you dance with me?
I'm fallin' in love with you

Just like you I'm wondrin' what I'm doin' here
Just like you I'm wondrin' what's goin' on

Wallflower, wallflower
Won't you dance with me?
The night will soon be gone

I have seen you standing in the smoky haze
And I know that you're gonna be mine one of these days
Mine alone

Wallflower, wallflower
Take a chance on me
Please let me ride you home

# George Jackson

I woke up this mornin'
There were tears in my bed
They killed a man I really loved
Shot him through the head
Lord, Lord
They cut George Jackson down
Lord, Lord
They laid him in the ground

Sent him off to prison
For a seventy-dollar robbery
Closed the door behind him
And they threw away the key
Lord, Lord
They cut George Jackson down
Lord, Lord
They laid him in the ground

He wouldn't take shit from no one
He wouldn't bow down or kneel
Authorities, they hated him
Because he was just too real
Lord, Lord
They cut George Jackson down
Lord, Lord
They laid him in the ground

Prison guards, they cursed him
As they watched him from above
But they were frightened of his power
They were scared of his love
Lord, Lord
So they cut George Jackson down
Lord, Lord
They laid him in the ground

Sometimes I think this whole world
Is one big prison yard
Some of us are prisoners
The rest of us are guards
Lord, Lord
They cut George Jackson down
Lord, Lord
They laid him in the ground

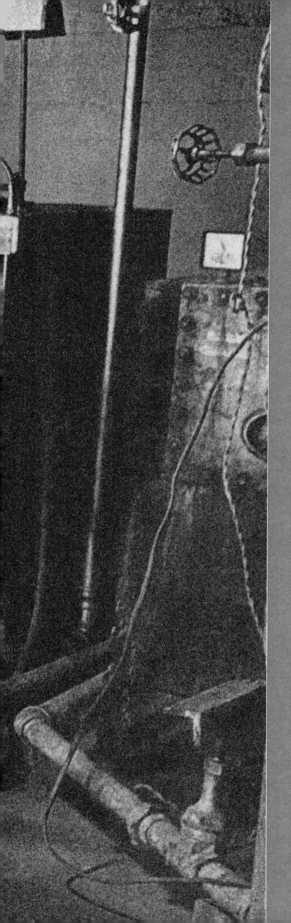

# The Basement Tapes

Odds and Ends
Million Dollar Bash
Goin' to Acapulco
Lo and Behold!
Clothes Line Saga
Apple Suckling Tree
Please, Mrs. Henry
Tears of Rage
Too Much of Nothing
Yea! Heavy and a Bottle of Bread
Down in the Flood
Tiny Montgomery
You Ain't Goin' Nowhere
Don't Ya Tell Henry
Nothing Was Delivered
Open the Door, Homer
Long-Distance Operator
This Wheel's on Fire

*additional lyrics*

Sign on the Cross
Quinn the Eskimo
  (The Mighty Quinn)
I Shall Be Released

Get Your Rocks Off!
Silent Weekend
Santa Fe

like a poor fool in his prime/trying to read your portrait
you can hear me talk

   is your heart made of stone/
                              or solid rock?


got fourteen fevers and five believers all dressed up ~~fifteen~~ so fine
   tell your mama and poppa not to worry cause theyre <u>friends</u> of mine

_dressed up like men_

THE
BASEMEN
TAPES

# Odds and Ends

I plan it all and I take my place
You break your promise all over the place
You promised to love me, but what do I see
Just you comin' and spillin' juice over me
Odds and ends, odds and ends
Lost time is not found again

Now, you take your file and you bend my head
I never can remember anything that you said
You promised to love me, but what do I know
You're always spillin' juice on me like you got someplace to go
Odds and ends, odds and ends
Lost time is not found again

Now, I've had enough, my box is clean
You know what I'm sayin' and you know what I mean
From now on you'd best get on someone else
While you're doin' it, keep that juice to yourself
Odds and ends, odds and ends
Lost time is not found again

# Million Dollar Bash

Well, that big dumb blonde
With her wheel in the gorge
And Turtle, that friend of theirs
With his checks all forged
And his cheeks in a chunk
With his cheese in the cash
They're all gonna be there
At that million dollar bash
Ooh, baby, ooh-ee
Ooh, baby, ooh-ee
It's that million dollar bash

Ev'rybody from right now
To over there and back
The louder they come
The harder they crack
Come now, sweet cream
Don't forget to flash
We're all gonna meet
At that million dollar bash
Ooh, baby, ooh-ee
Ooh, baby, ooh-ee
It's that million dollar bash

Well, I took my counselor
Out to the barn
Silly Nelly was there
She told him a yarn
Then along came Jones
Emptied the trash
Ev'rybody went down
To that million dollar bash
Ooh, baby, ooh-ee
Ooh, baby, ooh-ee
It's that million dollar bash

Well, I'm hittin' it too hard
My stones won't take
I get up in the mornin'
But it's too early to wake
First it's hello, goodbye
Then push and then crash
But we're all gonna make it
At that million dollar bash
Ooh, baby, ooh-ee
Ooh, baby, ooh-ee
It's that million dollar bash

Well, I looked at my watch
I looked at my wrist
Punched myself in the face
With my fist
I took my potatoes
Down to be mashed
Then I made it over
To that million dollar bash
Ooh, baby, ooh-ee
Ooh, baby, ooh-ee
It's that million dollar bash

# Goin' to Acapulco

I'm going down to Rose Marie's
She never does me wrong
She puts it to me plain as day
And gives it to me for a song

It's a wicked life but what the hell
The stars ain't falling down
I'm standing outside the Taj Mahal
I don't see no one around

Goin' to Acapulco—goin' on the run
Goin' down to see fat gut—goin' to have some fun
Yeah—goin' to have some fun

Now, whenever I get up
And I ain't got what I see
I just make it down to Rose Marie's
'Bout a quarter after three

There are worse ways of getting there
And I ain't complainin' none
If the clouds don't drop and the train don't stop
I'm bound to meet the sun

Goin' to Acapulco—goin' on the run
Goin' down to see fat gut—goin' to have some fun
Yeah—goin' to have some fun

Now, if someone offers me a joke
I just say no thanks
I try to tell it like it is
And keep away from pranks

Well, sometime you know when the well breaks down
I just go pump on it some
Rose Marie, she likes to go to big places
And just set there waitin' for me to come

Goin' to Acapulco—goin' on the run
Goin' down to see fat gut—goin' to have some fun
Yeah—goin' to have some fun

# Lo and Behold!

I pulled out for San Anton'
I never felt so good
My woman said she'd meet me there
And of course, I knew she would
The coachman, he hit me for my hook
And he asked me my name
I give it to him right away
Then I hung my head in shame
Lo and behold! Lo and behold!
Lookin' for my lo and behold
Get me outa here, my dear man!

I come into Pittsburgh
At six-thirty flat
I found myself a vacant seat
An' I put down my hat
"What's the matter, Molly, dear
What's the matter with your mound?"
"What's it to ya, Moby Dick?
This is chicken town!"
Lo and behold! Lo and behold!
Lookin' for my lo and behold
Get me outa here, my dear man!

I bought my girl
A herd of moose
One she could call her own
Well, she came out the very next day
To see where they had flown
I'm goin' down to Tennessee
Get me a truck 'r somethin'
Gonna save my money and rip it up!
Lo and behold! Lo and behold!
Lookin' for my lo and behold
Get me outa here, my dear man!

Now, I come in on a Ferris wheel
An' boys, I sure was slick
I come in like a ton of bricks
Laid a few tricks on 'em
Goin' back to Pittsburgh
Count up to thirty
Round that horn and ride that herd
Gonna thread up!
Lo and behold! Lo and behold!
Lookin' for my lo and behold
Get me outa here, my dear man!

# Clothes Line Saga

After a while we took in the clothes
Nobody said very much
Just some old wild shirts and a couple pairs of pants
Which nobody really wanted to touch
Mama come in and picked up a book
An' Papa asked her what it was
Someone else asked, "What do you care?"
Papa said, "Well, just because"
Then they started to take back their clothes
Hang 'em on the line
It was January the thirtieth
And everybody was feelin' fine

The next day everybody got up
Seein' if the clothes were dry
The dogs were barking, a neighbor passed
Mama, of course, she said, "Hi!"
"Have you heard the news?" he said, with a grin
"The Vice-President's gone mad!"
"Where?" "Downtown." "When?" "Last night"
"Hmm, say, that's too bad!"
"Well, there's nothin' we can do about it," said the neighbor
"It's just somethin' we're gonna have to forget"
"Yes, I guess so," said Ma
Then she asked me if the clothes was still wet

I reached up, touched my shirt
And the neighbor said, "Are those clothes yours?"
I said, "Some of 'em, not all of 'em"
He said, "Ya always help out around here with the chores?"
I said, "Sometime, not all the time"
Then my neighbor, he blew his nose
Just as Papa yelled outside
"Mama wants you t' come back in the house and bring them clothes"
Well, I just do what I'm told
So, I did it, of course
I went back in the house and Mama met me
And then I shut all the doors

# Apple Suckling Tree

Old man sailin' in a dinghy boat
Down there
Old man down is baitin' a hook
On there
Gonna pull man down on a suckling hook
Gonna pull man into the suckling brook
Oh yeah!

Now, he's underneath that apple suckling tree
Oh yeah!
Under that apple suckling tree
Oh yeah!
That's underneath that tree
There's gonna be just you and me
Underneath that apple suckling tree
Oh yeah!

I push him back and I stand in line
Oh yeah!
Then I hush my Sadie and stand in line
Oh yeah!
Then I hush my Sadie and stand in line
I get on board in two-eyed time
Oh yeah!

Under that apple suckling tree
Oh yeah!
Under that apple suckling tree
Oh yeah!
Underneath that tree
There's just gonna be you and me
Underneath that apple suckling tree
Oh yeah!

Now, who's on the table, who's to tell me?
Oh yeah!
Who's on the table, who's to tell me?
Oh yeah!
Who should I tell, oh, who should I tell?
The forty-nine of you like bats out of hell
Oh underneath that old apple suckling tree

# Please, Mrs. Henry

Well, I've already had two beers
I'm ready for the broom
Please, Missus Henry, won't you
Take me to my room?
I'm a good ol' boy
But I've been sniffin' too many eggs
Talkin' to too many people
Drinkin' too many kegs
Please, Missus Henry, Missus Henry, please!
Please, Missus Henry, Missus Henry, please!
I'm down on my knees
An' I ain't got a dime

Well, I'm groanin' in a hallway
Pretty soon I'll be mad
Please, Missus Henry, won't you
Take me to your dad?
I can drink like a fish
I can crawl like a snake
I can bite like a turkey
I can slam like a drake
Please, Missus Henry, Missus Henry, please!
Please, Missus Henry, Missus Henry, please!
I'm down on my knees
An' I ain't got a dime

Now, don't crowd me, lady
Or I'll fill up your shoe
I'm a sweet bourbon daddy
An' tonight I am blue
I'm a thousand years old
And I'm a generous bomb
I'm T-boned and punctured
But I'm known to be calm
Please, Missus Henry, Missus Henry, please!
Please, Missus Henry, Missus Henry, please!
I'm down on my knees
An' I ain't got a dime

Now, I'm startin' to drain
My stool's gonna squeak
If I walk too much farther
My crane's gonna leak
Look, Missus Henry
There's only so much I can do
Why don't you look my way
An' pump me a few?
Please, Missus Henry, Missus Henry, please!
Please, Missus Henry, Missus Henry, please!
I'm down on my knees
An' I ain't got a dime

# Tears of Rage

(with Richard Manuel)


We carried you in our arms
On Independence Day
And now you'd throw us all aside
And put us on our way
Oh what dear daughter 'neath the sun
Would treat a father so
To wait upon him hand and foot
And always tell him, "No"?
Tears of rage, tears of grief
Why must I always be the thief?
Come to me now, you know
We're so alone
And life is brief

We pointed out the way to go
And scratched your name in sand
Though you just thought it was nothing more
Than a place for you to stand
Now, I want you to know that while we watched
You discover there was no one true
Most ev'rybody really thought
It was a childish thing to do
Tears of rage, tears of grief
Must I always be the thief?
Come to me now, you know
We're so low
And life is brief

It was all very painless
When you went out to receive
All that false instruction
Which we never could believe
And now the heart is filled with gold
As if it was a purse
But, oh, what kind of love is this
Which goes from bad to worse?
Tears of rage, tears of grief
Must I always be the thief?
Come to me now, you know
We're so low
And life is brief

# Too Much of Nothing

Now, too much of nothing
Can make a man feel ill at ease
One man's temper might rise
While another man's temper might freeze
In the day of confession
We cannot mock a soul
Oh, when there's too much of nothing
No one has control

Say hello to Valerie
Say hello to Vivian
Send them all my salary
On the waters of oblivion

Too much of nothing
Can make a man abuse a king
He can walk the streets and boast like most
But he wouldn't know a thing
Now, it's all been done before
It's all been written in the book
But when there's too much of nothing
Nobody should look

Say hello to Valerie
Say hello to Vivian
Send them all my salary
On the waters of oblivion

Too much of nothing
Can turn a man into a liar
It can cause one man to sleep on nails
And another man to eat fire
Ev'rybody's doin' somethin'
I heard it in a dream
But when there's too much of nothing
It just makes a fella mean

Say hello to Valerie
Say hello to Vivian
Send them all my salary
On the waters of oblivion

# Yea! Heavy and a Bottle of Bread

Well, the comic book and me, just us, we caught the bus
The poor little chauffeur, though, she was back in bed
On the very next day, with a nose full of pus
Yea! Heavy and a bottle of bread
Yea! Heavy and a bottle of bread
Yea! Heavy and a bottle of bread

It's a one-track town, just brown, and a breeze, too
Pack up the meat, sweet, we're headin' out
For Wichita in a pile of fruit
Get the loot, don't be slow, we're gonna catch a trout
Get the loot, don't be slow, we're gonna catch a trout
Get the loot, don't be slow, we're gonna catch a trout

Now, pull that drummer out from behind that bottle
Bring me my pipe, we're gonna shake it
Slap that drummer with a pie that smells
Take me down to California, baby
Take me down to California, baby
Take me down to California, baby

Yes, the comic book and me, just us, we caught the bus
The poor little chauffeur, though, she was back in bed
On the very next day, with a nose full of pus
Yea! Heavy and a bottle of bread
Yea! Heavy and a bottle of bread
Yea! Heavy and a bottle of bread

# Down in the Flood

Crash on the levee, mama
Water's gonna overflow
Swamp's gonna rise
No boat's gonna row
Now, you can train on down
To Williams Point
You can bust your feet
You can rock this joint
But oh mama, ain't you gonna miss your best friend now?
You're gonna have to find yourself
Another best friend, somehow

Now, don't you try an' move me
You're just gonna lose
There's a crash on the levee
And, mama, you've been refused
Well, it's sugar for sugar
And salt for salt
If you go down in the flood
It's gonna be your own fault
Oh mama, ain't you gonna miss your best friend now?
You're gonna have to find yourself
Another best friend, somehow

Well, that high tide's risin'
Mama, don't you let me down
Pack up your suitcase
Mama, don't you make a sound
Now, it's king for king
Queen for queen
It's gonna be the meanest flood
That anybody's seen
Oh mama, ain't you gonna miss your best friend now?
Yes, you're gonna have to find yourself
Another best friend, somehow

# Tiny Montgomery

Well you can tell ev'rybody
Down in ol' Frisco
Tell 'em
Tiny Montgomery says hello

Now ev'ry boy and girl's
Gonna get their bang
'Cause Tiny Montgomery's
Gonna shake that thing
Tell ev'rybody
Down in ol' Frisco
That Tiny Montgomery's comin'
Down to say hello

Skinny Moo and
Half-track Frank
They're gonna both be gettin'
Outa the tank
One bird book
And a buzzard and a crow
Tell 'em all
That Tiny's gonna say hello

Scratch your dad
Do that bird
Suck that pig
And bring it on home
Pick that drip
And bake that dough
Tell 'em all
That Tiny says hello

Now he's king of the drunks
An' he squeezes, too
Watch out, Lester
Take it, Lou
Join the monks
The C.I.O.
Tell 'em all
That Tiny Montgomery says hello

Now grease that pig
And sing praise
Go on out
And gas that dog
Trick on in
Honk that stink
Take it on down
And watch it grow
Play it low
And pick it up
Take it on in
In a plucking cup
Three-legged man
And a hot-lipped hoe
Tell 'em all
Montgomery says hello

Well you can tell ev'rybody
Down in ol' Frisco
Tell 'em all
Montgomery says hello

# You Ain't Goin' Nowhere

Clouds so swift
Rain won't lift
Gate won't close
Railings froze
Get your mind off wintertime
You ain't goin' nowhere
Whoo-ee! Ride me high
Tomorrow's the day
My bride's gonna come
Oh, oh, are we gonna fly
Down in the easy chair!

I don't care
How many letters they sent
Morning came and morning went
Pick up your money
And pack up your tent
You ain't goin' nowhere
Whoo-ee! Ride me high
Tomorrow's the day
My bride's gonna come
Oh, oh, are we gonna fly
Down in the easy chair!

Buy me a flute
And a gun that shoots
Tailgates and substitutes
Strap yourself
To the tree with roots
You ain't goin' nowhere
Whoo-ee! Ride me high
Tomorrow's the day
My bride's gonna come
Oh, oh, are we gonna fly
Down in the easy chair!

Genghis Khan
He could not keep
All his kings
Supplied with sleep
We'll climb that hill no matter how steep
When we get up to it
Whoo-ee! Ride me high
Tomorrow's the day
My bride's gonna come
Oh, oh, are we gonna fly
Down in the easy chair!

# Don't Ya Tell Henry

Don't ya tell Henry
Apple's got your fly

I went down to the river on a Saturday morn
A-lookin' around just to see who's born
I found a little chicken down on his knees
I went up and yelled to him, "Please, please, please!"
He said, "Don't ya tell Henry
Don't ya tell Henry
Don't ya tell Henry
Apple's got your fly"

I went down to the corner at a-half past ten
I's lookin' around, I wouldn't say when
I looked down low, I looked above
And who did I see but the one I love
She said, "Don't ya tell Henry
Don't ya tell Henry
Don't ya tell Henry
Apple's got your fly"

Now, I went down to the beanery at half past twelve
A-lookin' around just to see myself
I spotted a horse and a donkey, too
I looked for a cow and I saw me a few
They said, "Don't ya tell Henry
Don't ya tell Henry
Don't ya tell Henry
Apple's got your fly"

Now, I went down to the pumphouse the other night
A-lookin' around, it was outa sight
I looked high and low for that big ol' tree
I did go upstairs but I didn't see nobody but me
I said, "Don't ya tell Henry
Don't ya tell Henry
Don't ya tell Henry
Apple's got your fly"

# Nothing Was Delivered

Nothing was delivered
And I tell this truth to you
Not out of spite or anger
But simply because it's true
Now, I hope you won't object to this
Giving back all of what you owe
The fewer words you have to waste on this
The sooner you can go

Nothing is better, nothing is best
Take heed of this and get plenty of rest

Nothing was delivered
But I can't say I sympathize
With what your fate is going to be
Yes, for telling all those lies
Now you must provide some answers
For what you sell has not been received
And the sooner you come up with them
The sooner you can leave

Nothing is better, nothing is best
Take heed of this and get plenty rest

(Now you know)
Nothing was delivered
And it's up to you to say
Just what you had in mind
When you made ev'rybody pay
No, nothing was delivered
Yes, 'n' someone must explain
That as long as it takes to do this
Then that's how long that you'll remain

Nothing is better, nothing is best
Take heed of this and get plenty rest

# Open the Door, Homer

Now, there's a certain thing
That I learned from Jim
That he'd always make sure I'd understand
And that is that there's a certain way
That a man must swim
If he expects to live off
Of the fat of the land
Open the door, Homer
I've heard it said before
Open the door, Homer
I've heard it said before
But I ain't gonna hear it said no more

Now, there's a certain thing
That I learned from my friend, Mouse
A fella who always blushes
And that is that ev'ryone
Must always flush out his house
If he don't expect to be
Goin' 'round housing flushes
Open the door, Homer
I've heard it said before
Open the door, Homer
I've heard it said before
But I ain't gonna hear it said no more

"Take care of all your memories"
Said my friend, Mick
"For you cannot relive them
And remember when you're out there
Tryin' to heal the sick
That you must always
First forgive them"
Open the door, Homer
I've heard it said before
Open the door, Homer
I've heard it said before
But I ain't gonna hear it said no more

# Long-Distance Operator

Long-distance operator
Place this call, it's not for fun
Long-distance operator
Please, place this call, you know it's not for fun
I gotta get a message to my baby
You know, she's not just anyone

There are thousands in the phone booth
Thousands at the gate
There are thousands in the phone booth
Thousands at the gate
Ev'rybody wants to make a long-distance call
But you know they're just gonna have to wait

If a call comes from Louisiana
Please, let it ride
If a call comes from Louisiana
Please, let it ride
This phone booth's on fire
It's getting hot inside

Ev'rybody wants to be my friend
But nobody wants to get higher
Ev'rybody wants to be my friend
But nobody wants to get higher
Long-distance operator
I believe I'm stranglin' on this telephone wire

# This Wheel's on Fire

(with Rick Danko)

If your mem'ry serves you well
We were goin' to meet again and wait
So I'm goin' to unpack all my things
And sit before it gets too late
No man alive will come to you
With another tale to tell
But you know that we shall meet again
If your mem'ry serves you well
This wheel's on fire
Rolling down the road
Best notify my next of kin
This wheel shall explode!

If your mem'ry serves you well
I was goin' to confiscate your lace
And wrap it up in a sailor's knot
And hide it in your case
If I knew for sure that it was yours . . .
But it was oh so hard to tell
But you knew that we would meet again
If your mem'ry serves you well
This wheel's on fire
Rolling down the road
Best notify my next of kin
This wheel shall explode!

If your mem'ry serves you well
You'll remember you're the one
That called on me to call on them
To get you your favors done
And after ev'ry plan had failed
And there was nothing more to tell
You knew that we would meet again
If your mem'ry served you well
This wheel's on fire
Rolling down the road
Best notify my next of kin
This wheel shall explode!

# Sign on the Cross

Now, I try, oh for so awf'ly long
And I just try to be
And now, oh it's a gold mine
But it's so fine
Yes, but I know in my head
That we're all so misled
And it's that ol' sign on the cross
That worries me

Now, when I was just a bawlin' child
I saw what I wanted to be
And it's all for the sake
Of that picture I should see
But I was lost on the moon
As I heard that front door slam
And that old sign on the cross
Still worries me

Well, it's that old sign on the cross
Well, it's that old key to the kingdom
Well, it's that old sign on the cross
Like you used to be
But, when I hold my head so high
As I see my ol' friends go by
And it's still that sign on the cross
That worries me

Well, it seem to be the sign on the cross. Ev'ry day,
ev'ry night, see the sign on the cross just layin' up
on top of the hill. Yes, we thought it might have
disappeared long ago, but I'm here to tell you, friends,
that I'm afraid it's lyin' there still. Yes, just a
little time is all you need, you might say, but I don't
know 'bout that any more, because the bird is here and
you might want to enter it, but, of course, the door might
be closed. But I just would like to tell you one time,
if I don't see you again, that the thing is, that the sign
on the cross is the thing you might need the most.

Yes, the sign on the cross
Is just a sign on the cross
Well, there is some on every chisel
And there is some in the championship, too
Oh, when your, when your days are numbered
And your nights are long
You might think you're weak
But I mean to say you're strong
Yes you are, if that sign on the cross
If it begins to worry you
Well, that's all right because sing a song
And all your troubles will pass right on through

# Quinn the Eskimo (The Mighty Quinn)

Ev'rybody's building the big ships and the boats
Some are building monuments
Others, jotting down notes
Ev'rybody's in despair
Ev'ry girl and boy
But when Quinn the Eskimo gets here
Ev'rybody's gonna jump for joy
Come all without, come all within
You'll not see nothing like the mighty Quinn

I like to do just like the rest, I like my sugar sweet
But guarding fumes and making haste
It ain't my cup of meat
Ev'rybody's 'neath the trees
Feeding pigeons on a limb
But when Quinn the Eskimo gets here
All the pigeons gonna run to him
Come all without, come all within
You'll not see nothing like the mighty Quinn

A cat's meow and a cow's moo, I can recite 'em all
Just tell me where it hurts yuh, honey
And I'll tell you who to call
Nobody can get no sleep
There's someone on ev'ryone's toes
But when Quinn the Eskimo gets here
Ev'rybody's gonna wanna doze
Come all without, come all within
You'll not see nothing like the mighty Quinn

# I Shall Be Released

They say ev'rything can be replaced
Yet ev'ry distance is not near
So I remember ev'ry face
Of ev'ry man who put me here
I see my light come shining
From the west unto the east
Any day now, any day now
I shall be released

They say ev'ry man needs protection
They say ev'ry man must fall
Yet I swear I see my reflection
Some place so high above this wall
I see my light come shining
From the west unto the east
Any day now, any day now
I shall be released

Standing next to me in this lonely crowd
Is a man who swears he's not to blame
All day long I hear him shout so loud
Crying out that he was framed
I see my light come shining
From the west unto the east
Any day now, any day now
I shall be released

# Get Your Rocks Off!

You know, there's two ol' maids layin' in the bed
One picked herself up an' the other one, she said:
"Get your rocks off!
Get your rocks off! (Get 'em off!)
Get your rocks off! (Get 'em off!)
Get your rocks off-a me! (Get 'em off!)"

Well, you know, there late one night up on Blueberry Hill
One man turned to the other man and said, with a blood-curdlin' chill, he said:
"Get your rocks off! (Get 'em off!)
Get your rocks off! (Get 'em off!)
Get your rocks off! (Get 'em off!)
Get your rocks off-a me! (Get 'em off!)"

Well, you know, we was layin' down around Mink Muscle Creek
One man said to the other man, he began to speak, he said:
"Get your rocks off! (Get 'em off!)
Get your rocks off! (Get 'em off!)
Get your rocks off! (Get 'em off!)
Get your rocks off-a me! (Get 'em off!)"

Well, you know, we was cruisin' down the highway in a Greyhound bus
All kinds-a children in the side road, they was hollerin' at us, sayin':
"Get your rocks off! (Get 'em off!)
Get your rocks off! (Get 'em off!)
Get your rocks off! (Get 'em off!)
Get your rocks off-a me!"

# Silent Weekend

Silent weekend
My baby she gave it to me
Silent weekend
My baby she gave it to me
She's actin' tough and hardy
She says it ain't my party
And she's leavin' me in misery

Silent weekend
My baby she took me by surprise
Silent weekend
My baby she took me by surprise
She's rockin' and a-reelin'
Head up to ceiling
An' swinging with some other guys

Silent weekend
Oh Lord, I wish Monday would come
Silent weekend
Oh Lord, I sure wish Monday would come
She's uppity, she's rollin'
She's in the groove, she's strolling
Over to the jukebox playin' deaf and dumb

Well, I done a whole lotta thinkin' 'bout a whole lot of cheatin'
And I, maybe I did some just to please
But I just walloped a lotta pizza after makin' our peace
Puts ya down on bended knees

Silent weekend
Man alive, I'm burnin' up on my brain
Silent weekend
Man alive, I'm burnin' up on my brain
She knows when I'm just teasin'
But it's not likely in the season
To open up a passenger train

# Santa Fe

Santa Fe, dear, dear, dear, dear, dear Santa Fe
My woman needs it ev'ryday
She promised this a-lad she'd stay
She's rollin' up a lotta bread to toss away

She's in Santa Fe, dear, dear, dear, dear, dear Santa Fe
Now she's opened up an old maid's home
She's proud, but she needs to roam
She's gonna write herself a roadside poem about Santa Fe

Santa Fe, dear, dear, dear, dear, dear Santa Fe
Since I'm never gonna cease to roam
I'm never, ever far from home
But I'll build a geodesic dome and sail away

Don't feel bad, no, no, no, no, don't feel bad
It's the best food I've ever had
Makes me feel so glad
That she's cooking in a homemade pad
She never caught a cold so bad when I'm away

Santa Fe, dear, dear, dear, dear, dear, dear Santa Fe
My shrimp boat's in the bay
I won't have my nature this way
And I'm leanin' on the wheel each day to drift away from

Santa Fe, dear, dear, dear, dear, dear Santa Fe
My sister looks good at home
She's lickin' on an ice cream cone
She's packin' her big white comb
What does it weigh?

# Pat Garrett & Billy the Kid

Billy
Knockin' on Heaven's Door

① Climbed upon the bell tower to gaze around at the terrain ②
I couldn't find you anywhere, you were gone like
a northern train

# Billy

There's guns across the river aimin' at ya
Lawman on your trail, he'd like to catch ya
Bounty hunters, too, they'd like to get ya
Billy, they don't like you to be so free

Campin' out all night on the berenda
Dealin' cards 'til dawn in the hacienda
Up to Boot Hill they'd like to send ya
Billy, don't you turn your back on me

Playin' around with some sweet señorita
Into her dark hallway she will lead ya
In some lonesome shadows she will greet ya
Billy, you're so far away from home

There's eyes behind the mirrors in empty places
Bullet holes and scars between the spaces
There's always one more notch and ten more paces
Billy, and you're walkin' all alone

They say that Pat Garrett's got your number
So sleep with one eye open when you slumber
Every little sound just might be thunder
Thunder from the barrel of his gun

Guitars will play your grand finale
Down in some Tularosa alley
Maybe in the Rio Pecos valley
Billy, you're so far away from home

There's always some new stranger sneakin' glances
Some trigger-happy fool willin' to take chances
And some old whore from San Pedro to make advances
Advances on your spirit and your soul

The businessmen from Taos want you to go down
They've hired Pat Garrett to force a showdown
Billy, don't it make ya feel so low-down
To be shot down by the man who was your friend?

Hang on to your woman if you got one
Remember in El Paso, once, you shot one
She may have been a whore, but she was a hot one
Billy, you been runnin' for so long

Guitars will play your grand finale
Down in some Tularosa alley
Maybe in the Rio Pecos valley
Billy, you're so far away from home

# Knockin' on Heaven's Door

Mama, take this badge off of me
I can't use it anymore
It's gettin' dark, too dark for me to see
I feel like I'm knockin' on heaven's door

Knock, knock, knockin' on heaven's door
Knock, knock, knockin' on heaven's door
Knock, knock, knockin' on heaven's door
Knock, knock, knockin' on heaven's door

Mama, put my guns in the ground
I can't shoot them anymore
That long black cloud is comin' down
I feel like I'm knockin' on heaven's door

Knock, knock, knockin' on heaven's door
Knock, knock, knockin' on heaven's door
Knock, knock, knockin' on heaven's door
Knock, knock, knockin' on heaven's door

# Planet Waves

Too soon
  an time behind

[with

early ~~an~~ one foggy mornin
upon the phantom sea I spied
tim finnigan's ship ~~to a statue drifted~~ a statue standing
~~from west to the lonesome tide~~
L in ~~the~~ shadows of the lonesome tide

~~[~~

~~[~~

eyes ~~that was~~ ~~blazing~~ wet
with ice box
        laughter, like blowing sleet
~~ice storm~~ ~~that~~ charged past
the open doorway
slammed the side of my head
an said

"you are hungry."
    (maybe)
"aint cha baby?"
but ~~that day I couldn't~~
    see past
    my own
        nose —
an such starving
times....
        indeed we
~~we all either~~
~~+~~ are all gobbling then—

CAST-IRON
SONGS
♥
TORCH
BALLAD

# On a Night Like This

On a night like this
So glad you came around
Hold on to me so tight
And heat up some coffee grounds
We got much to talk about
And much to reminisce
It sure is right
On a night like this

On a night like this
So glad you've come to stay
Hold on to me, pretty miss
Say you'll never go away to stray
Run your fingers down my spine
Bring me a touch of bliss
It sure feels right
On a night like this

On a night like this
I can't get any sleep
The air is so cold outside
And the snow's so deep
Build a fire, throw on logs
And listen to it hiss
And let it burn, burn, burn, burn
On a night like this

Put your body next to mine
And keep me company
There is plenty a-room for all
So please don't elbow me

Let the four winds blow
Around this old cabin door
If I'm not too far off
I think we did this once before
There's more frost on the window glass
With each new tender kiss
But it sure feels right
On a night like this

# Going, Going, Gone

I've just reached a place
Where the willow don't bend
There's not much more to be said
It's the top of the end
I'm going
I'm going
I'm gone

I'm closin' the book
On the pages and the text
And I don't really care
What happens next
I'm just going
I'm going
I'm gone

I been hangin' on threads
I been playin' it straight
Now, I've just got to cut loose
Before it gets late
So I'm going
I'm going
I'm gone

Grandma said, "Boy, go and follow your heart
And you'll be fine at the end of the line
All that's gold isn't meant to shine
Don't you and your one true love ever part"

I been walkin' the road
I been livin' on the edge
Now, I've just got to go
Before I get to the ledge
So I'm going
I'm just going
I'm gone

# Tough Mama

Tough Mama, meat shakin' on your bones
I'm gonna go down to the river and get some stones
Sister's on the highway with that steel-drivin' crew
Papa's in the big house, his workin' days are through
Tough Mama, can I blow a little smoke on you?

Dark Lady, won't you move it on over and make some room?
Rollin' steady, sweepin' through the country like a broom
Put your arms around me, like a circle 'round the sun
You got a pocket full of money but you can't help me none
Shady Lady, the dress that you are wearin' weighs a ton

Angel Baby, born of a blinding light and a changing wind
Drive me crazy, you know who you are and where you've been
Starin' at the ceiling, standin' on the chair
Big fires blazing, ashes in the air
Angel Baby, I wonder what you done back there

I'm crestfallen—the world of illusion is at my door
I hear you callin', same old thing like it was before
Crawlin' through the meadow like a lion in the den
Headin' for the round-up at the rainbow's end
Tough Mama, let's get on the road again

# Hazel

Hazel, dirty-blonde hair
I wouldn't be ashamed to be seen with you anywhere
You got something I want plenty of
Ooh, a little touch of your love

Hazel, stardust in your eye
You're goin' somewhere and so am I
I'd give you the sky high above
Ooh, for a little touch of your love

Oh no, I don't need any reminder
To know how much I really care
But it's just making me blinder and blinder
Because I'm up on a hill and still you're not there

Hazel, you called and I came
Now don't make me play this waiting game
You've got something I want plenty of
Ooh, a little touch of your love

# Something There Is About You

Something there is about you that strikes a match in me
Is it the way your body moves or is it the way your hair blows free?
Or is it because you remind me of something that used to be
Somethin' that crossed over from another century?

Thought I'd shaken the wonder and the phantoms of my youth
Rainy days on the Great Lakes, walkin' the hills of old Duluth
There was me and Danny Lopez, cold eyes, black night and then there was Ruth
Something there is about you that brings back a long-forgotten truth

Suddenly I found you and the spirit in me sings
Don't have to look no further, you're the soul of many things
I could say that I'd be faithful, I could say it in one sweet, easy breath
But to you that would be cruelty and to me it surely would be death

Something there is about you that moves with style and grace
I was in a whirlwind, now I'm in some better place
My hand's on the sabre and you've picked up the baton
Somethin' there is about you that I can't quite put my finger on

# Forever Young

May God bless and keep you always
May your wishes all come true
May you always do for others
And let others do for you
May you build a ladder to the stars
And climb on every rung
May you stay forever young
Forever young, forever young
May you stay forever young

May you grow up to be righteous
May you grow up to be true
May you always know the truth
And see the lights surrounding you
May you always be courageous
Stand upright and be strong
May you stay forever young
Forever young, forever young
May you stay forever young

May your hands always be busy
May your feet always be swift
May you have a strong foundation
When the winds of changes shift
May your heart always be joyful
May your song always be sung
May you stay forever young
Forever young, forever young
May you stay forever young

# Dirge

I hate myself for lovin' you and the weakness that it showed
You were just a painted face on a trip down Suicide Road
The stage was set, the lights went out all around the old hotel
I hate myself for lovin' you and I'm glad the curtain fell

I hate that foolish game we played and the need that was expressed
And the mercy that you showed to me, who ever would have guessed?
I went out on Lower Broadway and I felt that place within
That hollow place where martyrs weep and angels play with sin

Heard your songs of freedom and man forever stripped
Acting out his folly while his back is being whipped
Like a slave in orbit, he's beaten 'til he's tame
All for a moment's glory and it's a dirty, rotten shame

There are those who worship loneliness, I'm not one of them
In this age of fiberglass I'm searching for a gem
The crystal ball up on the wall hasn't shown me nothing yet
I've paid the price of solitude, but at last I'm out of debt

Can't recall a useful thing you ever did for me
'Cept pat me on the back one time when I was on my knees
We stared into each other's eyes 'til one of us would break
No use to apologize, what diff'rence would it make?

So sing your praise of progress and of the Doom Machine
The naked truth is still taboo whenever it can be seen
Lady Luck, who shines on me, will tell you where I'm at
I hate myself for lovin' you, but I should get over that

# You Angel You

You angel you
You got me under your wing
The way you walk and the way you talk
I feel I could almost sing

You angel you
You're as fine as anything's fine
The way you walk and the way you talk
It sure plays on my mind

You know I can't sleep at night for trying
Never did feel this way before
I get up at night and walk the floor
If this is love then gimme more
And more and more and more and more

You angel you
You're as fine as can be
The way you smile like a sweet baby child
It just falls all over me

You know I can't sleep at night for trying
Never did feel this way before
Never did get up and walk the floor
If this is love then gimme more
And more and more and more

You angel you
You got me under your wing
The way you walk and the way you talk
It says everything

# Never Say Goodbye

Twilight on the frozen lake
North wind about to break
On footprints in the snow
Silence down below

You're beautiful beyond words
You're beautiful to me
You can make me cry
Never say goodbye

Time is all I have to give
You can have it if you choose
With me you can live
Never say goodbye

My dreams are made of iron and steel
With a big bouquet
Of roses hanging down
From the heavens to the ground

The crashing waves roll over me
As I stand upon the sand
Wait for you to come
And grab hold of my hand

Oh, baby, baby, baby blue
You'll change your last name, too
You've turned your hair to brown
Love to see it hangin' down

# Wedding Song

I love you more than ever, more than time and more than love
I love you more than money and more than the stars above
Love you more than madness, more than waves upon the sea
Love you more than life itself, you mean that much to me

Ever since you walked right in, the circle's been complete
I've said goodbye to haunted rooms and faces in the street
To the courtyard of the jester which is hidden from the sun
I love you more than ever and I haven't yet begun

You breathed on me and made my life a richer one to live
When I was deep in poverty you taught me how to give
Dried the tears up from my dreams and pulled me from the hole
Quenched my thirst and satisfied the burning in my soul

You gave me babies one, two, three, what is more, you saved my life
Eye for eye and tooth for tooth, your love cuts like a knife
My thoughts of you don't ever rest, they'd kill me if I lie
I'd sacrifice the world for you and watch my senses die

The tune that is yours and mine to play upon this earth
We'll play it out the best we know, whatever it is worth
What's lost is lost, we can't regain what went down in the flood
But happiness to me is you and I love you more than blood

It's never been my duty to remake the world at large
Nor is it my intention to sound a battle charge
'Cause I love you more than all of that with a love that doesn't bend
And if there is eternity I'd love you there again

Oh, can't you see that you were born to stand by my side
And I was born to be with you, you were born to be my bride
You're the other half of what I am, you're the missing piece
And I love you more than ever with that love that doesn't cease

You turn the tide on me each day and teach my eyes to see
Just bein' next to you is a natural thing for me
And I could never let you go, no matter what goes on
'Cause I love you more than ever now that the past is gone

# Nobody 'Cept You

There's nothing 'round here I believe in
'Cept you, yeah you
And there's nothing to me that's sacred
'Cept you, yeah you

You're the one that reaches me
You're the one that I admire
Every time we meet together
My soul feels like it's on fire
Nothing matters to me
And there's nothing I desire
'Cept you, yeah you

Nothing 'round here I care to try for
'Cept you, yeah you
Got nothing left to live or die for
'Cept you, yeah you

There's a hymn I used to hear
In the churches all the time
Make me feel so good inside
So peaceful, so sublime
And there's nothing to remind me of that
Old familiar chime
'Cept you, uh huh you

Used to play in the cemetery
Dance and sing and run when I was a child
Never seemed strange
But now I just pass mournfully by
That place where the bones of life are piled
I know somethin' has changed
I'm a stranger here and no one sees me
'Cept you, yeah you

Nothing much matters or seems to please me
'Cept you, yeah you
Nothing hypnotizes me
Or holds me in a spell
Everything runs by me
Just like water from a well
Everybody wants my attention
Everybody's got something to sell
'Cept you, yeah you

# Blood on the Tracks

Tangled Up in Blue

Simple Twist of Fate

You're a Big Girl Now

Idiot Wind

You're Gonna Make Me Lonesome When You Go

Meet Me in the Morning

Lily, Rosemary and the Jack of Hearts

If You See Her, Say Hello

Shelter from the Storm

Buckets of Rain

*additional lyrics*
Up to Me
Call Letter Blues

① <u>5 in the</u>
<u>Early</u> one mornin, the sun was shining, he was
                                          Lyin in bed
Wonderin' if she'd changed at all, wondering if her hair
                              was still red
Her folks they said their lives together sure was gonna be
                                          rough
Never did like Mama's home-made dress, Papa's bankbook
                    wasn't big enough
                              by
And he was walking    the side of the road
Rain falling on his shoes
Heading out for the ol' East Coast
Lord knows he paid some dues
Tryin' tu get thr — Tangled up in BLUE

# Tangled Up in Blue

Early one mornin' the sun was shinin'
I was layin' in bed
Wond'rin' if she'd changed at all
If her hair was still red
Her folks they said our lives together
Sure was gonna be rough
They never did like Mama's homemade dress
Papa's bankbook wasn't big enough
And I was standin' on the side of the road
Rain fallin' on my shoes
Heading out for the East Coast
Lord knows I've paid some dues gettin' through
Tangled up in blue

She was married when we first met
Soon to be divorced
I helped her out of a jam, I guess
But I used a little too much force
We drove that car as far as we could
Abandoned it out West
Split up on a dark sad night
Both agreeing it was best
She turned around to look at me
As I was walkin' away
I heard her say over my shoulder
"We'll meet again someday on the avenue"
Tangled up in blue

I had a job in the great north woods
Working as a cook for a spell
But I never did like it all that much
And one day the ax just fell
So I drifted down to New Orleans
Where I happened to be employed
Workin' for a while on a fishin' boat
Right outside of Delacroix
But all the while I was alone
The past was close behind
I seen a lot of women
But she never escaped my mind, and I just grew
Tangled up in blue

She was workin' in a topless place
And I stopped in for a beer
I just kept lookin' at the side of her face
In the spotlight so clear
And later on as the crowd thinned out
I's just about to do the same
She was standing there in back of my chair
Said to me, "Don't I know your name?"
I muttered somethin' underneath my breath
She studied the lines on my face
I must admit I felt a little uneasy
When she bent down to tie the laces of my shoe
Tangled up in blue

She lit a burner on the stove
And offered me a pipe
"I thought you'd never say hello," she said
"You look like the silent type"
Then she opened up a book of poems
And handed it to me
Written by an Italian poet
From the thirteenth century
And every one of them words rang true
And glowed like burnin' coal
Pourin' off of every page
Like it was written in my soul from me to you
Tangled up in blue

I lived with them on Montague Street
In a basement down the stairs
There was music in the cafés at night
And revolution in the air
Then he started into dealing with slaves
And something inside of him died
She had to sell everything she owned
And froze up inside
And when finally the bottom fell out
I became withdrawn
The only thing I knew how to do
Was to keep on keepin' on like a bird that flew
Tangled up in blue

So now I'm goin' back again
I got to get to her somehow
All the people we used to know
They're an illusion to me now
Some are mathematicians
Some are carpenters' wives
Don't know how it all got started
I don't know what they're doin' with their lives
But me, I'm still on the road
Headin' for another joint
We always did feel the same
We just saw it from a different point of view
Tangled up in blue

# Simple Twist of Fate

They sat together in the park
As the evening sky grew dark
She looked at him and he felt a spark tingle to his bones
'Twas then he felt alone and wished that he'd gone straight
And watched out for a simple twist of fate

They walked along by the old canal
A little confused, I remember well
And stopped into a strange hotel with a neon burnin' bright
He felt the heat of the night hit him like a freight train
Moving with a simple twist of fate

A saxophone someplace far off played
As she was walkin' by the arcade
As the light bust through a beat-up shade where he was wakin' up
She dropped a coin into the cup of a blind man at the gate
And forgot about a simple twist of fate

He woke up, the room was bare
He didn't see her anywhere
He told himself he didn't care, pushed the window open wide
Felt an emptiness inside to which he just could not relate
Brought on by a simple twist of fate

He hears the ticking of the clocks
And walks along with a parrot that talks
Hunts her down by the waterfront docks where the sailors all come in
Maybe she'll pick him out again, how long must he wait
Once more for a simple twist of fate

People tell me it's a sin
To know and feel too much within
I still believe she was my twin, but I lost the ring
She was born in spring, but I was born too late
Blame it on a simple twist of fate

# You're a Big Girl Now

Our conversation was short and sweet
It nearly swept me off-a my feet
And I'm back in the rain, oh, oh
And you are on dry land
You made it there somehow
You're a big girl now

Bird on the horizon, sittin' on a fence
He's singin' his song for me at his own expense
And I'm just like that bird, oh, oh
Singin' just for you
I hope that you can hear
Hear me singin' through these tears

Time is a jet plane, it moves too fast
Oh, but what a shame if all we've shared can't last
I can change, I swear, oh, oh
See what you can do
I can make it through
You can make it too

Love is so simple, to quote a phrase
You've known it all the time, I'm learnin' it these days
Oh, I know where I can find you, oh, oh
In somebody's room
It's a price I have to pay
You're a big girl all the way

A change in the weather is known to be extreme
But what's the sense of changing horses in midstream?
I'm going out of my mind, oh, oh
With a pain that stops and starts
Like a corkscrew to my heart
Ever since we've been apart

# Idiot Wind

Someone's got it in for me, they're planting stories in the press
Whoever it is I wish they'd cut it out but when they will I can only guess
They say I shot a man named Gray and took his wife to Italy
She inherited a million bucks and when she died it came to me
I can't help it if I'm lucky

People see me all the time and they just can't remember how to act
Their minds are filled with big ideas, images and distorted facts
Even you, yesterday you had to ask me where it was at
I couldn't believe after all these years, you didn't know me better than that
Sweet lady

Idiot wind, blowing every time you move your mouth
Blowing down the backroads headin' south
Idiot wind, blowing every time you move your teeth
You're an idiot, babe
It's a wonder that you still know how to breathe

I ran into the fortune-teller, who said beware of lightning that might strike
I haven't known peace and quiet for so long I can't remember what it's like
There's a lone soldier on the cross, smoke pourin' out of a boxcar door
You didn't know it, you didn't think it could be done, in the final end he won the wars
After losin' every battle

I woke up on the roadside, daydreamin' 'bout the way things sometimes are
Visions of your chestnut mare shoot through my head and are makin' me see stars
You hurt the ones that I love best and cover up the truth with lies
One day you'll be in the ditch, flies buzzin' around your eyes
Blood on your saddle

Idiot wind, blowing through the flowers on your tomb
Blowing through the curtains in your room
Idiot wind, blowing every time you move your teeth
You're an idiot, babe
It's a wonder that you still know how to breathe

It was gravity which pulled us down and destiny which broke us apart
You tamed the lion in my cage but it just wasn't enough to change my heart
Now everything's a little upside down, as a matter of fact the wheels have stopped
What's good is bad, what's bad is good, you'll find out when you reach the top
You're on the bottom

I noticed at the ceremony, your corrupt ways had finally made you blind
I can't remember your face anymore, your mouth has changed, your eyes
    don't look into mine
The priest wore black on the seventh day and sat stone-faced while the
    building burned
I waited for you on the running boards, near the cypress trees, while the
    springtime turned
Slowly into autumn

Idiot wind, blowing like a circle around my skull
From the Grand Coulee Dam to the Capitol
Idiot wind, blowing every time you move your teeth
You're an idiot, babe
It's a wonder that you still know how to breathe

I can't feel you anymore, I can't even touch the books you've read
Every time I crawl past your door, I been wishin' I was somebody else instead
Down the highway, down the tracks, down the road to ecstasy
I followed you beneath the stars, hounded by your memory
And all your ragin' glory

I been double-crossed now for the very last time and now I'm finally free
I kissed goodbye the howling beast on the borderline which separated you from me
You'll never know the hurt I suffered nor the pain I rise above
And I'll never know the same about you, your holiness or your kind of love
And it makes me feel so sorry

Idiot wind, blowing through the buttons of our coats
Blowing through the letters that we wrote
Idiot wind, blowing through the dust upon our shelves
We're idiots, babe
It's a wonder we can even feed ourselves

# You're Gonna Make Me Lonesome When You Go

I've seen love go by my door
It's never been this close before
Never been so easy or so slow
Been shooting in the dark too long
When somethin's not right it's wrong
Yer gonna make me lonesome when you go

Dragon clouds so high above
I've only known careless love
It's always hit me from below
This time around it's more correct
Right on target, so direct
Yer gonna make me lonesome when you go

Purple clover, Queen Anne's lace
Crimson hair across your face
You could make me cry if you don't know
Can't remember what I was thinkin' of
You might be spoilin' me too much, love
Yer gonna make me lonesome when you go

Flowers on the hillside, bloomin' crazy
Crickets talkin' back and forth in rhyme
Blue river runnin' slow and lazy
I could stay with you forever and never realize the time

Situations have ended sad
Relationships have all been bad
Mine've been like Verlaine's and Rimbaud
But there's no way I can compare
All those scenes to this affair
Yer gonna make me lonesome when you go

Yer gonna make me wonder what I'm doin'
Stayin' far behind without you
Yer gonna make me wonder what I'm sayin'
Yer gonna make me give myself a good talkin' to

I'll look for you in old Honolulu
San Francisco, Ashtabula
Yer gonna have to leave me now, I know
But I'll see you in the sky above
In the tall grass, in the ones I love
Yer gonna make me lonesome when you go

# Meet Me in the Morning

Meet me in the morning, 56th and Wabasha
Meet me in the morning, 56th and Wabasha
Honey, we could be in Kansas
By time the snow begins to thaw

They say the darkest hour is right before the dawn
They say the darkest hour is right before the dawn
But you wouldn't know it by me
Every day's been darkness since you been gone

Little rooster crowin', there must be something on his mind
Little rooster crowin', there must be something on his mind
Well, I feel just like that rooster
Honey, ya treat me so unkind

The birds are flyin' low babe, honey I feel so exposed
Well, the birds are flyin' low babe, honey I feel so exposed
Well now, I ain't got any matches
And the station doors are closed

Well, I struggled through barbed wire, felt the hail fall from above
Well, I struggled through barbed wire, felt the hail fall from above
Well, you know I even outran the hound dogs
Honey, you know I've earned your love

Look at the sun sinkin' like a ship
Look at the sun sinkin' like a ship
Ain't that just like my heart, babe
When you kissed my lips?

# Lily, Rosemary and the Jack of Hearts

The festival was over, the boys were all plannin' for a fall
The cabaret was quiet except for the drillin' in the wall
The curfew had been lifted and the gamblin' wheel shut down
Anyone with any sense had already left town
He was standin' in the doorway lookin' like the Jack of Hearts

He moved across the mirrored room, "Set it up for everyone," he said
Then everyone commenced to do what they were doin' before he turned their heads
Then he walked up to a stranger and he asked him with a grin
"Could you kindly tell me, friend, what time the show begins?"
Then he moved into the corner, face down like the Jack of Hearts

Backstage the girls were playin' five-card stud by the stairs
Lily had two queens, she was hopin' for a third to match her pair
Outside the streets were fillin' up, the window was open wide
A gentle breeze was blowin', you could feel it from inside
Lily called another bet and drew up the Jack of Hearts

Big Jim was no one's fool, he owned the town's only diamond mine
He made his usual entrance lookin' so dandy and so fine
With his bodyguards and silver cane and every hair in place
He took whatever he wanted to and he laid it all to waste
But his bodyguards and silver cane were no match for the Jack of Hearts

Rosemary combed her hair and took a carriage into town
She slipped in through the side door lookin' like a queen without a crown
She fluttered her false eyelashes and whispered in his ear
"Sorry, darlin', that I'm late," but he didn't seem to hear
He was starin' into space over at the Jack of Hearts

"I know I've seen that face before," Big Jim was thinkin' to himself
"Maybe down in Mexico or a picture up on somebody's shelf"
But then the crowd began to stamp their feet and the houselights did dim
And in the darkness of the room there was only Jim and him
Starin' at the butterfly who just drew the Jack of Hearts

Lily was a princess, she was fair-skinned and precious as a child
She did whatever she had to do, she had that certain flash every time she smiled
She'd come away from a broken home, had lots of strange affairs
With men in every walk of life which took her everywhere
But she'd never met anyone quite like the Jack of Hearts

The hangin' judge came in unnoticed and was being wined and dined
The drillin' in the wall kept up but no one seemed to pay it any mind
It was known all around that Lily had Jim's ring
And nothing would ever come between Lily and the king
No, nothin' ever would except maybe the Jack of Hearts

Rosemary started drinkin' hard and seein' her reflection in the knife
She was tired of the attention, tired of playin' the role of Big Jim's wife
She had done a lot of bad things, even once tried suicide
Was lookin' to do just one good deed before she died
She was gazin' to the future, riding on the Jack of Hearts

Lily washed her face, took her dress off and buried it away
"Has your luck run out?" she laughed at him, "Well, I guess you must
    have known it would someday
Be careful not to touch the wall, there's a brand-new coat of paint
I'm glad to see you're still alive, you're lookin' like a saint"
Down the hallway footsteps were comin' for the Jack of Hearts

The backstage manager was pacing all around by his chair
"There's something funny going on," he said, "I can just feel it in the air"
He went to get the hangin' judge, but the hangin' judge was drunk
As the leading actor hurried by in the costume of a monk
There was no actor anywhere better than the Jack of Hearts

Lily's arms were locked around the man that she dearly loved to touch
She forgot all about the man she couldn't stand who hounded her so much
"I've missed you so," she said to him, and he felt she was sincere
But just beyond the door he felt jealousy and fear
Just another night in the life of the Jack of Hearts

No one knew the circumstance but they say that it happened pretty quick
The door to the dressing room burst open and a cold revolver clicked
And Big Jim was standin' there, ya couldn't say surprised
Rosemary right beside him, steady in her eyes
She was with Big Jim but she was leanin' to the Jack of Hearts

Two doors down the boys finally made it through the wall
And cleaned out the bank safe, it's said that they got off with quite a haul
In the darkness by the riverbed they waited on the ground
For one more member who had business back in town
But they couldn't go no further without the Jack of Hearts

The next day was hangin' day, the sky was overcast and black
Big Jim lay covered up, killed by a penknife in the back
And Rosemary on the gallows, she didn't even blink
The hangin' judge was sober, he hadn't had a drink
The only person on the scene missin' was the Jack of Hearts

---

The cabaret was empty now, a sign said, "Closed for repair"
Lily had already taken all of the dye out of her hair
She was thinkin' 'bout her father, who she very rarely saw
Thinkin' 'bout Rosemary and thinkin' about the law
But most of all she was thinkin' 'bout the Jack of Hearts

# If You See Her, Say Hello

If you see her, say hello, she might be in Tangier
It's the city 'cross the water, not too far from here
Say for me that I'm all right though things are kind of slow
She might think that I've forgotten her. Don't tell her it isn't so

We had a falling-out, like lovers sometimes do
But to think of how she left that night, it hurts me through and through
And though our situation pierced me to the bone
I got to find someone to take her place. I don't like to be alone

I see a lot of people as I make the rounds
And I hear her name here and there as I go from town to town
And I've never gotten used to it, I've just learned to turn it off
Her eyes were blue, her hair was too, her skin so sweet and soft

Sundown, yellow moon, I replay the past
I know every scene by heart, they all went by so fast
If she's passin' back this way, and I sure hope she don't
Tell her she can look me up. I'll either be here or I won't

# Shelter from the Storm

'Twas in another lifetime, one of toil and blood
When blackness was a virtue and the road was full of mud
I came in from the wilderness, a creature void of form
"Come in," she said, "I'll give you shelter from the storm"

And if I pass this way again, you can rest assured
I'll always do my best for her, on that I give my word
In a world of steel-eyed death, and men who are fighting to be warm
"Come in," she said, "I'll give you shelter from the storm"

Not a word was spoke between us, there was little risk involved
Everything up to that point had been left unresolved
Try imagining a place where it's always safe and warm
"Come in," she said, "I'll give you shelter from the storm"

I was burned out from exhaustion, buried in the hail
Poisoned in the bushes an' blown out on the trail
Hunted like a crocodile, ravaged in the corn
"Come in," she said, "I'll give you shelter from the storm"

Suddenly I turned around and she was standin' there
With silver bracelets on her wrists and flowers in her hair
She walked up to me so gracefully and took my crown of thorns
"Come in," she said, "I'll give you shelter from the storm"

Now there's a wall between us, somethin' there's been lost
I took too much for granted, got my signals crossed
Just to think that it all began on a long-forgotten morn
"Come in," she said, "I'll give you shelter from the storm"

Well, the deputy walks on hard nails and the preacher rides a mount
But nothing really matters much, it's doom alone that counts
And the one-eyed undertaker, he blows a futile horn
"Come in," she said, "I'll give you shelter from the storm"

I've heard newborn babies wailin' like a mournin' dove
And old men with broken teeth stranded without love
Do I understand your question, man, is it hopeless and forlorn?
"Come in," she said, "I'll give you shelter from the storm"

In a little hilltop village, they gambled for my clothes
I bargained for salvation an' they gave me a lethal dose
I offered up my innocence and got repaid with scorn
"Come in," she said, "I'll give you shelter from the storm"

Well, I'm livin' in a foreign country but I'm bound to cross the line
Beauty walks a razor's edge, someday I'll make it mine
If I could only turn back the clock to when God and her were born
"Come in," she said, "I'll give you shelter from the storm"

# Buckets of Rain

Buckets of rain
Buckets of tears
Got all them buckets comin' out of my ears
Buckets of moonbeams in my hand
I got all the love, honey baby
You can stand

I been meek
And hard like an oak
I seen pretty people disappear like smoke
Friends will arrive, friends will disappear
If you want me, honey baby
I'll be here

Like your smile
And your fingertips
Like the way that you move your lips
I like the cool way you look at me
Everything about you is bringing me
Misery

Little red wagon
Little red bike
I ain't no monkey but I know what I like
I like the way you love me strong and slow
I'm takin' you with me, honey baby
When I go

Life is sad
Life is a bust
All ya can do is do what you must
You do what you must do and ya do it well
I'll do it for you, honey baby
Can't you tell?

# Up to Me

Everything went from bad to worse, money never changed a thing
Death kept followin', trackin' us down, at least I heard your bluebird sing
Now somebody's got to show their hand, time is an enemy
I know you're long gone, I guess it must be up to me

If I'd thought about it I never would've done it, I guess I would've let it slide
If I'd lived my life by what others were thinkin', the heart inside me would've died
I was just too stubborn to ever be governed by enforced insanity
Someone had to reach for the risin' star, I guess it was up to me

Oh, the Union Central is pullin' out and the orchids are in bloom
I've only got me one good shirt left and it smells of stale perfume
In fourteen months I've only smiled once and I didn't do it consciously
Somebody's got to find your trail, I guess it must be up to me

It was like a revelation when you betrayed me with your touch
I'd just about convinced myself that nothin' had changed that much
The old Rounder in the iron mask slipped me the master key
Somebody had to unlock your heart, he said it was up to me

Well, I watched you slowly disappear down into the officers' club
I would've followed you in the door but I didn't have a ticket stub
So I waited all night 'til the break of day, hopin' one of us could get free
When the dawn came over the river bridge, I knew it was up to me

Oh, the only decent thing I did when I worked as a postal clerk
Was to haul your picture down off the wall near the cage where I used to work
Was I a fool or not to try to protect your identity?
You looked a little burned out, my friend, I thought it might be up to me

Well, I met somebody face to face and I had to remove my hat
She's everything I need and love but I can't be swayed by that
It frightens me, the awful truth of how sweet life can be
But she ain't a-gonna make me move, I guess it must be up to me

We heard the Sermon on the Mount and I knew it was too complex
It didn't amount to anything more than what the broken glass reflects
When you bite off more than you can chew you pay the penalty
Somebody's got to tell the tale, I guess it must be up to me

Well, Dupree came in pimpin' tonight to the Thunderbird Café
Crystal wanted to talk to him, I had to look the other way
Well, I just can't rest without you, love, I need your company
But you ain't a-gonna cross the line, I guess it must be up to me

There's a note left in the bottle, you can give it to Estelle
She's the one you been wond'rin' about, but there's really nothin' much to tell
We both heard voices for a while, now the rest is history
Somebody's got to cry some tears, I guess it must be up to me

So go on, boys, and play your hands, life is a pantomime
The ringleaders from the county seat say you don't have all that much time
And the girl with me behind the shades, she ain't my property
One of us has got to hit the road, I guess it must be up to me

And if we never meet again, baby, remember me
How my lone guitar played sweet for you that old-time melody
And the harmonica around my neck, I blew it for you, free
No one else could play that tune, you know it was up to me

# Call Letter Blues

Well, I walked all night long
Listenin' to them church bells tone
Yes, I walked all night long
Listenin' to them church bells tone
Either someone needing mercy
Or maybe something I've done wrong

Well, your friends come by for you
I don't know what to say
Well, your friends come by for you
I don't know what to say
I just can't face up to tell 'em
Honey you just went away

Well, children cry for mother
I tell them, "Mother took a trip"
Well, children cry for mother
I tell them, "Mother took a trip"
Well, I walk on pins and needles
I hope my tongue don't slip

Well, I gaze at passing strangers
In case I might see you
Yes, I gaze at passing strangers
In case I might see you
But the sun goes around the heavens
And another day just drives on through

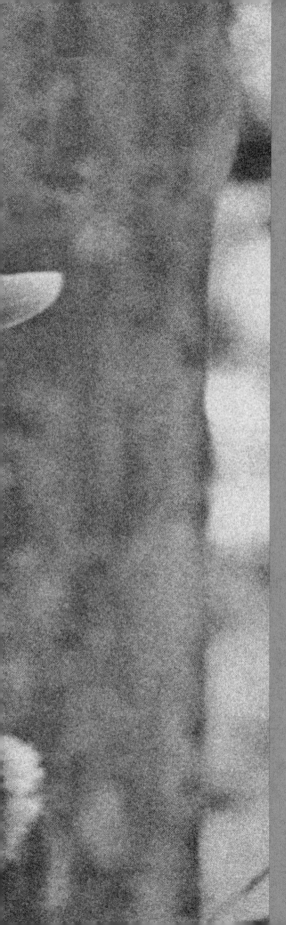

# Desire

Carolina born and bred
Love to hunt the little quail
Got a hundred-acre spread
Got some huntin dogs for sale
    CHORUS
Reggie Jackson at the plate
Seein' nothin' but the curve
Swing too early or too late
Got to eat what Catfish serve.
    CHORUS
Even Billy Virdon grins
When the Fish is in the game
Every season twenty wins
Gonna make the Hall of Fame.

# Hurricane

(with Jacques Levy)

Pistol shots ring out in the barroom night
Enter Patty Valentine from the upper hall
She sees the bartender in a pool of blood
Cries out, "My God, they killed them all!"
Here comes the story of the Hurricane
The man the authorities came to blame
For somethin' that he never done
Put in a prison cell, but one time he could-a been
The champion of the world

Three bodies lyin' there does Patty see
And another man named Bello, movin' around mysteriously
"I didn't do it," he says, and he throws up his hands
"I was only robbin' the register, I hope you understand
I saw them leavin'," he says, and he stops
"One of us had better call up the cops"
And so Patty calls the cops
And they arrive on the scene with their red lights flashin'
In the hot New Jersey night

Meanwhile, far away in another part of town
Rubin Carter and a couple of friends are drivin' around
Number one contender for the middleweight crown
Had no idea what kinda shit was about to go down
When a cop pulled him over to the side of the road
Just like the time before and the time before that
In Paterson that's just the way things go
If you're black you might as well not show up on the street
'Less you wanna draw the heat

Alfred Bello had a partner and he had a rap for the cops
Him and Arthur Dexter Bradley were just out prowlin' around
He said, "I saw two men runnin' out, they looked like middleweights
They jumped into a white car with out-of-state plates"
And Miss Patty Valentine just nodded her head
Cop said, "Wait a minute, boys, this one's not dead"
So they took him to the infirmary
And though this man could hardly see
They told him that he could identify the guilty men

Four in the mornin' and they haul Rubin in
Take him to the hospital and they bring him upstairs
The wounded man looks up through his one dyin' eye
Says, "Wha'd you bring him in here for? He ain't the guy!"
Yes, here's the story of the Hurricane
The man the authorities came to blame
For somethin' that he never done
Put in a prison cell, but one time he could-a been
The champion of the world

Four months later, the ghettos are in flame
Rubin's in South America, fightin' for his name
While Arthur Dexter Bradley's still in the robbery game
And the cops are puttin' the screws to him, lookin' for somebody to blame
"Remember that murder that happened in a bar?"
"Remember you said you saw the getaway car?"
"You think you'd like to play ball with the law?"
"Think it might-a been that fighter that you saw runnin' that night?"
"Don't forget that you are white"

Arthur Dexter Bradley said, "I'm really not sure"
Cops said, "A poor boy like you could use a break
We got you for the motel job and we're talkin' to your friend Bello
Now you don't wanta have to go back to jail, be a nice fellow
You'll be doin' society a favor
That sonofabitch is brave and gettin' braver
We want to put his ass in stir
We want to pin this triple murder on him
He ain't no Gentleman Jim"

Rubin could take a man out with just one punch
But he never did like to talk about it all that much
It's my work, he'd say, and I do it for pay
And when it's over I'd just as soon go on my way
Up to some paradise
Where the trout streams flow and the air is nice
And ride a horse along a trail
But then they took him to the jailhouse
Where they try to turn a man into a mouse

All of Rubin's cards were marked in advance
The trial was a pig-circus, he never had a chance
The judge made Rubin's witnesses drunkards from the slums
To the white folks who watched he was a revolutionary bum
And to the black folks he was just a crazy nigger
No one doubted that he pulled the trigger
And though they could not produce the gun
The D.A. said he was the one who did the deed
And the all-white jury agreed

———

Rubin Carter was falsely tried
The crime was murder "one," guess who testified?
Bello and Bradley and they both baldly lied
And the newspapers, they all went along for the ride
How can the life of such a man
Be in the palm of some fool's hand?
To see him obviously framed
Couldn't help but make me feel ashamed to live in a land
Where justice is a game

Now all the criminals in their coats and their ties
Are free to drink martinis and watch the sun rise
While Rubin sits like Buddha in a ten-foot cell
An innocent man in a living hell
That's the story of the Hurricane
But it won't be over till they clear his name
And give him back the time he's done
Put in a prison cell, but one time he could-a been
The champion of the world

# Isis

(with Jacques Levy)

I married Isis on the fifth day of May
But I could not hold on to her very long
So I cut off my hair and I rode straight away
For the wild unknown country where I could not go wrong

I came to a high place of darkness and light
The dividing line ran through the center of town
I hitched up my pony to a post on the right
Went in to a laundry to wash my clothes down

A man in the corner approached me for a match
I knew right away he was not ordinary
He said, "Are you lookin' for somethin' easy to catch?"
I said, "I got no money." He said, "That ain't necessary"

We set out that night for the cold in the North
I gave him my blanket, he gave me his word
I said, "Where are we goin'?" He said we'd be back by the fourth
I said, "That's the best news that I've ever heard"

I was thinkin' about turquoise, I was thinkin' about gold
I was thinkin' about diamonds and the world's biggest necklace
As we rode through the canyons, through the devilish cold
I was thinkin' about Isis, how she thought I was so reckless

How she told me that one day we would meet up again
And things would be different the next time we wed
If I only could hang on and just be her friend
I still can't remember all the best things she said

We came to the pyramids all embedded in ice
He said, "There's a body I'm tryin' to find
If I carry it out it'll bring a good price"
'Twas then that I knew what he had on his mind

The wind it was howlin' and the snow was outrageous
We chopped through the night and we chopped through the dawn
When he died I was hopin' that it wasn't contagious
But I made up my mind that I had to go on

I broke into the tomb, but the casket was empty
There was no jewels, no nothin', I felt I'd been had
When I saw that my partner was just bein' friendly
When I took up his offer I must-a been mad

I picked up his body and I dragged him inside
Threw him down in the hole and I put back the cover
I said a quick prayer and I felt satisfied
Then I rode back to find Isis just to tell her I love her

She was there in the meadow where the creek used to rise
Blinded by sleep and in need of a bed
I came in from the East with the sun in my eyes
I cursed her one time then I rode on ahead

She said, "Where ya been?" I said, "No place special"
She said, "You look different." I said, "Well, not quite"
She said, "You been gone." I said, "That's only natural"
She said, "You gonna stay?" I said, "Yeah, I jes might"

Isis, oh, Isis, you mystical child
What drives me to you is what drives me insane
I still can remember the way that you smiled
On the fifth day of May in the drizzlin' rain

# Mozambique

(with Jacques Levy)

I like to spend some time in Mozambique
The sunny sky is aqua blue
And all the couples dancing cheek to cheek
It's very nice to stay a week or two

There's lot of pretty girls in Mozambique
And plenty time for good romance
And everybody likes to stop and speak
To give the special one you seek a chance
Or maybe say hello with just a glance

Lying next to her by the ocean
Reaching out and touching her hand
Whispering your secret emotion
Magic in a magical land

And when it's time for leaving Mozambique
To say goodbye to sand and sea
You turn around to take a final peek
And you see why it's so unique to be
Among the lovely people living free
Upon the beach of sunny Mozambique

# One More Cup of Coffee (Valley Below)

Your breath is sweet
Your eyes are like two jewels in the sky
Your back is straight, your hair is smooth
On the pillow where you lie
But I don't sense affection
No gratitude or love
Your loyalty is not to me
But to the stars above

One more cup of coffee for the road
One more cup of coffee 'fore I go
To the valley below

Your daddy he's an outlaw
And a wanderer by trade
He'll teach you how to pick and choose
And how to throw the blade
He oversees his kingdom
So no stranger does intrude
His voice it trembles as he calls out
For another plate of food

One more cup of coffee for the road
One more cup of coffee 'fore I go
To the valley below

Your sister sees the future
Like your mama and yourself
You've never learned to read or write
There's no books upon your shelf
And your pleasure knows no limits
Your voice is like a meadowlark
But your heart is like an ocean
Mysterious and dark

One more cup of coffee for the road
One more cup of coffee 'fore I go
To the valley below

# Oh, Sister

(with Jacques Levy)

Oh, sister, when I come to lie in your arms
You should not treat me like a stranger
Our Father would not like the way that you act
And you must realize the danger

Oh, sister, am I not a brother to you
And one deserving of affection?
And is our purpose not the same on this earth
To love and follow His direction?

We grew up together
From the cradle to the grave
We died and were reborn
And then mysteriously saved

Oh, sister, when I come to knock on your door
Don't turn away, you'll create sorrow
Time is an ocean but it ends at the shore
You may not see me tomorrow

# Joey

(with Jacques Levy)

Born in Red Hook, Brooklyn, in the year of who knows when
Opened up his eyes to the tune of an accordion
Always on the outside of whatever side there was
When they asked him why it had to be that way, "Well," he answered,
   "just because"

Larry was the oldest, Joey was next to last
They called Joe "Crazy," the baby they called "Kid Blast"
Some say they lived off gambling and runnin' numbers too
It always seemed they got caught between the mob and the men in blue

Joey, Joey
King of the streets, child of clay
Joey, Joey
What made them want to come and blow you away?

There was talk they killed their rivals, but the truth was far from that
No one ever knew for sure where they were really at
When they tried to strangle Larry, Joey almost hit the roof
He went out that night to seek revenge, thinkin' he was bulletproof

The war broke out at the break of dawn, it emptied out the streets
Joey and his brothers suffered terrible defeats
Till they ventured out behind the lines and took five prisoners
They stashed them away in a basement, called them amateurs

The hostages were tremblin' when they heard a man exclaim
"Let's blow this place to kingdom come, let Con Edison take the blame"
But Joey stepped up, he raised his hand, said, "We're not those kind of men
It's peace and quiet that we need to go back to work again"

Joey, Joey
King of the streets, child of clay
Joey, Joey
What made them want to come and blow you away?

The police department hounded him, they called him Mr. Smith
They got him on conspiracy, they were never sure who with
"What time is it?" said the judge to Joey when they met
"Five to ten," said Joey. The judge says, "That's exactly what you get"

He did ten years in Attica, reading Nietzsche and Wilhelm Reich
They threw him in the hole one time for tryin' to stop a strike
His closest friends were black men 'cause they seemed to understand
What it's like to be in society with a shackle on your hand

When they let him out in '71 he'd lost a little weight
But he dressed like Jimmy Cagney and I swear he did look great
He tried to find the way back into the life he left behind
To the boss he said, "I have returned and now I want what's mine"

Joey, Joey
King of the streets, child of clay
Joey, Joey
Why did they have to come and blow you away?

It was true that in his later years he would not carry a gun
"I'm around too many children," he'd say, "they should never know of one"
Yet he walked right into the clubhouse of his lifelong deadly foe
Emptied out the register, said, "Tell 'em it was Crazy Joe"

One day they blew him down in a clam bar in New York
He could see it comin' through the door as he lifted up his fork
He pushed the table over to protect his family
Then he staggered out into the streets of Little Italy

Joey, Joey
King of the streets, child of clay
Joey, Joey
What made them want to come and blow you away?

Sister Jacqueline and Carmela and mother Mary all did weep
I heard his best friend Frankie say, "He ain't dead, he's just asleep"
Then I saw the old man's limousine head back towards the grave
I guess he had to say one last goodbye to the son that he could not save

The sun turned cold over President Street and the town of Brooklyn mourned
They said a mass in the old church near the house where he was born
And someday if God's in heaven overlookin' His preserve
I know the men that shot him down will get what they deserve

Joey, Joey
King of the streets, child of clay
Joey, Joey
What made them want to come and blow you away?

# Romance in Durango

(with Jacques Levy)

Hot chili peppers in the blistering sun
Dust on my face and my cape
Me and Magdalena on the run
I think this time we shall escape

Sold my guitar to the baker's son
For a few crumbs and a place to hide
But I can get another one
And I'll play for Magdalena as we ride

No llores, mi querida
Dios nos vigila
Soon the horse will take us to Durango
Agarrame, mi vida
Soon the desert will be gone
Soon you will be dancing the fandango

Past the Aztec ruins and the ghosts of our people
Hoofbeats like castanets on stone
At night I dream of bells in the village steeple
Then I see the bloody face of Ramon

Was it me that shot him down in the cantina
Was it my hand that held the gun?
Come, let us fly, my Magdalena
The dogs are barking and what's done is done

No llores, mi querida
Dios nos vigila
Soon the horse will take us to Durango
Agarrame, mi vida
Soon the desert will be gone
Soon you will be dancing the fandango

At the corrida we'll sit in the shade
And watch the young torero stand alone
We'll drink tequila where our grandfathers stayed
When they rode with Villa into Torreón

Then the padre will recite the prayers of old
In the little church this side of town
I will wear new boots and an earring of gold
You'll shine with diamonds in your wedding gown

The way is long but the end is near
Already the fiesta has begun
The face of God will appear
With His serpent eyes of obsidian

No llores, mi querida
Dio nos vigila
Soon the horse will take us to Durango
Agarrame, mi vida
Soon the desert will be gone
Soon you will be dancing the fandango

Was that the thunder that I heard?
My head is vibrating, I feel a sharp pain
Come sit by me, don't say a word
Oh, can it be that I am slain?

Quick, Magdalena, take my gun
Look up in the hills, that flash of light
Aim well my little one
We may not make it through the night

No llores, mi querida
Dios nos vigila
Soon the horse will take us to Durango
Agarrame, mi vida
Soon the desert will be gone
Soon you will be dancing the fandango

# Black Diamond Bay

(with Jacques Levy)


Up on the white veranda
She wears a necktie and a Panama hat
Her passport shows a face
From another time and place
She looks nothin' like that
And all the remnants of her recent past
Are scattered in the wild wind
She walks across the marble floor
Where a voice from the gambling room is callin' her to come on in
She smiles, walks the other way
As the last ship sails and the moon fades away
From Black Diamond Bay

As the mornin' light breaks open, the Greek comes down
And he asks for a rope and a pen that will write
"Pardon, monsieur," the desk clerk says
Carefully removes his fez
"Am I hearin' you right?"
And as the yellow fog is liftin'
The Greek is quickly headin' for the second floor
She passes him on the spiral staircase
Thinkin' he's the Soviet Ambassador
She starts to speak, but he walks away
As the storm clouds rise and the palm branches sway
On Black Diamond Bay

A soldier sits beneath the fan
Doin' business with a tiny man who sells him a ring
Lightning strikes, the lights blow out
The desk clerk wakes and begins to shout
"Can you see anything?"
Then the Greek appears on the second floor
In his bare feet with a rope around his neck
While a loser in the gambling room lights up a candle
Says, "Open up another deck"
But the dealer says, "Attendez-vous, s'il vous plaît"
As the rain beats down and the cranes fly away
From Black Diamond Bay

The desk clerk heard the woman laugh
As he looked around the aftermath and the soldier got tough
He tried to grab the woman's hand
Said, "Here's a ring, it cost a grand"
She said, "That ain't enough"
Then she ran upstairs to pack her bags
While a horse-drawn taxi waited at the curb
She passed the door that the Greek had locked
Where a handwritten sign read, "Do Not Disturb"
She knocked upon it anyway
As the sun went down and the music did play
On Black Diamond Bay

"I've got to talk to someone quick!"
But the Greek said, "Go away," and he kicked the chair to the floor
He hung there from the chandelier
She cried, "Help, there's danger near
Please open up the door!"
Then the volcano erupted
And the lava flowed down from the mountain high above
The soldier and the tiny man were crouched in the corner
Thinking of forbidden love
But the desk clerk said, "It happens every day"
As the stars fell down and the fields burned away
On Black Diamond Bay

As the island slowly sank
The loser finally broke the bank in the gambling room
The dealer said, "It's too late now
You can take your money, but I don't know how
You'll spend it in the tomb"
The tiny man bit the soldier's ear
As the floor caved in and the boiler in the basement blew
While she's out on the balcony, where a stranger tells her
"My darling, je vous aime beaucoup"
She sheds a tear and then begins to pray
As the fire burns on and the smoke drifts away
From Black Diamond Bay

I was sittin' home alone one night in L.A.
Watchin' old Cronkite on the seven o'clock news
It seems there was an earthquake that
Left nothin' but a Panama hat
And a pair of old Greek shoes
Didn't seem like much was happenin'
So I turned it off and went to grab another beer
Seems like every time you turn around
There's another hard-luck story that you're gonna hear
And there's really nothin' anyone can say
And I never did plan to go anyway
To Black Diamond Bay

———

368

# Sara

I laid on a dune, I looked at the sky
When the children were babies and played on the beach
You came up behind me, I saw you go by
You were always so close and still within reach

Sara, Sara
Whatever made you want to change your mind?
Sara, Sara
So easy to look at, so hard to define

I can still see them playin' with their pails in the sand
They run to the water their buckets to fill
I can still see the shells fallin' out of their hands
As they follow each other back up the hill

Sara, Sara
Sweet virgin angel, sweet love of my life
Sara, Sara
Radiant jewel, mystical wife

Sleepin' in the woods by a fire in the night
Drinkin' white rum in a Portugal bar
Them playin' leapfrog and hearin' about Snow White
You in the marketplace in Savanna-la-Mar

Sara, Sara
It's all so clear, I could never forget
Sara, Sara
Lovin' you is the one thing I'll never regret

I can still hear the sounds of those Methodist bells
I'd taken the cure and had just gotten through
Stayin' up for days in the Chelsea Hotel
Writin' "Sad-Eyed Lady of the Lowlands" for you

Sara, Sara
Wherever we travel we're never apart
Sara, oh Sara
Beautiful lady, so dear to my heart

How did I meet you? I don't know
A messenger sent me in a tropical storm
You were there in the winter, moonlight on the snow
And on Lily Pond Lane when the weather was warm

Sara, oh Sara
Scorpio Sphinx in a calico dress
Sara, Sara
You must forgive me my unworthiness

Now the beach is deserted except for some kelp
And a piece of an old ship that lies on the shore
You always responded when I needed your help
You gimme a map and a key to your door

Sara, oh Sara
Glamorous nymph with an arrow and bow
Sara, oh Sara
Don't ever leave me, don't ever go

# Abandoned Love

I can hear the turning of the key
I've been deceived by the clown inside of me
I thought that he was righteous but he's vain
Oh, something's a-telling me I wear the ball and chain

My patron saint is a-fighting with a ghost
He's always off somewhere when I need him most
The Spanish moon is rising on the hill
But my heart is a-tellin' me I love ya still

I come back to the town from the flaming moon
I see you in the streets, I begin to swoon
I love to see you dress before the mirror
Won't you let me in your room one time 'fore I finally disappear?

Everybody's wearing a disguise
To hide what they've got left behind their eyes
But me, I can't cover what I am
Wherever the children go I'll follow them

I march in the parade of liberty
But as long as I love you I'm not free
How long must I suffer such abuse
Won't you let me see you smile one time before I turn you loose?

I've given up the game, I've got to leave
The pot of gold is only make-believe
The treasure can't be found by men who search
Whose gods are dead and whose queens are in the church

We sat in an empty theater and we kissed
I asked ya please to cross me off-a your list
My head tells me it's time to make a change
But my heart is telling me I love ya but you're strange

One more time at midnight, near the wall
Take off your heavy makeup and your shawl
Won't you descend from the throne, from where you sit?
Let me feel your love one more time before I abandon it

—

# Catfish

(with Jacques Levy)

Lazy stadium night
Catfish on the mound
"Strike three," the umpire said
Batter have to go back and sit down

Catfish, million-dollar-man
Nobody can throw the ball like Catfish can

Used to work on Mr. Finley's farm
But the old man wouldn't pay
So he packed his glove and took his arm
An' one day he just ran away

Catfish, million-dollar-man
Nobody can throw the ball like Catfish can

Come up where the Yankees are
Dress up in a pinstripe suit
Smoke a custom-made cigar
Wear an alligator boot

Catfish, million-dollar-man
Nobody can throw the ball like Catfish can

Carolina born and bred
Love to hunt the little quail
Got a hundred-acre spread
Got some huntin' dogs for sale

Catfish, million-dollar-man
Nobody can throw the ball like Catfish can

Reggie Jackson at the plate
Seein' nothin' but the curve
Swing too early or too late
Got to eat what Catfish serve

Catfish, million-dollar-man
Nobody can throw the ball like Catfish can

Even Billy Martin grins
When the Fish is in the game
Every season twenty wins
Gonna make the Hall of Fame

Catfish, million-dollar-man
Nobody can throw the ball like Catfish can

# Golden Loom

Smoky autumn night, stars up in the sky
I see the sailin' boats across the bay go by
Eucalyptus trees hang above the street
And then I turn my head, for you're approachin' me
Moonlight on the water, fisherman's daughter, floatin' in to my room
With a golden loom

First we wash our feet near the immortal shrine
And then our shadows meet and then we drink the wine
I see the hungry clouds up above your face
And then the tears roll down, what a bitter taste
And then you drift away on a summer's day where the wildflowers bloom
With your golden loom

I walk across the bridge in the dismal light
Where all the cars are stripped between the gates of night
I see the trembling lion with the lotus flower tail
And then I kiss your lips as I lift your veil
But you're gone and then all I seem to recall is the smell of perfume
And your golden loom

# Rita May

(with Jacques Levy)

Rita May, Rita May
You got your body in the way
You're so damn nonchalant
But it's your mind that I want
You got me huffin' and a-puffin'
Next to you I feel like nothin'
Rita May

Rita May, Rita May
How'd you ever get that way?
When do you ever see the light?
Don't you ever feel a fright?
You got me burnin' and I'm turnin'
But I know I must be learnin'
Rita May

All my friends have told me
If I hang around with you
That I'll go blind
But I know that when you hold me
That there really must be somethin'
On your mind

Rita May, Rita May
Laying in a stack of hay
Do you remember where you been?
What's that crazy place you're in?
I'm gonna have to go to college
'Cause you are the book of knowledge
Rita May

# Seven Days

Seven days, seven more days she'll be comin'
I'll be waiting at the station for her to arrive
Seven more days, all I gotta do is survive

She been gone ever since I been a child
Ever since I seen her smile, I ain't forgotten her eyes
She had a face that could outshine the sun in the skies

I been good, I been good while I been waitin'
Maybe guilty of hesitatin', I just been holdin' on
Seven more days, all that'll be gone

There's kissing in the valley
Thieving in the alley
Fighting every inch of the way
Trying to be tender
With somebody I remember
In a night that's always brighter'n the day

Seven days, seven more days that are connected
Just like I expected, she'll be comin' on forth
My beautiful comrade from the north

There's kissing in the valley
Thieving in the alley
Fighting every inch of the way
Trying to be tender
With somebody I remember
In a night that's always brighter'n the day

# Sign Language

You speak to me
In sign language
As I'm eating a sandwich
In a small café
At a quarter to three
But I can't respond
To your sign language
You're taking advantage
Bringing me down
Can't you make any sound?

'Twas there by the bakery
Surrounded by fakery
Tell her my story
Still I'm still there
Does she know I still care?

Link Wray was playin'
On a jukebox I was payin'
For the words I was sayin'
So misunderstood
He didn't do me no good

You speak to me
In sign language
As I'm eating a sandwich
In a small café
At a quarter to three
But I can't respond
To your sign language
You're taking advantage
Bringing me down
Can't you make any sound?

# Money Blues

(with Jacques Levy)

Sittin' here thinkin'
Where does the money go
Sittin' here thinkin'
Where does the money go
Well, I give it to my woman
She ain't got it no more

Went out last night
Bought two eggs and a slice of ham
Went out last night
Bought two eggs and a slice of ham
Bill came to three dollars and ten cents
And I didn't even get no jam

Man came around
Askin' for the rent
Man came around
Askin' for the rent
Well, I looked into the drawer
But the money's all been spent

Well, well
Ain't got no bank account
Well, well
Ain't got no bank account
Went down to start one
But I didn't have the right amount

Everything's inflated
Like a tire on a car
Everything's inflated
Like a tire on a car
Well, the man came and took my Chevy back
I'm glad I hid my old guitar

Come to me, mama
Ease my money crisis now
Come to me, mama
Ease my money crisis now
I need something to support me
And only you know how

# Street Legal

Midwives stroll   between jupiter & apollo
Struggling babes   past   (Between the sheets of...
A messenger arrives with a blck nightengale
~~There~~ I see her on the square & | I cannot help but follow
Follow her down to the fountain | where she's lifting her veil

*I stared into the eyes* ~ Ages roll - up on Jupiter & Apollo
*Destiny's faces*
~ lifted her veil
*on the steppes*
*lifted*

~~Here I am~~ *Baby be still* she said, can y spare me a moment's passion
Can I shine yr shoes, print yr money or mark yr cards
What ~~frozen~~ truths ~~can~~ yr brave ~~me~~ souls imagine
Does yr hearts have the courage for the changing of the guards

# Changing of the Guards

Sixteen years
Sixteen banners united over the field
Where the good shepherd grieves
Desperate men, desperate women divided
Spreading their wings 'neath the falling leaves

Fortune calls
I stepped forth from the shadows, to the marketplace
Merchants and thieves, hungry for power, my last deal gone down
She's smelling sweet like the meadows where she was born
On midsummer's eve, near the tower

The cold-blooded moon
The captain waits above the celebration
Sending his thoughts to a beloved maid
Whose ebony face is beyond communication
The captain is down but still believing that his love will be repaid

They shaved her head
She was torn between Jupiter and Apollo
A messenger arrived with a black nightingale
I seen her on the stairs and I couldn't help but follow
Follow her down past the fountain where they lifted her veil

I stumbled to my feet
I rode past destruction in the ditches
With the stitches still mending 'neath a heart-shaped tattoo
Renegade priests and treacherous young witches
Were handing out the flowers that I'd given to you

The palace of mirrors
Where dog soldiers are reflected
The endless road and the wailing of chimes
The empty rooms where her memory is protected
Where the angels' voices whisper to the souls of previous times

She wakes him up
Forty-eight hours later, the sun is breaking
Near broken chains, mountain laurel and rolling rocks
She's begging to know what measures he now will be taking
He's pulling her down and she's clutching on to his long golden locks

---

Gentlemen, he said
I don't need your organization, I've shined your shoes
I've moved your mountains and marked your cards
But Eden is burning, either brace yourself for elimination
Or else your hearts must have the courage for the changing of the guards

Peace will come
With tranquillity and splendor on the wheels of fire
But will bring us no reward when her false idols fall
And cruel death surrenders with its pale ghost retreating
Between the King and the Queen of Swords

# New Pony

Once I had a pony, her name was Lucifer
I had a pony, her name was Lucifer
She broke her leg and she needed shooting
I swear it hurt me more than it could ever have hurted her

Sometimes I wonder what's going on in the mind of Miss X
Sometimes I wonder what's going on in the mind of Miss X
You know she got such a sweet disposition
I never know what the poor girl's gonna do to me next

I got a new pony, she knows how to fox-trot, lope and pace
Well, I got a new pony, she knows how to fox-trot, lope and pace
She got great big hind legs
And long black shaggy hair above her face

Well now, it was early in the mornin', I seen your shadow in the door
It was early in the mornin', I seen your shadow in the door
Now, I don't have to ask nobody
I know what you come here for

They say you're usin' voodoo, your feet walk by themselves
They say you're usin' voodoo, I seen your feet walk by themselves
Oh, baby, that god you been prayin' to
Is gonna give ya back what you're wishin' on someone else

Come over here pony, I, I wanna climb up one time on you
Come over here pony, I, I wanna climb up one time on you
Well, you're so bad and nasty
But I love you, yes I do

# No Time to Think

In death, you face life with a child and a wife
Who sleep-walks through your dreams into walls
You're a soldier of mercy, you're cold and you curse
"He who cannot be trusted must fall"

Loneliness, tenderness, high society, notoriety
You fight for the throne and you travel alone
Unknown as you slowly sink
And there's no time to think

In the Federal City you been blown and shown pity
In secret, for pieces of change
The empress attracts you but oppression distracts you
And it makes you feel violent and strange

Memory, ecstasy, tyranny, hypocrisy
Betrayed by a kiss on a cool night of bliss
In the valley of the missing link
And you have no time to think

Judges will haunt you, the country priestess will want you
Her worst is better than best
I've seen all these decoys through a set of deep turquoise eyes
And I feel so depressed

China doll, alcohol, duality, mortality
Mercury rules you and destiny fools you
Like the plague, with a dangerous wink
And there's no time to think

Your conscience betrayed you when some tyrant waylaid you
Where the lion lies down with the lamb
I'd have paid off the traitor and killed him much later
But that's just the way that I am

Paradise, sacrifice, mortality, reality
But the magician is quicker and his game
Is much thicker than blood and blacker than ink
And there's no time to think

Anger and jealousy's all that he sells us
He's content when you're under his thumb
Madmen oppose him, but your kindness throws him
To survive it you play deaf and dumb

Equality, liberty, humility, simplicity
You glance through the mirror and there's eyes staring clear
At the back of your head as you drink
And there's no time to think

Warlords of sorrow and queens of tomorrow
Will offer their heads for a prayer
You can't find no salvation, you have no expectations
Anytime, anyplace, anywhere

Mercury, gravity, nobility, humility
You know you can't keep her and the water gets deeper
That is leading you onto the brink
But there's no time to think

You've murdered your vanity, buried your sanity
For pleasure you must now resist
Lovers obey you but they cannot sway you
They're not even sure you exist

Socialism, hypnotism, patriotism, materialism
Fools making laws for the breaking of jaws
And the sound of the keys as they clink
But there's no time to think

The bridge that you travel on goes to the Babylon girl
With the rose in her hair
Starlight in the East and you're finally released
You're stranded but with nothing to share

Loyalty, unity, epitome, rigidity
You turn around for one real last glimpse of Camille
'Neath the moon shinin' bloody and pink
And there's no time to think

Bullets can harm you and death can disarm you
But no, you will not be deceived
Stripped of all virtue as you crawl through the dirt
You can give but you cannot receive

No time to choose when the truth must die
No time to lose or say goodbye
No time to prepare for the victim that's there
No time to suffer or blink
And no time to think

# Baby, Stop Crying

You been down to the bottom with a bad man, babe
But you're back where you belong
Go get me my pistol, babe
Honey, I can't tell right from wrong

Baby, please stop crying, stop crying, stop crying
Baby, please stop crying, stop crying, stop crying
Baby, please stop crying
You know, I know, the sun will always shine
So baby, please stop crying 'cause it's tearing up my mind

Go down to the river, babe
Honey, I will meet you there
Go down to the river, babe
Honey, I will pay your fare

Baby, please stop crying, stop crying, stop crying
Baby, please stop crying, stop crying, stop crying
Baby, please stop crying
You know, I know, the sun will always shine
So baby, please stop crying 'cause it's tearing up my mind

If you're looking for assistance, babe
Or if you just want some company
Or if you just want a friend you can talk to
Honey, come and see about me

Baby, please stop crying, stop crying, stop crying
Baby, please stop crying, stop crying, stop crying
Baby, please stop crying
You know, I know, the sun will always shine
So baby, please stop crying 'cause it's tearing up my mind

You been hurt so many times
And I know what you're thinking of
Well, I don't have to be no doctor, babe
To see that you're madly in love

Baby, please stop crying, stop crying, stop crying
Baby, please stop crying, stop crying, stop crying
Baby, please stop crying
You know, I know, the sun will always shine
So baby, please stop crying 'cause it's tearing up my mind

# Is Your Love in Vain?

Do you love me, or are you just extending goodwill?
Do you need me half as bad as you say, or are you just feeling guilt?
I've been burned before and I know the score
So you won't hear me complain
Will I be able to count on you
Or is your love in vain?

Are you so fast that you cannot see that I must have solitude?
When I am in the darkness, why do you intrude?
Do you know my world, do you know my kind
Or must I explain?
Will you let me be myself
Or is your love in vain?

Well I've been to the mountain and I've been in the wind
I've been in and out of happiness
I have dined with kings, I've been offered wings
And I've never been too impressed

All right, I'll take a chance, I will fall in love with you
If I'm a fool you can have the night, you can have the morning too
Can you cook and sew, make flowers grow
Do you understand my pain?
Are you willing to risk it all
Or is your love in vain?

# Señor
# (Tales of Yankee Power)

Señor, señor, do you know where we're headin'?
Lincoln County Road or Armageddon?
Seems like I been down this way before
Is there any truth in that, señor?

Señor, señor, do you know where she is hidin'?
How long are we gonna be ridin'?
How long must I keep my eyes glued to the door?
Will there be any comfort there, señor?

There's a wicked wind still blowin' on that upper deck
There's an iron cross still hanging down from around her neck
There's a marchin' band still playin' in that vacant lot
Where she held me in her arms one time and said, "Forget me not"

Señor, señor, I can see that painted wagon
I can smell the tail of the dragon
Can't stand the suspense anymore
Can you tell me who to contact here, señor?

Well, the last thing I remember before I stripped and kneeled
Was that trainload of fools bogged down in a magnetic field
A gypsy with a broken flag and a flashing ring
Said, "Son, this ain't a dream no more, it's the real thing"

Señor, señor, you know their hearts is as hard as leather
Well, give me a minute, let me get it together
I just gotta pick myself up off the floor
I'm ready when you are, señor

Señor, señor, let's disconnect these cables
Overturn these tables
This place don't make sense to me no more
Can you tell me what we're waiting for, señor?

# True Love Tends to Forget

I'm getting weary looking in my baby's eyes
When she's near me she's so hard to recognize
I finally realize there's no room for regret
True love, true love, true love tends to forget

Hold me, baby be near
You told me that you'd be sincere
Every day of the year's like playin' Russian roulette
True love, true love, true love tends to forget

I was lyin' down in the reeds without any oxygen
I saw you in the wilderness among the men
Saw you drift into infinity and come back again
All you got to do is wait and I'll tell you when

You're a tearjerker, baby, but I'm under your spell
You're a hard worker, baby, and I know you well
But this weekend in hell is making me sweat
True love, true love, true love tends to forget

I was lyin' down in the reeds without any oxygen
I saw you in the wilderness among the men
Saw you drift into infinity and come back again
All you got to do is wait and I'll tell you when

You belong to me, baby, without any doubt
Don't forsake me, baby, don't sell me out
Don't keep me knockin' about from Mexico to Tibet
True love, true love, true love tends to forget

# We Better Talk This Over

I think we better talk this over
Maybe when we both get sober
You'll understand I'm only a man
Doin' the best that I can

This situation can only get rougher
Why should we needlessly suffer?
Let's call it a day, go our own different ways
Before we decay

You don't have to be afraid of looking into my face
We've done nothing to each other time will not erase

I feel displaced, I got a low-down feeling
You been two-faced, you been double-dealing
I took a chance, got caught in the trance
Of a downhill dance

Oh, child, why you wanna hurt me?
I'm exiled, you can't convert me
I'm lost in the haze of your delicate ways
With both eyes glazed

You don't have to yearn for love, you don't have to be alone
Somewheres in this universe there's a place that you can call home

I guess I'll be leaving tomorrow
If I have to beg, steal or borrow
It'd be great to cross paths in a day and a half
Look at each other and laugh

But I don't think it's liable to happen
Like the sound of one hand clappin'
The vows that we kept are now broken and swept
'Neath the bed where we slept

Don't think of me and fantasize on what we never had
Be grateful for what we've shared together and be glad
Why should we go on watching each other through a telescope?
Eventually we'll hang ourselves on all this tangled rope

Oh, babe, time for a new transition
I wish I was a magician
I would wave a wand and tie back the bond
That we've both gone beyond

# Where Are You Tonight? (Journey Through Dark Heat)

There's a long-distance train rolling through the rain
Tears on the letter I write
There's a woman I long to touch and I miss her so much
But she's drifting like a satellite

There's a neon light ablaze in this green smoky haze
Laughter down on Elizabeth Street
And a lonesome bell tone in that valley of stone
Where she bathed in a stream of pure heat

Her father would emphasize you got to be more than streetwise
But he practiced what he preached from the heart
A full-blooded Cherokee, he predicted to me
The time and the place that the trouble would start

There's a babe in the arms of a woman in a rage
And a longtime golden-haired stripper onstage
And she winds back the clock and she turns back the page
Of a book that no one can write
Oh, where are you tonight?

The truth was obscure, too profound and too pure
To live it you have to explode
In that last hour of need, we entirely agreed
Sacrifice was the code of the road

I left town at dawn, with Marcel and St. John
Strong men belittled by doubt
I couldn't tell her what my private thoughts were
But she had some way of finding them out

He took dead-center aim but he missed just the same
She was waiting, putting flowers on the shelf
She could feel my despair as I climbed up her hair
And discovered her invisible self

There's a lion in the road, there's a demon escaped
There's a million dreams gone, there's a landscape being raped
As her beauty fades and I watch her undrape
I won't but then again, maybe I might
Oh, if I could just find you tonight

I fought with my twin, that enemy within
'Til both of us fell by the way
Horseplay and disease is killing me by degrees
While the law looks the other way

Your partners in crime hit me up for nickels and dimes
The guy you were lovin' couldn't stay clean
It felt outa place, my foot in his face
But he should-a stayed where his money was green

I bit into the root of forbidden fruit
With the juice running down my leg
Then I dealt with your boss, who'd never known about loss
And who always was too proud to beg

There's a white diamond gloom on the dark side of this room
And a pathway that leads up to the stars
If you don't believe there's a price for this sweet paradise
Remind me to show you the scars

There's a new day at dawn and I've finally arrived
If I'm there in the morning, baby, you'll know I've survived
I can't believe it, I can't believe I'm alive
But without you it just doesn't seem right
Oh, where are you tonight?

# Legionnaire's Disease

Some say it was radiation, some say there was acid on the microphone
Some say a combination that turned their hearts to stone
But whatever it was, it drove them to their knees
Oh, Legionnaire's disease

I wish I had a dollar for everyone that died within that year
Got 'em hot by the collar, plenty an old maid shed a tear
Now within my heart, it sure put on a squeeze
Oh, that Legionnaire's disease

Granddad fought in a revolutionary war, father in the War of 1812
Uncle fought in Vietnam and then he fought a war all by himself
But whatever it was, it came out of the trees
Oh, that Legionnaire's disease

# Slow Train Coming

Gotta Serve Somebody

Precious Angel

I Believe in You

Slow Train

Gonna Change My Way of Thinking

Do Right to Me Baby
   (Do Unto Others)

When You Gonna Wake Up?

Man Gave Names to All the Animals

When He Returns

*additional lyrics*
Ain't No Man Righteous, No Not One
Trouble in Mind
Ye Shall Be Changed

Suddenly I turned around, she was standing there
with bracelets on wrists and flowers in her hair
She walked up to me so gracefully and took my crown
of thorns
"Come in" she said "I'll give you shelter

# Gotta Serve Somebody

You may be an ambassador to England or France
You may like to gamble, you might like to dance
You may be the heavyweight champion of the world
You may be a socialite with a long string of pearls

But you're gonna have to serve somebody, yes indeed
You're gonna have to serve somebody
Well, it may be the devil or it may be the Lord
But you're gonna have to serve somebody

You might be a rock 'n' roll addict prancing on the stage
You might have drugs at your command, women in a cage
You may be a businessman or some high-degree thief
They may call you Doctor or they may call you Chief

But you're gonna have to serve somebody, yes indeed
You're gonna have to serve somebody
Well, it may be the devil or it may be the Lord
But you're gonna have to serve somebody

You may be a state trooper, you might be a young Turk
You may be the head of some big TV network
You may be rich or poor, you may be blind or lame
You may be living in another country under another name

But you're gonna have to serve somebody, yes indeed
You're gonna have to serve somebody
Well, it may be the devil or it may be the Lord
But you're gonna have to serve somebody

You may be a construction worker working on a home
You may be living in a mansion or you might live in a dome
You might own guns and you might even own tanks
You might be somebody's landlord, you might even own banks

But you're gonna have to serve somebody, yes indeed
You're gonna have to serve somebody
Well, it may be the devil or it may be the Lord
But you're gonna have to serve somebody

You may be a preacher with your spiritual pride
You may be a city councilman taking bribes on the side
You may be workin' in a barbershop, you may know how to cut hair
You may be somebody's mistress, may be somebody's heir

---

But you're gonna have to serve somebody, yes indeed
You're gonna have to serve somebody
Well, it may be the devil or it may be the Lord
But you're gonna have to serve somebody

Might like to wear cotton, might like to wear silk
Might like to drink whiskey, might like to drink milk
You might like to eat caviar, you might like to eat bread
You may be sleeping on the floor, sleeping in a king-sized bed

But you're gonna have to serve somebody, yes indeed
You're gonna have to serve somebody
Well, it may be the devil or it may be the Lord
But you're gonna have to serve somebody

You may call me Terry, you may call me Timmy
You may call me Bobby, you may call me Zimmy
You may call me R.J., you may call me Ray
You may call me anything but no matter what you say

You're gonna have to serve somebody, yes indeed
You're gonna have to serve somebody
Well, it may be the devil or it may be the Lord
But you're gonna have to serve somebody

# Precious Angel

Precious angel, under the sun
How was I to know you'd be the one
To show me I was blinded, to show me I was gone
How weak was the foundation I was standing upon?

Now there's spiritual warfare and flesh and blood breaking down
Ya either got faith or ya got unbelief and there ain't no neutral ground
The enemy is subtle, how be it we are so deceived
When the truth's in our hearts and we still don't believe?

Shine your light, shine your light on me
Shine your light, shine your light on me
Shine your light, shine your light on me
Ya know I just couldn't make it by myself
I'm a little too blind to see

My so-called friends have fallen under a spell
They look me squarely in the eye and they say, "All is well"
Can they imagine the darkness that will fall from on high
When men will beg God to kill them and they won't be able to die?

Sister, lemme tell you about a vision I saw
You were drawing water for your husband, you were suffering under the law
You were telling him about Buddha, you were telling him about Mohammed
    in the same breath
You never mentioned one time the Man who came and died a criminal's death

Shine your light, shine your light on me
Shine your light, shine your light on me
Shine your light, shine your light on me
Ya know I just couldn't make it by myself
I'm a little too blind to see

Precious angel, you believe me when I say
What God has given to us no man can take away
We are covered in blood, girl, you know our forefathers were slaves
Let us hope they've found mercy in their bone-filled graves

You're the queen of my flesh, girl, you're my woman, you're my delight
You're the lamp of my soul, girl, and you torch up the night
But there's violence in the eyes, girl, so let us not be enticed
On the way out of Egypt, through Ethiopia, to the judgment hall of Christ

Shine your light, shine your light on me
Shine your light, shine your light on me
Shine your light, shine your light on me
Ya know I just couldn't make it by myself
I'm a little too blind to see

# I Believe in You

They ask me how I feel
And if my love is real
And how I know I'll make it through
And they, they look at me and frown
They'd like to drive me from this town
They don't want me around
'Cause I believe in you

They show me to the door
They say don't come back no more
'Cause I don't be like they'd like me to
And I walk out on my own
A thousand miles from home
But I don't feel alone
'Cause I believe in you

I believe in you even through the tears and the laughter
I believe in you even though we be apart
I believe in you even on the morning after
Oh, when the dawn is nearing
Oh, when the night is disappearing
Oh, this feeling is still here in my heart

Don't let me drift too far
Keep me where you are
Where I will always be renewed
And that which you've given me today
Is worth more than I could pay
And no matter what they say
I believe in you

I believe in you when winter turn to summer
I believe in you when white turn to black
I believe in you even though I be outnumbered
Oh, though the earth may shake me
Oh, though my friends forsake me
Oh, even that couldn't make me go back

Don't let me change my heart
Keep me set apart
From all the plans they do pursue
And I, I don't mind the pain
Don't mind the driving rain
I know I will sustain
'Cause I believe in you

# Slow Train

Sometimes I feel so low-down and disgusted
Can't help but wonder what's happenin' to my companions
Are they lost or are they found
Have they counted the cost it'll take to bring down
All their earthly principles they're gonna have to abandon?
There's a slow, slow train comin' up around the bend

I had a woman down in Alabama
She was a backwoods girl, but she sure was realistic
She said, "Boy, without a doubt
Have to quit your mess and straighten out
You could die down here, be just another accident statistic"
There's a slow, slow train comin' up around the bend

All that foreign oil controlling American soil
Look around you, it's just bound to make you embarrassed
Sheiks walkin' around like kings
Wearing fancy jewels and nose rings
Deciding America's future from Amsterdam and to Paris
And there's a slow, slow train comin' up around the bend

Man's ego is inflated, his laws are outdated, they don't apply no more
You can't rely no more to be standin' around waitin'
In the home of the brave
Jefferson turnin' over in his grave
Fools glorifying themselves, trying to manipulate Satan
And there's a slow, slow train comin' up around the bend

Big-time negotiators, false healers and woman haters
Masters of the bluff and masters of the proposition
But the enemy I see
Wears a cloak of decency
All nonbelievers and men stealers talkin' in the name of religion
And there's a slow, slow train comin' up around the bend

People starving and thirsting, grain elevators are bursting
Oh, you know it costs more to store the food than it do to give it
They say lose your inhibitions
Follow your own ambitions
They talk about a life of brotherly love show me someone who knows how to live it
There's a slow, slow train comin' up around the bend

Well, my baby went to Illinois with some bad-talkin' boy she could destroy
A real suicide case, but there was nothin' I could do to stop it
I don't care about economy
I don't care about astronomy
But it sure do bother me to see my loved ones turning into puppets
There's a slow, slow train comin' up around the bend

# Gonna Change My Way of Thinking

Gonna change my way of thinking
Make myself a different set of rules
Gonna change my way of thinking
Make myself a different set of rules
Gonna put my good foot forward
And stop being influenced by fools

So much oppression
Can't keep track of it no more
So much oppression
Can't keep track of it no more
Sons becoming husbands to their mothers
And old men turning young daughters into whores

Stripes on your shoulders
Stripes on your back and on your hands
Stripes on your shoulders
Stripes on your back and on your hands
Swords piercing your side
Blood and water flowing through the land

Well don't know which one is worse
Doing your own thing or just being cool
Well don't know which one is worse
Doing your own thing or just being cool
You remember only about the brass ring
You forget all about the golden rule

You can mislead a man
You can take ahold of his heart with your eyes
You can mislead a man
You can take ahold of his heart with your eyes
But there's only one authority
And that's the authority on high

I got a God-fearing woman
One I can easily afford
I got a God-fearing woman
One I can easily afford
She can do the Georgia crawl
She can walk in the spirit of the Lord

Jesus said, "Be ready
For you know not the hour in which I come"
Jesus said, "Be ready
For you know not the hour in which I come"
He said, "He who is not for Me is against Me"
Just so you know where He's coming from

There's a kingdom called Heaven
A place where there is no pain of birth
There's a kingdom called Heaven
A place where there is no pain of birth
Well the Lord created it, mister
About the same time He made the earth

# Gonna Change My Way of Thinking

(Alternate Version)

Change my way of thinking, make myself a different set of rules
Change my way of thinking, make myself a different set of rules
Put my best foot forward, stop being influenced by fools

I'm sittin' at the welcome table, I'm so hungry I could eat a horse
I'm sittin' at the welcome table, I'm so hungry I could eat a horse
I'm gonna revitalize my thinking, I'm gonna let the law take its course

Jesus is calling, He's coming back to gather up his jewels
Jesus is calling, He's coming back to gather up his jewels
We living by the golden rule, whoever got the gold rules

The sun is shining, ain't but one train on this track
The sun is shining, ain't but one train on this track
I'm stepping out of the dark woods, I'm jumping on the monkey's back

I'm all dressed up, I'm going to the county dance
I'm all dressed up, I'm going to the county dance
Every day you got to pray for guidance
Every day you got to give yourself a chance

Storms are on the ocean, storms out on the mountain, too
Storms are on the ocean, storms out on the mountain, too
Oh Lord, you know I have no friend like you

I'll tell you something, things you never had you'll never miss
I'll tell you something, things you never had you'll never miss
A brave man will kill you with a sword, a coward with a kiss

# Do Right to Me Baby (Do Unto Others)

Don't wanna judge nobody, don't wanna be judged
Don't wanna touch nobody, don't wanna be touched
Don't wanna hurt nobody, don't wanna be hurt
Don't wanna treat nobody like they was dirt

But if you do right to me, baby
I'll do right to you, too
Ya got to do unto others
Like you'd have them, like you'd have them, do unto you

Don't wanna shoot nobody, don't wanna be shot
Don't wanna buy nobody, don't wanna be bought
Don't wanna bury nobody, don't wanna be buried
Don't wanna marry nobody if they're already married

But if you do right to me, baby
I'll do right to you, too
Ya got to do unto others
Like you'd have them, like you'd have them, do unto you

Don't wanna burn nobody, don't wanna be burned
Don't wanna learn from nobody what I gotta unlearn
Don't wanna cheat nobody, don't wanna be cheated
Don't wanna defeat nobody if they already been defeated

But if you do right to me, baby
I'll do right to you, too
Ya got to do unto others
Like you'd have them, like you'd have them, do unto you

Don't wanna wink at nobody, don't wanna be winked at
Don't wanna be used by nobody for a doormat
Don't wanna confuse nobody, don't wanna be confused
Don't wanna amuse nobody, don't wanna be amused

But if you do right to me, baby
I'll do right to you, too
Ya got to do unto others
Like you'd have them, like you'd have them, do unto you

Don't wanna betray nobody, don't wanna be betrayed
Don't wanna play with nobody, don't wanna be waylaid
Don't wanna miss nobody, don't wanna be missed
Don't put my faith in nobody, not even a scientist

But if you do right to me, baby
I'll do right to you, too
Ya got to do unto others
Like you'd have them, like you'd have them, do unto you

# When You Gonna Wake Up?

God don't make no promises that He don't keep
You got some big dreams, baby, but in order to dream you gotta still be asleep

When you gonna wake up, when you gonna wake up
When you gonna wake up and strengthen the things that remain?

Counterfeit philosophies have polluted all of your thoughts
Karl Marx has got ya by the throat, Henry Kissinger's got you tied up in knots

When you gonna wake up, when you gonna wake up
When you gonna wake up and strengthen the things that remain?

You got innocent men in jail, your insane asylums are filled
You got unrighteous doctors dealing drugs that'll never cure your ills

When you gonna wake up, when you gonna wake up
When you gonna wake up and strengthen the things that remain?

You got men who can't hold their peace and women who can't control their tongues
The rich seduce the poor and the old are seduced by the young

When you gonna wake up, when you gonna wake up
When you gonna wake up and strengthen the things that remain?

Adulterers in churches and pornography in the schools
You got gangsters in power and lawbreakers making rules

When you gonna wake up, when you gonna wake up
When you gonna wake up and strengthen the things that remain?

Spiritual advisors and gurus to guide your every move
Instant inner peace and every step you take has got to be approved

When you gonna wake up, when you gonna wake up
When you gonna wake up and strengthen the things that remain?

Do you ever wonder just what God requires?
You think He's just an errand boy to satisfy your wandering desires

When you gonna wake up, when you gonna wake up
When you gonna wake up and strengthen the things that remain?

You can't take it with you and you know that it's too worthless to be sold
They tell you, "Time is money," as if your life was worth its weight in gold

When you gonna wake up, when you gonna wake up
When you gonna wake up and strengthen the things that remain?

There's a Man up on a cross and He's been crucified
Do you have any idea why or for who He died?

When you gonna wake up, when you gonna wake up
When you gonna wake up and strengthen the things that remain?

# Man Gave Names to All the Animals

Man gave names to all the animals
In the beginning, in the beginning
Man gave names to all the animals
In the beginning, long time ago

He saw an animal that liked to growl
Big furry paws and he liked to howl
Great big furry back and furry hair
"Ah, think I'll call it a bear"

Man gave names to all the animals
In the beginning, in the beginning
Man gave names to all the animals
In the beginning, long time ago

He saw an animal up on a hill
Chewing up so much grass until she was filled
He saw milk comin' out but he didn't know how
"Ah, think I'll call it a cow"

Man gave names to all the animals
In the beginning, in the beginning
Man gave names to all the animals
In the beginning, long time ago

He saw an animal that liked to snort
Horns on his head and they weren't too short
It looked like there wasn't nothin' that he couldn't pull
"Ah, think I'll call it a bull"

Man gave names to all the animals
In the beginning, in the beginning
Man gave names to all the animals
In the beginning, long time ago

He saw an animal leavin' a muddy trail
Real dirty face and a curly tail
He wasn't too small and he wasn't too big
"Ah, think I'll call it a pig"

Man gave names to all the animals
In the beginning, in the beginning
Man gave names to all the animals
In the beginning, long time ago

Next animal that he did meet
Had wool on his back and hooves on his feet
Eating grass on a mountainside so steep
"Ah, think I'll call it a sheep"

Man gave names to all the animals
In the beginning, in the beginning
Man gave names to all the animals
In the beginning, long time ago

He saw an animal as smooth as glass
Slithering his way through the grass
Saw him disappear by a tree near a lake . . .

# When He Returns

The iron hand it ain't no match for the iron rod
The strongest wall will crumble and fall to a mighty God
For all those who have eyes and all those who have ears
It is only He who can reduce me to tears
Don't you cry and don't you die and don't you burn
For like a thief in the night, He'll replace wrong with right
When He returns

Truth is an arrow and the gate is narrow that it passes through
He unleashed His power at an unknown hour that no one knew
How long can I listen to the lies of prejudice?
How long can I stay drunk on fear out in the wilderness?
Can I cast it aside, all this loyalty and this pride?
Will I ever learn that there'll be no peace, that the war won't cease
Until He returns?

Surrender your crown on this blood-stained ground, take off your mask
He sees your deeds, He knows your needs even before you ask
How long can you falsify and deny what is real?
How long can you hate yourself for the weakness you conceal?
Of every earthly plan that be known to man, He is unconcerned
He's got plans of His own to set up His throne
When He returns

# Ain't No Man Righteous, No Not One

When a man he serves the Lord, it makes his life worthwhile
It don't matter 'bout his position, it don't matter 'bout his lifestyle
Talk about perfection, I ain't never seen none
And there ain't no man righteous, no not one

Sometimes the devil likes to drive you from the neighborhood
He'll even work his ways through those whose intentions are good
Some like to worship on the moon, others are worshipping the sun
And there ain't no man righteous, no not one

Look around, ya see so many social hypocrites
Like to make rules for others while they do just the opposite

You can't get to glory by the raising and the lowering of no flag
Put your goodness next to God's and it comes out like a filthy rag
In a city of darkness there's no need of the sun
And there ain't no man righteous, no not one

Done so many evil things in the name of love, it's a crying shame
I never did see no fire that could put out a flame

Pull your hat down, baby, pull the wool down over your eyes
Keep a-talking, baby, 'til you run right out of alibis
Someday you'll account for all the deeds that you done
Well, there ain't no man righteous, no not one

God got the power, man has got his vanity
Man gotta choose before God can set him free
Don't you know there's nothing new that's under the sun?
Well, there ain't no man righteous, no not one

When I'm gone don't wonder where I be
Just say that I trusted in God and that Christ was in me
Say He defeated the devil, He was God's chosen Son
And that there ain't no man righteous, no not one

# Trouble in Mind

I got to know, Lord, when to pull back on the reins
Death can be the result of the most underrated pain
Satan whispers to ya, "Well, I don't want to bore ya
But when ya get tired of the Miss So-and-so I got another woman for ya"

Trouble in mind, Lord, trouble in mind
Lord, take away this trouble in mind

When the deeds that you do don't add up to zero
It's what's inside that counts, ask any war hero
You think you can hide but you're never alone
Ask Lot what he thought when his wife turned to stone

Trouble in mind, Lord, trouble in mind
Lord, take away this trouble in mind

Here comes Satan, prince of the power of the air
He's gonna make you a law unto yourself, gonna build a bird's nest in your hair
He's gonna deaden your conscience 'til you worship the work of your own hands
You'll be serving strangers in a strange, forsaken land

Trouble in mind, Lord, trouble in mind
Lord, take away this trouble in mind

Well, your true love has caught you where you don't belong
You say, "Baby, everybody's doing it so I guess it can't be wrong"
The truth is far from you, so you know you got to lie
Then you're all the time defending what you can never justify

Trouble in mind, Lord, trouble in mind
Lord, take away this trouble in mind

So many of my brothers, they still want to be the boss
They can't relate to the Lord's kingdom, they can't relate to the cross
They self-inflict punishment on their own broken lives
Put their faith in their possessions, in their jobs or their wives

Trouble in mind, Lord, trouble in mind
Lord, take away this trouble in mind

When my life is over, it'll be like a puff of smoke
How long must I suffer, Lord, how long must I be provoked?
Satan will give you a little taste, then he'll move in with rapid speed
Lord, keep my blind side covered and see that I don't bleed

# Ye Shall Be Changed

You harbor resentment
You know there ain't too much of a thrill
You wish for contentment
But you got an emptiness that can't be filled
You've had enough of hatred
Your bones are breaking, can't find nothing sacred

Ye shall be changed, ye shall be changed
In a twinkling of an eye, when the last trumpet blows
The dead will arise and burst out of your clothes
And ye shall be changed

Everything you've gotten
You've gotten by sweat, blood and muscle
From early in the morning 'til way past dark
All you ever do is hustle
All your loved ones have walked out the door
You're not even sure 'bout your wife and kids no more, but

Ye shall be changed, ye shall be changed
In a twinkling of an eye, when the last trumpet blows
The dead will arise and burst out of your clothes
And ye shall be changed

The past don't control you
But the future's like a roulette wheel spinning
Deep down inside
You know you need a whole new beginning
Don't have to go to Russia or Iran
Just surrender to God and He'll move you right here where you stand, and

Ye shall be changed, ye shall be changed
In a twinkling of an eye, when the last trumpet blows
The dead will arise and burst out of your clothes
And ye shall be changed

You drink bitter water
And you been eating the bread of sorrow
You can't live for today
When all you're ever thinking of is tomorrow
The path you've endured has been rough
When you've decided that you've had enough, then

Ye shall be changed, ye shall be changed
In a twinkling of an eye, when the last trumpet blows
The dead will arise and burst out of your clothes
And ye shall be changed

# Saved

like a poor fool in his prime/trying to read your portrait
you can hear me talk

   is your heart made of stone/
                    or solid rock?

# Saved

(with Tim Drummond)

I was blinded by the devil
Born already ruined
Stone-cold dead
As I stepped out of the womb
By His grace I have been touched
By His word I have been healed
By His hand I've been delivered
By His spirit I've been sealed

I've been saved
By the blood of the lamb
Saved
By the blood of the lamb
Saved
Saved
And I'm so glad
Yes, I'm so glad
I'm so glad
So glad
I want to thank You, Lord
I just want to thank You, Lord
Thank You, Lord

By His truth I can be upright
By His strength I do endure
By His power I've been lifted
In His love I am secure
He bought me with a price
Freed me from the pit
Full of emptiness and wrath
And the fire that burns in it

I've been saved
By the blood of the lamb
Saved
By the blood of the lamb
Saved
Saved
And I'm so glad
Yes, I'm so glad
I'm so glad
So glad
I want to thank You, Lord
I just want to thank You, Lord
Thank You, Lord

Nobody to rescue me
Nobody would dare
I was going down for the last time
But by His mercy I've been spared
Not by works
But by faith in Him who called
For so long I've been hindered
For so long I've been stalled

I've been saved
By the blood of the lamb
Saved
By the blood of the lamb
Saved
Saved
And I'm so glad
Yes, I'm so glad
I'm so glad
So glad
I want to thank You, Lord
I just want to thank You, Lord
Thank You, Lord

# Covenant Woman

Covenant woman got a contract with the Lord
Way up yonder, great will be her reward
Covenant woman, shining like a morning star
I know I can trust you to stay where you are

And I just got to tell you
I do intend
To stay closer than any friend
I just got to thank you
Once again
For making your prayers known
Unto heaven for me
And to you, always, so grateful
I will forever be

I've been broken, shattered like an empty cup
I'm just waiting on the Lord to rebuild and fill me up
And I know He will do it 'cause He's faithful and He's true
He must have loved me so much to send me someone as fine as you

And I just got to tell you
I do intend
To stay closer than any friend
I just got to thank you
Once again
For making your prayers known
Unto heaven for me
And to you, always, so grateful
I will forever be

Covenant woman, intimate little girl
Who knows those most secret things of me that are hidden from the world
You know we are strangers in a land we're passing through
I'll always be right by your side, I've got a covenant too

And I just got to tell you
I do intend
To stay closer than any friend
I just got to thank you
Once again
For making your prayers known
Unto heaven for me
And to you, always, so grateful
I will forever be

# What Can I Do for You?

You have given everything to me
What can I do for You?
You have given me eyes to see
What can I do for You?

Pulled me out of bondage and You made me renewed inside
Filled up a hunger that had always been denied
Opened up a door no man can shut and You opened it up so wide
And You've chosen me to be among the few
What can I do for You?

You have laid down Your life for me
What can I do for You?
You have explained every mystery
What can I do for You?

Soon as a man is born, you know the sparks begin to fly
He gets wise in his own eyes and he's made to believe a lie
Who would deliver him from the death he's bound to die?
Well, You've done it all and there's no more anyone can pretend to do
What can I do for You?

You have given all there is to give
What can I do for You?
You have given me life to live
How can I live for You?

I know all about poison, I know all about fiery darts
I don't care how rough the road is, show me where it starts
Whatever pleases You, tell it to my heart
Well, I don't deserve it but I sure did make it through
What can I do for You?

# Solid Rock

Well, I'm hangin' on to a solid rock
Made before the foundation of the world
And I won't let go, and I can't let go, won't let go
And I can't let go, won't let go and I can't let go no more

For me He was chastised, for me He was hated
For me He was rejected by a world that He created
Nations are angry, cursed are some
People are expecting a false peace to come

Well, I'm hangin' on to a solid rock
Made before the foundation of the world
And I won't let go and I can't let go, won't let go
And I can't let go, won't let go and I can't let go no more

It's the ways of the flesh to war against the spirit
Twenty-four hours a day you can feel it and you can hear it
Using all the devices under the sun
And He never give up 'til the battle's lost or won

Well, I'm hangin' on to a solid rock
Made before the foundation of the world
And I won't let go and I can't let go, won't let go
And I can't let go, won't let go and I can't let go no more

# Pressing On

Well I'm pressing on
Yes, I'm pressing on
Well I'm pressing on
To the higher calling of my Lord

Many try to stop me, shake me up in my mind
Say, "Prove to me that He is Lord, show me a sign"
What kind of sign they need when it all come from within
When what's lost has been found, what's to come has already been?

Well I'm pressing on
Yes, I'm pressing on
Well I'm pressing on
To the higher calling of my Lord

Shake the dust off of your feet, don't look back
Nothing now can hold you down, nothing that you lack
Temptation's not an easy thing, Adam given the devil reign
Because he sinned I got no choice, it run in my vein

Well I'm pressing on
Yes, I'm pressing on
Well I'm pressing on
To the higher calling of my Lord

# In the Garden

When they came for Him in the garden, did they know?
When they came for Him in the garden, did they know?
Did they know He was the Son of God, did they know that He was Lord?
Did they hear when He told Peter, "Peter, put up your sword"?
When they came for Him in the garden, did they know?
When they came for Him in the garden, did they know?

When He spoke to them in the city, did they hear?
When He spoke to them in the city, did they hear?
Nicodemus came at night so he wouldn't be seen by men
Saying, "Master, tell me why a man must be born again"
When He spoke to them in the city, did they hear?
When He spoke to them in the city, did they hear?

When He healed the blind and crippled, did they see?
When He healed the blind and crippled, did they see?
When He said, "Pick up your bed and walk, why must you criticize?
Same thing My Father do, I can do likewise"
When He healed the blind and crippled, did they see?
When He healed the blind and crippled, did they see?

Did they speak out against Him, did they dare?
Did they speak out against Him, did they dare?
The multitude wanted to make Him king, put a crown upon His head
Why did He slip away to a quiet place instead?
Did they speak out against Him, did they dare?
Did they speak out against Him, did they dare?

When He rose from the dead, did they believe?
When He rose from the dead, did they believe?
He said, "All power is given to Me in heaven and on earth"
Did they know right then and there what the power was worth?
When He rose from the dead, did they believe?
When He rose from the dead, did they believe?

# Saving Grace

If you find it in Your heart, can I be forgiven?
Guess I owe You some kind of apology
I've escaped death so many times, I know I'm only living
By the saving grace that's over me

By this time I'd-a thought I would be sleeping
In a pine box for all eternity
My faith keeps me alive, but I still be weeping
For the saving grace that's over me

Well, the death of life, then come the resurrection
Wherever I am welcome is where I'll be
I put all my confidence in Him, my sole protection
Is the saving grace that's over me

Well, the devil's shining light, it can be most blinding
But to search for love, that ain't no more than vanity
As I look around this world all that I'm finding
Is the saving grace that's over me

The wicked know no peace and you just can't fake it
There's only one road and it leads to Calvary
It gets discouraging at times, but I know I'll make it
By the saving grace that's over me

# Are You Ready?

Are you ready, are you ready?
Are you ready, are you ready?

Are you ready to meet Jesus?
Are you where you ought to be?
Will He know you when He sees you
Or will He say, "Depart from Me"?

Are you ready, hope you're ready
Am I ready, am I ready?
Am I ready, am I ready?

Am I ready to lay down my life for the brethren
And to take up my cross?
Have I surrendered to the will of God
Or am I still acting like the boss?

Am I ready, hope I'm ready

When destruction cometh swiftly
And there's no time to say a fare-thee-well
Have you decided whether you want to be
In heaven or in hell?

Are you ready, are you ready?

Have you got some unfinished business?
Is there something holding you back?
Are you thinking for yourself
Or are you following the pack?

Are you ready, hope you're ready
Are you ready?

Are you ready for the judgment?
Are you ready for that terrible swift sword?
Are you ready for Armageddon?
Are you ready for the day of the Lord?

Are you ready, I hope you're ready

# City of Gold

There is a City of Gold
Far from the rat race that eats at your soul
Far from the madness and the bars that hold
There is a City of Gold

There is a City of Light
Raised up in the heavens and the streets are bright
Glory to God—not by deeds or by might
There is a City of Light

There is a City of Love
Surrounded by stars and the powers above
Far from this world and the stuff dreams are made of
There is a City of Love

There is a City of Grace
You drink holy water in sanctified space
No one is afraid to show their face
In the City of Grace

There is a City of Peace
Where all foul forms of destruction cease
Where the mighty have fallen and there are no police
There is a City of Peace

There is a City of Hope
Above the ravine on the green sunlit slope
All I need is an axe and a rope
To get to the City of Hope

I'm heading for the City of Gold
Before it's too late, before it gets too cold
Before I'm too tired, before I'm too old
I'm heading for the City of Gold

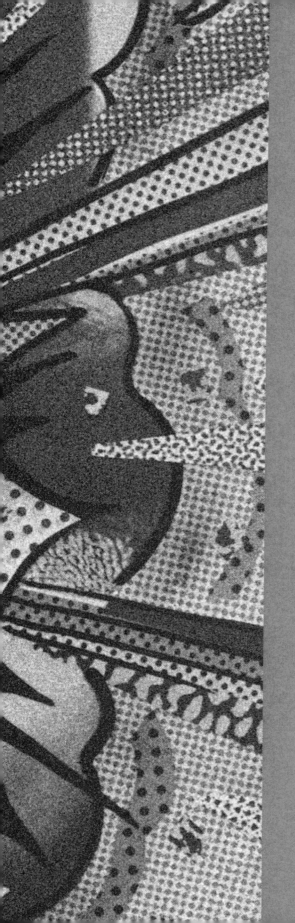

# Shot of Love

People tell me it's a sin
To know and see too much within
But I still believe she was my twin
I still can feel the string (It was all so everyth.)
She was born in the Spring (But I lost the ring)
But I was born too late)
Blame it on a Simple Twist of Fate

# Shot of Love

I need a shot of love, I need a shot of love

Don't need a shot of heroin to kill my disease
Don't need a shot of turpentine, only bring me to my knees
Don't need a shot of codeine to help me to repent
Don't need a shot of whiskey, help me be president

I need a shot of love, I need a shot of love

Doctor, can you hear me? I need some Medicaid
I seen the kingdoms of the world and it's makin' me feel afraid
What I got ain't painful, it's just bound to kill me dead
Like the men that followed Jesus when they put a price upon His head

I need a shot of love, I need a shot of love

I don't need no alibi when I'm spending time with you
I've heard all of them rumors and you have heard 'em too
Don't show me no picture show or give me no book to read
It don't satisfy the hurt inside nor the habit that it feeds

I need a shot of love, I need a shot of love

Why would I want to take your life?
You've only murdered my father, raped his wife
Tattooed my babies with a poison pen
Mocked my God, humiliated my friends

I need a shot of love, I need a shot of love

Don't wanna be with nobody tonight
Veronica not around nowhere, Mavis just ain't right
There's a man that hates me and he's swift, smooth and near
Am I supposed to set back and wait until he's here?

I need a shot of love, I need a shot of love

What makes the wind wanna blow tonight?
Don't even feel like crossing the street and my car ain't actin' right
Called home, everybody seemed to have moved away
My conscience is beginning to bother me today

I need a shot of love, I need a shot of love

I need a shot of love, I need a shot of love
If you're a doctor, I need a shot of love

# Heart of Mine

Heart of mine be still
You can play with fire but you'll get the bill
Don't let her know
Don't let her know that you love her
Don't be a fool, don't be blind
Heart of mine

Heart of mine go back home
You got no reason to wander, you got no reason to roam
Don't let her see
Don't let her see that you need her
Don't put yourself over the line
Heart of mine

Heart of mine go back where you been
It'll only be trouble for you if you let her in
Don't let her hear
Don't let her hear you want her
Don't let her think you think she's fine
Heart of mine

Heart of mine you know that she'll never be true
She'll only give to others the love that she's gotten from you
Don't let her know
Don't let her know where you're going
Don't untie the ties that bind
Heart of mine

Heart of mine so malicious and so full of guile
Give you an inch and you'll take a mile
Don't let yourself fall
Don't let yourself stumble
If you can't do the time, don't do the crime
Heart of mine

# Property of Jesus

Go ahead and talk about him because he makes you doubt
Because he has denied himself the things that you can't live without
Laugh at him behind his back just like the others do
Remind him of what he used to be when he comes walkin' through

He's the property of Jesus
Resent him to the bone
You got something better
You've got a heart of stone

Stop your conversation when he passes on the street
Hope he falls upon himself, oh, won't that be sweet
Because he can't be exploited by superstition anymore
Because he can't be bribed or bought by the things that you adore

He's the property of Jesus
Resent him to the bone
You got something better
You've got a heart of stone

When the whip that's keeping you in line doesn't make him jump
Say he's hard-of-hearin', say that he's a chump
Say he's out of step with reality as you try to test his nerve
Because he doesn't pay no tribute to the king that you serve

He's the property of Jesus
Resent him to the bone
You got something better
You've got a heart of stone

Say that he's a loser 'cause he got no common sense
Because he don't increase his worth at someone else's expense
Because he's not afraid of trying, 'cause he don't look at you and smile
'Cause he doesn't tell you jokes or fairy tales, say he's got no style

He's the property of Jesus
Resent him to the bone
You got something better
You've got a heart of stone

You can laugh at salvation, you can play Olympic games
You think that when you rest at last you'll go back from where you came
But you've picked up quite a story and you've changed since the womb
What happened to the real you, you've been captured but by whom?

He's the property of Jesus
Resent him to the bone
You got something better
You've got a heart of stone

# Lenny Bruce

Lenny Bruce is dead but his ghost lives on and on
Never did get any Golden Globe award, never made it to Synanon
He was an outlaw, that's for sure
More of an outlaw than you ever were
Lenny Bruce is gone but his spirit's livin' on and on

Maybe he had some problems, maybe some things that he couldn't work out
But he sure was funny and he sure told the truth and he knew what he was
    talkin' about
Never robbed any churches nor cut off any babies' heads
He just took the folks in high places and he shined a light in their beds
He's on some other shore, he didn't wanna live anymore

Lenny Bruce is dead but he didn't commit any crime
He just had the insight to rip off the lid before its time
I rode with him in a taxi once
Only for a mile and a half, seemed like it took a couple of months
Lenny Bruce moved on and like the ones that killed him, gone

They said that he was sick 'cause he didn't play by the rules
He just showed the wise men of his day to be nothing more than fools
They stamped him and they labeled him like they do with pants and shirts
He fought a war on a battlefield where every victory hurts
Lenny Bruce was bad, he was the brother that you never had

# Watered-Down Love

Love that's pure hopes all things
Believes all things, won't pull no strings
Won't sneak up into your room, tall, dark and handsome
Capture your heart and hold it for ransom

You don't want a love that's pure
You wanna drown love
You want a watered-down love

Love that's pure, it don't make no false claims
Intercedes for you 'stead of casting you blame
Will not deceive you or lead you into transgression
Won't write it up and make you sign a false confession

You don't want a love that's pure
You wanna drown love
You want a watered-down love

Love that's pure won't lead you astray
Won't hold you back, won't mess up your day
Won't pervert you, corrupt you with stupid wishes
It don't make you envious, it don't make you suspicious

You don't want a love that's pure
You wanna drown love
You want a watered-down love

Love that's pure ain't no accident
Always on time, is always content
An eternal flame, quietly burning
Never needs to be proud, restlessly yearning

You don't want a love that's pure
You wanna drown love
You want a watered-down love

# The Groom's Still Waiting at the Altar

Prayed in the ghetto with my face in the cement
Heard the last moan of a boxer, seen the massacre of the innocent
Felt around for the light switch, became nauseated
She was walking down the hallway while the walls deteriorated

West of the Jordan, east of the Rock of Gibraltar
I see the turning of the page
Curtain risin' on a new age
See the groom still waitin' at the altar

Try to be pure at heart, they arrest you for robbery
Mistake your shyness for aloofness, your silence for snobbery
Got the message this morning, the one that was sent to me
About the madness of becomin' what one was never meant to be

West of the Jordan, east of the Rock of Gibraltar
I see the burning of the stage
Curtain risin' on a new age
See the groom still waitin' at the altar

Don't know what I can say about Claudette that wouldn't come back to haunt me
Finally had to give her up 'bout the time she began to want me
But I know God has mercy on them who are slandered and humiliated
I'd a-done anything for that woman if she didn't make me feel so obligated

West of the Jordan, east of the Rock of Gibraltar
I see the burning of the cage
Curtain risin' on a new stage
See the groom still waitin' at the altar

Put your hand on my head, baby, do I have a temperature?
I see people who are supposed to know better standin' around like furniture
There's a wall between you and what you want and you got to leap it
Tonight you got the power to take it, tomorrow you won't have the power to keep it

West of the Jordan, east of the Rock of Gibraltar
I see the burning of the stage
Curtain risin' on a new age
See the groom still waitin' at the altar

Cities on fire, phones out of order
They're killing nuns and soldiers, there's fighting on the border
What can I say about Claudette? Ain't seen her since January
She could be respectfully married or running a whorehouse in Buenos Aires

West of the Jordan, east of the Rock of Gibraltar
I see the burning of the stage
Curtain risin' on a new age
See the groom still waitin' at the altar

# Dead Man, Dead Man

Uttering idle words from a reprobate mind
Clinging to strange promises, dying on the vine
Never bein' able to separate the good from the bad
Ooh, I can't stand it, I can't stand it
It's makin' me feel so sad

Dead man, dead man
When will you arise?
Cobwebs in your mind
Dust upon your eyes

Satan got you by the heel, there's a bird's nest in your hair
Do you have any faith at all? Do you have any love to share?
The way that you hold your head, cursin' God with every move
Ooh, I can't stand it, I can't stand it
What are you tryin' to prove?

Dead man, dead man
When will you arise?
Cobwebs in your mind
Dust upon your eyes

The glamour and the bright lights and the politics of sin
The ghetto that you build for me is the one you end up in
The race of the engine that overrules your heart
Ooh, I can't stand it, I can't stand it
Pretending that you're so smart

Dead man, dead man
When will you arise?
Cobwebs in your mind
Dust upon your eyes

What are you tryin' to overpower me with, the doctrine or the gun?
My back is already to the wall, where can I run?
The tuxedo that you're wearin', the flower in your lapel
Ooh, I can't stand it, I can't stand it
You wanna take me down to hell

Dead man, dead man
When will you arise?
Cobwebs in your mind
Dust upon your eyes

# In the Summertime

I was in your presence for an hour or so
Or was it a day? I truly don't know
Where the sun never set, where the trees hung low
By that soft and shining sea
Did you respect me for what I did
Or for what I didn't do, or for keeping it hid?
Did I lose my mind when I tried to get rid
Of everything you see?

In the summertime, ah in the summertime
In the summertime, when you were with me

I got the heart and you got the blood
We cut through iron and we cut through mud
Then came the warnin' that was before the flood
That set everybody free
Fools they made a mock of sin
Our loyalty they tried to win
But you were closer to me than my next of kin
When they didn't want to know or see

In the summertime, ah in the summertime
In the summertime when you were with me

Strangers, they meddled in our affairs
Poverty and shame was theirs
But all that sufferin' was not to be compared
With the glory that is to be
And I'm still carrying the gift you gave
It's a part of me now, it's been cherished and saved
It'll be with me unto the grave
And then unto eternity

In the summertime, ah in the summertime
In the summertime when you were with me

# Trouble

Trouble in the city, trouble in the farm
You got your rabbit's foot, you got your good-luck charm
But they can't help you none when there's trouble

Trouble
Trouble, trouble, trouble
Nothin' but trouble

Trouble in the water, trouble in the air
Go all the way to the other side of the world, you'll find trouble there
Revolution even ain't no solution for trouble

Trouble
Trouble, trouble, trouble
Nothin' but trouble

Drought and starvation, packaging of the soul
Persecution, execution, governments out of control
You can see the writing on the wall inviting trouble

Trouble
Trouble, trouble, trouble
Nothin' but trouble

Put your ear to the train tracks, put your ear to the ground
You ever feel like you're never alone even when there's nobody else around?
Since the beginning of the universe man's been cursed by trouble

Trouble
Trouble, trouble, trouble
Nothin' but trouble

Nightclubs of the broken-hearted, stadiums of the damned
Legislature, perverted nature, doors that are rudely slammed
Look into infinity, all you see is trouble

Trouble
Trouble, trouble, trouble
Nothin' but trouble

# Every Grain of Sand

In the time of my confession, in the hour of my deepest need
When the pool of tears beneath my feet flood every newborn seed
There's a dyin' voice within me reaching out somewhere
Toiling in the danger and in the morals of despair

Don't have the inclination to look back on any mistake
Like Cain, I now behold this chain of events that I must break
In the fury of the moment I can see the Master's hand
In every leaf that trembles, in every grain of sand

Oh, the flowers of indulgence and the weeds of yesteryear
Like criminals, they have choked the breath of conscience and good cheer
The sun beat down upon the steps of time to light the way
To ease the pain of idleness and the memory of decay

I gaze into the doorway of temptation's angry flame
And every time I pass that way I always hear my name
Then onward in my journey I come to understand
That every hair is numbered like every grain of sand

I have gone from rags to riches in the sorrow of the night
In the violence of a summer's dream, in the chill of a wintry light
In the bitter dance of loneliness fading into space
In the broken mirror of innocence on each forgotten face

I hear the ancient footsteps like the motion of the sea
Sometimes I turn, there's someone there, other times it's only me
I am hanging in the balance of the reality of man
Like every sparrow falling, like every grain of sand

# Let's Keep It Between Us

Let's keep it between us
These people meddlin' in our affairs, they're not our friends
Let's keep it between us
Before doors close and our togetherness comes to an end
They'll turn you against me and me against you
'Til we don't know who to trust
Oh, darlin', can we keep it between us?

Let's keep it between us
We've been through too much tough times that they never shared
They've had nothing to say to us before
Now all of a sudden it's as if they've always cared
All we need is honesty
A little humility and trust
Oh, darlin', can we keep it between us?

I know we're not perfect
Then again, neither are they
They act like we got to live for them
As if there just ain't no other way
And it's makin' me kind of tired

Can we just lay back for a moment
Before we wake up and find ourselves in a daze that's got us out of our minds?
There must be something we're overlooking here
We better drop down now and get back behind the lines
There's some things not fit for human ears
Some things don't need to be discussed
Oh, darlin', can we keep it between us?

They'll tell you one thing and me another
'Til we don't know who to trust
Oh, darlin', can we keep it between us?

Let's keep it between us
Before it all snaps and goes too far
If we can't deal with this by ourselves
Tell me we ain't worse off than they think we are
Backseat drivers don't know the feel of the wheel
But they sure know how to make a fuss
Oh, darlin', can we keep it between us?

Can we keep it between us?

# Caribbean Wind

She was the rose of Sharon from paradise lost
From the city of seven hills near the place of the cross
I was playing a show in Miami in the theater of divine comedy
Told about Jesus, told about the rain
She told me about the jungle where her brothers were slain
By a man who danced on the roof of the embassy

Was she a child or a woman, I can't say which
From one to another she could easily switch
We went into the wall to where the long arm of the law could not reach
Could I been used and played as a pawn?
It certainly was possible as the gay night wore on
Where men bathed in perfume and celebrated free speech

And them Caribbean winds still blow from Nassau to Mexico
Fanning the flames in the furnace of desire
And them distant ships of liberty on them iron waves so bold and free
Bringing everything that's near to me nearer to the fire

She looked into my soul through the clothes that I wore
She said, "We got a mutual friend over by the door
And you know he's got our best interest in mind"
He was well connected but her heart was a snare
And she had left him to die in there
There were payments due and he was a little behind

The cry of the peacock, flies buzz my head
Ceiling fan broken, there's a heat in my bed
Street band playing "Nearer My God to Thee"
We met at the steeple where the mission bells ring
She said, "I know what you're thinking, but there ain't a thing
You can do about it, so let us just agree to agree"

And them Caribbean winds still blow from Nassau to Mexico
Fanning the flames in the furnace of desire
And them distant ships of liberty on them iron waves so bold and free
Bringing everything that's near to me nearer to the fire

Atlantic City by the cold grey sea
I hear a voice crying, "Daddy," I always think it's for me
But it's only the silence in the buttermilk hills that call
Every new messenger brings evil report
'Bout armies on the march and time that is short
And famines and earthquakes and hatred written upon walls

---

Would I have married her? I don't know, I suppose
She had bells in her braids and they hung to her toes
But I kept hearing my name and had to be movin' on
I saw screws break loose, saw the devil pound tin
I saw a house in the country being torn from within
I heard my ancestors calling from the land far beyond

And them Caribbean winds still blow from Nassau to Mexico
Fanning the flames in the furnace of desire
And them distant ships of liberty on them iron waves so bold and free
Bringing everything that's near to me nearer to the fire

———

# Need a Woman

It's been raining in the trenches all day long, dripping down to my clothes
My patience is wearing thin, got a fire inside my nose
Searching for the truth the way God designed it
The truth is I might drown before I find it

Well I need a woman, yes I do
Need a woman, yes I do
Someone who can see me as I am
Somebody who just don't give a damn
And I want you to be that woman every night
Be that woman

I've had my eyes on you baby for about five long years
You probably don't know me at all, but I have seen your laughter and tears
Now you don't frighten me, my heart is jumping
And you look like it wouldn't hurt you none to have a man
    who could give ya something

Well I need a woman, oh don't I
Need a woman, bring it home safe at last
Seen you turn the corner, seen your boot heels spark
Seen you in the daylight, and watched you in the dark
And I want you to be that woman, all right
Be that woman every night

Well, if you believe in something long enough you just naturally
    come to think it's true
There ain't no wall you can't cross over, ain't no fire you can't walk through
Well, believing is all right, just don't let the wrong people know what it's all about
They might put the evil eye on you, use their hidden powers to try to turn you out

Well I need a woman, just to be my queen
Need a woman, know what I mean?

# Angelina

Well, it's always been my nature to take chances
My right hand drawing back while my left hand advances
Where the current is strong and the monkey dances
To the tune of a concertina

Blood dryin' in my yellow hair as I go from shore to shore
I know what it is that has drawn me to your door
But whatever it could be, makes me think you've seen me before
Angelina

Oh, Angelina. Oh, Angelina

His eyes were two slits that would make a snake proud
With a face that any painter would paint as he walked through the crowd
Worshipping a god with the body of a woman well endowed
And the head of a hyena

Do I need your permission to turn the other cheek?
If you can read my mind, why must I speak?
No, I have heard nothing about the man that you seek
Angelina

Oh, Angelina. Oh, Angelina

In the valley of the giants where the stars and stripes explode
The peaches they were sweet and the milk and honey flowed
I was only following instructions when the judge sent me down the road
With your subpoena

When you cease to exist, then who will you blame
I've tried my best to love you but I cannot play this game
Your best friend and my worst enemy is one and the same
Angelina

Oh, Angelina. Oh, Angelina

There's a black Mercedes rollin' through the combat zone
Your servants are half dead, you're down to the bone
Tell me, tall men, where would you like to be overthrown
Maybe down in Jerusalem or Argentina?

She was stolen from her mother when she was three days old
Now her vengeance has been satisfied and her possessions have been sold
He's surrounded by God's angels and she's wearin' a blindfold
And so are you, Angelina

Oh, Angelina. Oh, Angelina

I see pieces of men marching, trying to take heaven by force
I can see the unknown rider, I can see the pale white horse
In God's truth tell me what you want and you'll have it of course
Just step into the arena

Beat a path of retreat up them spiral staircases
Pass the tree of smoke, pass the angel with four faces
Begging God for mercy and weepin' in unholy places
Angelina

Oh, Angelina. Oh, Angelina

# You Changed My Life

I was listening to the voices of death on parade
Singing about conspiracy, wanted me to be afraid
Working for a system I couldn't understand or trust
Suffered ridicule and wanting to give it all up in disgust

But you changed my life
Came along in a time of strife
In hunger and need, you made my heart bleed
You changed my life

Talk about salvation, people suddenly get tired
They got a million things to do, they're all so inspired
You do the work of the devil, you got a million friends
They'll be there when you got something, they'll take it all in the end

But you changed my life
Came along in a time of strife
I was under the gun, clouds blocking the sun
You changed my life

Well, the nature of man is to beg and to steal
I do it myself, it's not so unreal
The call of the wild is forever at my door
Wants me to fly like an eagle while being chained to the floor

But you changed my life
Came along in a time of strife
From silver and gold to what man cannot hold
You changed my life

I was eating with the pigs off a fancy tray
I was told I was looking good and to have a nice day
It all seemed so proper, it all seemed so elite
Eating that absolute garbage while being so discreet

But you changed my life
Came along in a time of strife
From silver and gold to what man cannot hold
You changed my life

You were glowing in the sun while being peaceably calm
While orphans of man danced to the beat of the palm
Your eyes were on fire, your feet were of brass
In the world you had made they made you an outcast

You changed my life
Came along in a time of strife
From silver and gold to what man cannot hold
You changed my life

There was someone in my body that I could hardly see
Invading my privacy making my decisions for me
Holding me back, not letting me stand
Making me feel like a stranger in a strange land

But you changed my life
Came along in a time of strife
You come down the line, gave me a new mind
You changed my life

My Lord and my Savior, my companion, my friend
Heart fixer, mind regulator, true to the end
My creator, my comforter, my cause for joy
What the world is set against but will never destroy

You changed my life
Came along in a time of strife
You came in like the wind, like Errol Flynn
You changed my life

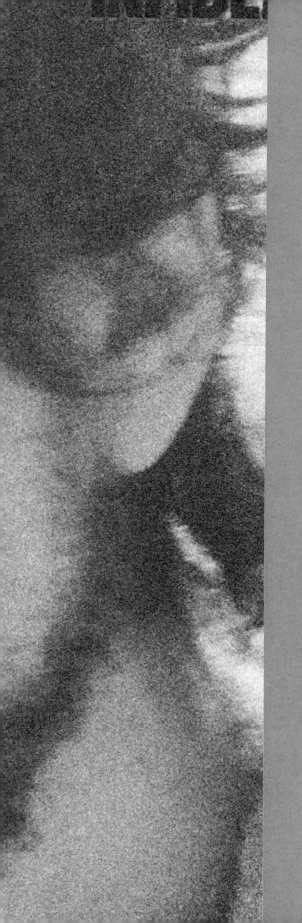

# Infidels

---

Jokerman

Sweetheart Like You

Neighborhood Bully

License to Kill

Man of Peace

Union Sundown

I and I

Don't Fall Apart on Me Tonight

*additional lyrics*

Blind Willie McTell

Foot of Pride

Lord Protect My Child

Someone's Got a Hold of My Heart (Early version
   of "Tight Connection to My Heart")

Tell Me

They say that oppression is a cruel tutor YOU KNOW NEWS OF YOU HAS COME
And injustice is a nurse DOWN THE LINE EVEN BEFORE YA CAME IN THE DOOR!
You can put your hand in the hand of a man with a nose that can't smell THEY SAY
But you put your confidence in him and that's worse IN YOUR FATHER'S HOUSE,
Snap out of it, baby THERE'S MANY MANSIONS — EACH ONE OF 'M GOT A
People are jealous of you
They smile in your face, but behind your back they hiss FIRE PROOF FLOOR!
What's a sweetheart like you doin' in a dump like this

# Jokerman

Standing on the waters casting your bread
While the eyes of the idol with the iron head are glowing
Distant ships sailing into the mist
You were born with a snake in both of your fists while a hurricane was blowing
Freedom just around the corner for you
But with the truth so far off, what good will it do?

Jokerman dance to the nightingale tune
Bird fly high by the light of the moon
Oh, oh, oh, Jokerman

So swiftly the sun sets in the sky
You rise up and say goodbye to no one
Fools rush in where angels fear to tread
Both of their futures, so full of dread, you don't show one
Shedding off one more layer of skin
Keeping one step ahead of the persecutor within

Jokerman dance to the nightingale tune
Bird fly high by the light of the moon
Oh, oh, oh, Jokerman

You're a man of the mountains, you can walk on the clouds
Manipulator of crowds, you're a dream twister
You're going to Sodom and Gomorrah
But what do you care? Ain't nobody there would want to marry your sister
Friend to the martyr, a friend to the woman of shame
You look into the fiery furnace, see the rich man without any name

Jokerman dance to the nightingale tune
Bird fly high by the light of the moon
Oh, oh, oh, Jokerman

Well, the Book of Leviticus and Deuteronomy
The law of the jungle and the sea are your only teachers
In the smoke of the twilight on a milk-white steed
Michelangelo indeed could've carved out your features
Resting in the fields, far from the turbulent space
Half asleep near the stars with a small dog licking your face

Jokerman dance to the nightingale tune
Bird fly high by the light of the moon
Oh, oh, oh, Jokerman

Well, the rifleman's stalking the sick and the lame
Preacherman seeks the same, who'll get there first is uncertain
Nightsticks and water cannons, tear gas, padlocks
Molotov cocktails and rocks behind every curtain
False-hearted judges dying in the webs that they spin
Only a matter of time 'til night comes steppin' in

Jokerman dance to the nightingale tune
Bird fly high by the light of the moon
Oh, oh, oh, Jokerman

It's a shadowy world, skies are slippery grey
A woman just gave birth to a prince today and dressed him in scarlet
He'll put the priest in his pocket, put the blade to the heat
Take the motherless children off the street and place them at the feet of a harlot
Oh, Jokerman, you know what he wants
Oh, Jokerman, you don't show any response

Jokerman dance to the nightingale tune
Bird fly high by the light of the moon
Oh, oh, oh, Jokerman

# Sweetheart Like You

Well, the pressure's down, the boss ain't here
He gone North, he ain't around
They say that vanity got the best of him
But he sure left here after sundown
By the way, that's a cute hat
And that smile's so hard to resist
But what's a sweetheart like you doin' in a dump like this?

You know, I once knew a woman who looked like you
She wanted a whole man, not just a half
She used to call me sweet daddy when I was only a child
You kind of remind me of her when you laugh
In order to deal in this game, got to make the queen disappear
It's done with a flick of the wrist
What's a sweetheart like you doin' in a dump like this?

You know, a woman like you should be at home
That's where you belong
Watching out for someone who loves you true
Who would never do you wrong
Just how much abuse will you be able to take?
Well, there's no way to tell by that first kiss
What's a sweetheart like you doin' in a dump like this?

You know you can make a name for yourself
You can hear them tires squeal
You can be known as the most beautiful woman
Who ever crawled across cut glass to make a deal

You know, news of you has come down the line
Even before ya came in the door
They say in your father's house, there's many mansions
Each one of them got a fireproof floor
Snap out of it, baby, people are jealous of you
They smile to your face, but behind your back they hiss
What's a sweetheart like you doin' in a dump like this?

Got to be an important person to be in here, honey
Got to have done some evil deed
Got to have your own harem when you come in the door
Got to play your harp until your lips bleed

They say that patriotism is the last refuge
To which a scoundrel clings
Steal a little and they throw you in jail
Steal a lot and they make you king
There's only one step down from here, baby
It's called the land of permanent bliss
What's a sweetheart like you doin' in a dump like this?

# Neighborhood Bully

Well, the neighborhood bully, he's just one man
His enemies say he's on their land
They got him outnumbered about a million to one
He got no place to escape to, no place to run
He's the neighborhood bully

The neighborhood bully just lives to survive
He's criticized and condemned for being alive
He's not supposed to fight back, he's supposed to have thick skin
He's supposed to lay down and die when his door is kicked in
He's the neighborhood bully

The neighborhood bully been driven out of every land
He's wandered the earth an exiled man
Seen his family scattered, his people hounded and torn
He's always on trial for just being born
He's the neighborhood bully

Well, he knocked out a lynch mob, he was criticized
Old women condemned him, said he should apologize
Then he destroyed a bomb factory, nobody was glad
The bombs were meant for him. He was supposed to feel bad
He's the neighborhood bully

Well, the chances are against it and the odds are slim
That he'll live by the rules that the world makes for him
'Cause there's a noose at his neck and a gun at his back
And a license to kill him is given out to every maniac
He's the neighborhood bully

He got no allies to really speak of
What he gets he must pay for, he don't get it out of love
He buys obsolete weapons and he won't be denied
But no one sends flesh and blood to fight by his side
He's the neighborhood bully

Well, he's surrounded by pacifists who all want peace
They pray for it nightly that the bloodshed must cease
Now, they wouldn't hurt a fly. To hurt one they would weep
They lay and they wait for this bully to fall asleep
He's the neighborhood bully

Every empire that's enslaved him is gone
Egypt and Rome, even the great Babylon
He's made a garden of paradise in the desert sand
In bed with nobody, under no one's command
He's the neighborhood bully

Now his holiest books have been trampled upon
No contract he signed was worth what it was written on
He took the crumbs of the world and he turned it into wealth
Took sickness and disease and he turned it into health
He's the neighborhood bully

What's anybody indebted to him for?
Nothin', they say. He just likes to cause war
Pride and prejudice and superstition indeed
They wait for this bully like a dog waits to feed
He's the neighborhood bully

What has he done to wear so many scars?
Does he change the course of rivers? Does he pollute the moon and stars?
Neighborhood bully, standing on the hill
Running out the clock, time standing still
Neighborhood bully

# License to Kill

Man thinks 'cause he rules the earth he can do with it as he please
And if things don't change soon, he will
Oh, man has invented his doom
First step was touching the moon

Now, there's a woman on my block
She just sit there as the night grows still
She say who gonna take away his license to kill?

Now, they take him and they teach him and they groom him for life
And they set him on a path where he's bound to get ill
Then they bury him with stars
Sell his body like they do used cars

Now, there's a woman on my block
She just sit there facin' the hill
She say who gonna take away his license to kill?

Now, he's hell-bent for destruction, he's afraid and confused
And his brain has been mismanaged with great skill
All he believes are his eyes
And his eyes, they just tell him lies

But there's a woman on my block
Sitting there in a cold chill
She say who gonna take away his license to kill?

Ya may be a noisemaker, spirit maker
Heartbreaker, backbreaker
Leave no stone unturned
May be an actor in a plot
That might be all that you got
'Til your error you clearly learn

Now he worships at an altar of a stagnant pool
And when he sees his reflection, he's fulfilled
Oh, man is opposed to fair play
He wants it all and he wants it his way

Now, there's a woman on my block
She just sit there as the night grows still
She say who gonna take away his license to kill?

# Man of Peace

Look out your window, baby, there's a scene you'd like to catch
The band is playing "Dixie," a man got his hand outstretched
Could be the Führer
Could be the local priest
You know sometimes Satan comes as a man of peace

He got a sweet gift of gab, he got a harmonious tongue
He knows every song of love that ever has been sung
Good intentions can be evil
Both hands can be full of grease
You know that sometimes Satan comes as a man of peace

Well, first he's in the background, then he's in the front
Both eyes are looking like they're on a rabbit hunt
Nobody can see through him
No, not even the Chief of Police
You know that sometimes Satan comes as a man of peace

Well, he catch you when you're hoping for a glimpse of the sun
Catch you when your troubles feel like they weigh a ton
He could be standing next to you
The person that you'd notice least
I hear that sometimes Satan comes as a man of peace

Well, he can be fascinating, he can be dull
He can ride down Niagara Falls in the barrels of your skull
I can smell something cooking
I can tell there's going to be a feast
You know that sometimes Satan comes as a man of peace

He's a great humanitarian, he's a great philanthropist
He knows just where to touch you, honey, and how you like to be kissed
He'll put both his arms around you
You can feel the tender touch of the beast
You know that sometimes Satan comes as a man of peace

Well, the howling wolf will howl tonight, the king snake will crawl
Trees that've stood for a thousand years suddenly will fall
Wanna get married? Do it now
Tomorrow all activity will cease
You know that sometimes Satan comes as a man of peace

Somewhere Mama's weeping for her blue-eyed boy
She's holding them little white shoes and that little broken toy
And he's following a star
The same one them three men followed from the East
I hear that sometimes Satan comes as a man of peace

# Union Sundown

Well, my shoes, they come from Singapore
My flashlight's from Taiwan
My tablecloth's from Malaysia
My belt buckle's from the Amazon
You know, this shirt I wear comes from the Philippines
And the car I drive is a Chevrolet
It was put together down in Argentina
By a guy makin' thirty cents a day

Well, it's sundown on the union
And what's made in the U.S.A.
Sure was a good idea
'Til greed got in the way

Well, this silk dress is from Hong Kong
And the pearls are from Japan
Well, the dog collar's from India
And the flower pot's from Pakistan
All the furniture, it says "Made in Brazil"
Where a woman, she slaved for sure
Bringin' home thirty cents a day to a family of twelve
You know, that's a lot of money to her

Well, it's sundown on the union
And what's made in the U.S.A.
Sure was a good idea
'Til greed got in the way

Well, you know, lots of people complainin' that there is no work
I say, "Why you say that for
When nothin' you got is U.S.–made?"
They don't make nothin' here no more
You know, capitalism is above the law
It say, "It don't count 'less it sells"
When it costs too much to build it at home
You just build it cheaper someplace else

Well, it's sundown on the union
And what's made in the U.S.A.
Sure was a good idea
'Til greed got in the way

Well, the job that you used to have
They gave it to somebody down in El Salvador
The unions are big business, friend
And they're goin' out like a dinosaur
They used to grow food in Kansas
Now they want to grow it on the moon and eat it raw
I can see the day coming when even your home garden
Is gonna be against the law

Well, it's sundown on the union
And what's made in the U.S.A.
Sure was a good idea
'Til greed got in the way

Democracy don't rule the world
You'd better get that in your head
This world is ruled by violence
But I guess that's better left unsaid
From Broadway to the Milky Way
That's a lot of territory indeed
And a man's gonna do what he has to do
When he's got a hungry mouth to feed

Well, it's sundown on the union
And what's made in the U.S.A.
Sure was a good idea
'Til greed got in the way

# I and I

Been so long since a strange woman has slept in my bed
Look how sweet she sleeps, how free must be her dreams
In another lifetime she must have owned the world, or been faithfully wed
To some righteous king who wrote psalms beside moonlit streams

I and I
In creation where one's nature neither honors nor forgives
I and I
One says to the other, no man sees my face and lives

Think I'll go out and go for a walk
Not much happenin' here, nothin' ever does
Besides, if she wakes up now, she'll just want me to talk
I got nothin' to say, 'specially about whatever was

I and I
In creation where one's nature neither honors nor forgives
I and I
One says to the other, no man sees my face and lives

Took an untrodden path once, where the swift don't win the race
It goes to the worthy, who can divide the word of truth
Took a stranger to teach me, to look into justice's beautiful face
And to see an eye for an eye and a tooth for a tooth

I and I
In creation where one's nature neither honors nor forgives
I and I
One says to the other, no man sees my face and lives

Outside of two men on a train platform there's nobody in sight
They're waiting for spring to come, smoking down the track
The world could come to an end tonight, but that's all right
She should still be there sleepin' when I get back

I and I
In creation where one's nature neither honors nor forgives
I and I
One says to the other, no man sees my face and lives

Noontime, and I'm still pushin' myself along the road, the darkest part
Into the narrow lanes, I can't stumble or stay put
Someone else is speakin' with my mouth, but I'm listening only to my heart
I've made shoes for everyone, even you, while I still go barefoot

I and I
In creation where one's nature neither honors nor forgives
I and I
One says to the other, no man sees my face and lives

# Don't Fall Apart on Me Tonight

Just a minute before you leave, girl
Just a minute before you touch the door
What is it that you're trying to achieve, girl?
Do you think we can talk about it some more?
You know, the streets are filled with vipers
Who've lost all ray of hope
You know, it ain't even safe no more
In the palace of the Pope

Don't fall apart on me tonight
I just don't think that I could handle it
Don't fall apart on me tonight
Yesterday's just a memory
Tomorrow is never what it's supposed to be
And I need you, yeah

Come over here from over there, girl
Sit down here. You can have my chair
I can't see us goin' anywhere, girl
The only place open is a thousand miles away and I can't take you there
I wish I'd have been a doctor
Maybe I'd have saved some life that had been lost
Maybe I'd have done some good in the world
'Stead of burning every bridge I crossed

Don't fall apart on me tonight
I just don't think that I could handle it
Don't fall apart on me tonight
Yesterday's just a memory
Tomorrow is never what it's supposed to be
And I need you, oh, yeah

I ain't too good at conversation, girl
So you might not know exactly how I feel
But if I could, I'd bring you to the mountaintop, girl
And build you a house made out of stainless steel
But it's like I'm stuck inside a painting
That's hanging in the Louvre
My throat start to tickle and my nose itches
But I know that I can't move

Don't fall apart on me tonight
I just don't think that I could handle it
Don't fall apart on me tonight
Yesterday's gone but the past lives on
Tomorrow's just one step beyond
And I need you, oh, yeah

Who are these people who are walking towards you?
Do you know them or will there be a fight?
With their humorless smiles so easy to see through
Can they tell you what's wrong from what's right?
Do you remember St. James Street
Where you blew Jackie P.'s mind?
You were so fine, Clark Gable would have fell at your feet
And laid his life on the line

Let's try to get beneath the surface waste, girl
No more booby traps and bombs
No more decadence and charm
No more affection that's misplaced, girl
No more mudcake creatures lying in your arms
What about that millionaire with the drumsticks in his pants?
He looked so baffled and so bewildered
When he played and we didn't dance

Don't fall apart on me tonight
I just don't think that I could handle it
Don't fall apart on me tonight
Yesterday's just a memory
Tomorrow is never what it's supposed to be
And I need you, yeah

# Blind Willie McTell

Seen the arrow on the doorpost
Saying, "This land is condemned
All the way from New Orleans
To new Jerusalem"
I traveled through East Texas
Where many martyrs fell
And I can tell you one thing
Nobody can sing the blues
Like Blind Willie McTell

Well, I heard that hoot owl singing
As they were taking down the tents
The stars above the barren trees
Were his only audience
Them charcoal gypsy maidens
Can strut their feathers well
And I can tell you one thing
Nobody can sing the blues
Like Blind Willie McTell

There's a woman by the river
With some fine young handsome man
He's dressed up like a squire
Bootlegged whiskey in his hand
Some of them died in the battle
Some of them survived as well
And I can tell you one thing
Nobody can sing the blues
Like Blind Willie McTell

Well, God is in His heaven
And we all want what's His
But power and greed and corruptible seed
Seem to be all that there is
I'm gazing out the window
Of the St. James Hotel
And I can tell you one thing
Nobody can sing the blues
Like Blind Willie McTell

# Foot of Pride

Like the lion tears the flesh off of a man
So can a woman who passes herself off as a male
They sang "Danny Boy" at his funeral and the Lord's Prayer
Preacher talking 'bout Christ betrayed
It's like the earth just opened and swallowed him up
He reached too high, was thrown back to the ground
You know what they say about bein' nice to the right people on the way up
Sooner or later you gonna meet them comin' down

Well, there ain't no goin' back
When your foot of pride come down
Ain't no goin' back

Hear ya got a brother named James, don't forget faces or names
Sunken cheeks and his blood is mixed
He looked straight into the sun and said revenge is mine
But he drinks, and drinks can be fixed
Sing me one more song, about ya love me to the moon and the stranger
And your fall-by-the sword love affair with Errol Flynn
In these times of compassion when conformity's in fashion
Say one more stupid thing to me before the final nail is driven in

Well, there ain't no goin' back
When your foot of pride come down
Ain't no goin' back

There's a retired businessman named Red
Cast down from heaven and he's out of his head
He feeds off of everyone that he can touch
He said he only deals in cash or sells tickets to a plane crash
He's not somebody that you play around with much
Miss Delilah is his, a Phillistine is what she is
She'll do wondrous works with your fate, feed you coconut bread,
    spice buns in your bed
If you don't mind sleepin' with your head face down in a grave

Well, there ain't no goin' back
When your foot of pride come down
Ain't no goin' back

———

Well, they'll choose a man for you to meet tonight
You'll play the fool and learn how to walk through doors
How to enter into the gates of paradise
No, how to carry a burden too heavy to be yours
Yeah, from the stage they'll be tryin' to get water outa rocks
A whore will pass the hat, collect a hundred grand and say thanks
They like to take all this money from sin, build big universities to study in
Sing "Amazing Grace" all the way to the Swiss banks

Well, there ain't no goin' back
When your foot of pride come down
Ain't no goin' back

They got some beautiful people out there, man
They can be a terror to your mind and show you how to hold your tongue
They got mystery written all over their forehead
They kill babies in the crib and say only the good die young
They don't believe in mercy
Judgement on them is something that you'll never see
They can exalt you up or bring you down main route
Turn you into anything that they want you to be

Well, there ain't no goin' back
When your foot of pride come down
Ain't no goin' back

Yes, I guess I loved him too
I can still see him in my mind climbin' that hill
Did he make it to the top, well he probably did and dropped
Struck down by the strength of the will
Ain't nothin' left here partner, just the dust of a plague
    that has left this whole town afraid
From now on, this'll be where you're from
Let the dead bury the dead. Your time will come
Let hot iron blow as he raised the shade

Well, there ain't no goin' back
When your foot of pride come down
Ain't no goin' back

# Lord Protect My Child

For his age, he's wise
He's got his mother's eyes
There's gladness in his heart
He's young and he's wild
My only prayer is, if I can't be there
Lord, protect my child

As his youth now unfolds
He is centuries old
Just to see him at play makes me smile
No matter what happens to me
No matter what my destiny
Lord, protect my child

The whole world is asleep
You can look at it and weep
Few things you find are worthwhile
And though I don't ask for much
No material things to touch
Lord, protect my child

He's young and on fire
Full of hope and desire
In a world that's been raped and defiled
If I fall along the way
And can't see another day
Lord, protect my child

There'll be a time I hear tell
When all will be well
When God and man will be reconciled
But until men lose their chains
And righteousness reigns
Lord, protect my child

# Someone's Got a Hold of My Heart

(Early version of "Tight Connection to My Heart")

They say, "Eat, drink and be merry"
"Take the bull by the horns"
I keep seeing visions of you, a lily among thorns
Everything looks a little far away to me

Gettin' harder and harder to recognize the trap
Too much information about nothin'
Too much educated rap
It's just like you told me, just like you said it would be

The moon rising like wildfire
I feel the breath of a storm
Something I got to do tonight
You go inside and stay warm

Someone's got a hold of my heart
Someone's got a hold of my heart
Someone's got a hold of my heart
You—
Yeah, you got a hold of my heart

Just got back from a city of flaming red skies
Everybody thinks with their stomach
There's plenty of spies
Every street is crooked, they just wind around till they disappear

Madame Butterfly, she lulled me to sleep
Like an ancient river
So wide and deep
She said, "Be easy, baby, ain't nothin' worth stealin' here"

You're the one I've been waitin' for
You're the one I desire
But you must first realize
I'm not another man for hire

Someone's got a hold of my heart
Someone's got a hold of my heart
Someone's got a hold of my heart
You, you, you, you
Yeah, you got a hold of my heart

Hear that hot-blooded singer
On the bandstand croon
September song, Memphis in June
While they're beating the devil out of a guy who's wearing a powder blue wig

I been to Babylon
I gotta confess
I could still hear the voice crying in the wilderness
What looks large from a distance, close up is never that big
Never could learn to drink that blood and call it wine
Never could learn to look at your face and call it mine

Someone's got a hold of my heart
Someone's got a hold of my heart
Someone's got a hold of my heart
You—
Yeah, you got a hold of my heart

# Tell Me

Tell me—I've got to know
Tell me—Tell me before I go
Does that flame still burn, does that fire still glow
Or has it died out and melted like the snow
Tell me
Tell me

Tell me—what are you focused upon
Tell me—will it come to me after you're gone
Tell me quick with a glance on the side
Shall I hold you close or shall I let you go by
Tell me
Tell me

Are you lookin' at me and thinking of somebody else
Can you feel the heat and the beat of my pulse
Do you have any secrets
That will only come out in time
Do you lay in bed and stare at the stars
Is your main friend someone who's an old acquaintance of ours
Tell me
Tell me

Tell me—what's in back of them pretty brown eyes
Tell me—behind what door your treasure lies
Ever gone broke in a big way
Ever done the opposite of what the experts say
Tell me
Tell me

Is it some kind of game that you're playin' with me
Am I imagining something that never can be
Do you have any morals
Do you have any point of view
Is that a smile I see on your face
Will it take you to glory or to disgrace
Tell me
Tell me

Tell me—is my name in your book
Tell me—will you go back and take another look
Tell me the truth, tell me no lies
Are you someone whom anyone prays for or cries
Tell me
Tell me

---

# Empire Burlesque

Tight Connection to My Heart
  (Has Anybody Seen My Love)
Seeing the Real You at Last
I'll Remember You
Clean-Cut Kid
Never Gonna Be the Same Again
Trust Yourself
Emotionally Yours
When the Night Comes Falling from the Sky
Something's Burning, Baby
Dark Eyes

If I'd a thought about, I wouldn't 've done it, (hesitated) I think I
                                                    woulda let it slide
If I'd a lived my life by what others ~~know~~ think, the heart
(ya been asked (~~~~~~~~~~) them inside me would've died
but I moaned for men's ..... how his cheap morality,
Some one had to reach for the rising star, it looked like it
                                                    was up to me

# Tight Connection to My Heart (Has Anybody Seen My Love)

Well, I had to move fast
And I couldn't with you around my neck
I said I'd send for you and I did
What did you expect?
My hands are sweating
And we haven't even started yet
I'll go along with the charade
Until I can think my way out
I know it was all a big joke
Whatever it was about
Someday maybe
I'll remember to forget

I'm gonna get my coat
I feel the breath of a storm
There's something I've got to do tonight
You go inside and stay warm

Has anybody seen my love
Has anybody seen my love
Has anybody seen my love
I don't know
Has anybody seen my love?

You want to talk to me
Go ahead and talk
Whatever you got to say to me
Won't come as any shock
I must be guilty of something
You just whisper it into my ear
Madame Butterfly
She lulled me to sleep
In a town without pity
Where the water runs deep
She said, "Be easy, baby
There ain't nothin' worth stealin' in here"

You're the one I've been looking for
You're the one that's got the key
But I can't figure out whether I'm too good for you
Or you're too good for me

Has anybody seen my love
Has anybody seen my love
Has anybody seen my love
I don't know
Has anybody seen my love?

Well, they're not showing any lights tonight
And there's no moon
There's just a hot-blooded singer
Singing "Memphis in June"
While they're beatin' the devil out of a guy
Who's wearing a powder-blue wig
Later he'll be shot
For resisting arrest
I can still hear his voice crying
In the wilderness
What looks large from a distance
Close up ain't never that big

Never could learn to drink that blood
And call it wine
Never could learn to hold you, love
And call you mine

# Seeing the Real You at Last

Well, I thought that the rain would cool things down
But it looks like it don't
I'd like to get you to change your mind
But it looks like you won't

From now on I'll be busy
Ain't goin' nowhere fast
I'm just glad it's over
And I'm seeing the real you at last

Well, didn't I risk my neck for you
Didn't I take chances?
Didn't I rise above it all for you
The most unfortunate circumstances?

Well, I have had some rotten nights
Didn't think that they would pass
I'm just thankful and grateful
To be seeing the real you at last

I'm hungry and I'm irritable
And I'm tired of this bag of tricks
At one time there was nothing wrong with me
That you could not fix

Well, I sailed through the storm
Strapped to the mast
But the time has come
And I'm seeing the real you at last

When I met you, baby
You didn't show no visible scars
You could ride like Annie Oakley
You could shoot like Belle Starr

Well, I don't mind a reasonable amount of trouble
Trouble always comes to pass
But all I care about now
Is that I'm seeing the real you at last

Well, I'm gonna quit this baby talk now
I guess I should have known
I got troubles, I think maybe you got troubles
I think maybe we'd better leave each other alone

Whatever you gonna do
Please do it fast
I'm still trying to get used to
Seeing the real you at last

# I'll Remember You

I'll remember you
When I've forgotten all the rest
You to me were true
You to me were the best
When there is no more
You cut to the core
Quicker than anyone I knew
When I'm all alone
In the great unknown
I'll remember you

I'll remember you
At the end of the trail
I had so much left to do
I had so little time to fail
There's some people that
You don't forget
Even though you've only seen 'm one time or two
When the roses fade
And I'm in the shade
I'll remember you

Didn't I, didn't I try to love you?
Didn't I, didn't I try to care?
Didn't I sleep, didn't I weep beside you
With the rain blowing in your hair?

I'll remember you
When the wind blows through the piney wood
It was you who came right through
It was you who understood
Though I'd never say
That I done it the way
That you'd have liked me to
In the end
My dear sweet friend
I'll remember you

# Clean-Cut Kid

Everybody wants to know why he couldn't adjust
Adjust to what, a dream that bust?

He was a clean-cut kid
But they made a killer out of him
That's what they did

They said what's up is down, they said what isn't is
They put ideas in his head he thought were his

He was a clean-cut kid
But they made a killer out of him
That's what they did

He was on the baseball team, he was in the marching band
When he was ten years old he had a watermelon stand

He was a clean-cut kid
But they made a killer out of him
That's what they did

He went to church on Sunday, he was a Boy Scout
For his friends he would turn his pockets inside out

He was a clean-cut kid
But they made a killer out of him
That's what they did

They said, "Listen boy, you're just a pup"
They sent him to a napalm health spa to shape up

They gave him dope to smoke, drinks and pills
A jeep to drive, blood to spill

They said "Congratulations, you got what it takes"
They sent him back into the rat race without any brakes

He was a clean-cut kid
But they made a killer out of him
That's what they did

He bought the American dream but it put him in debt
The only game he could play was Russian roulette

He drank Coca-Cola, he was eating Wonder Bread
Ate Burger Kings, he was well fed

He went to Hollywood to see Peter O'Toole
He stole a Rolls-Royce and drove it in a swimming pool

They took a clean-cut kid
And they made a killer out of him
That's what they did

He could've sold insurance, owned a restaurant or bar
Could've been an accountant or a tennis star

He was wearing boxing gloves, took a dive one day
Off the Golden Gate Bridge into China Bay

His mama walks the floor, his daddy weeps and moans
They gotta sleep together in a home they don't own

They took a clean-cut kid
And they made a killer out of him
That's what they did

Well, everybody's asking why he couldn't adjust
All he ever wanted was somebody to trust

They took his head and turned it inside out
He never did know what it was all about

He had a steady job, he joined the choir
He never did plan to walk the high wire

They took a clean-cut kid
And they made a killer out of him
That's what they did

# Never Gonna Be the Same Again

Now you're here beside me, baby
You're a living dream
And every time you get this close
It makes me want to scream
You touched me and you knew
That I was warm for you and then
I ain't never gonna be the same again

Sorry if I hurt you, baby
Sorry if I did
Sorry if I touched the place
Where your secrets are hid
But you meant more than everything
And I could not pretend
I ain't never gonna be the same again

You give me something to think about, baby
Every time I see ya
Don't worry, baby, I don't mind leaving
I'd just like it to be my idea

You taught me how to love you, baby
You taught me, oh, so well
Now, I can't go back to what was, baby
I can't unring the bell
You took my reality
And cast it to the wind
And I ain't never gonna be the same again

# Trust Yourself

Trust yourself
Trust yourself to do the things that only you know best
Trust yourself
Trust yourself to do what's right and not be second-guessed
Don't trust me to show you beauty
When beauty may only turn to rust
If you need somebody you can trust, trust yourself

Trust yourself
Trust yourself to know the way that will prove true in the end
Trust yourself
Trust yourself to find the path where there is no if and when
Don't trust me to show you the truth
When the truth may only be ashes and dust
If you want somebody you can trust, trust yourself

Well, you're on your own, you always were
In a land of wolves and thieves
Don't put your hope in ungodly man
Or be a slave to what somebody else believes

Trust yourself
And you won't be disappointed when vain people let you down
Trust yourself
And look not for answers where no answers can be found
Don't trust me to show you love
When my love may be only lust
If you want somebody you can trust, trust yourself

# Emotionally Yours

Come baby, find me, come baby, remind me of where I once begun
Come baby, show me, show me you know me, tell me you're the one
I could be learning, you could be yearning to see behind closed doors
But I will always be emotionally yours

Come baby, rock me, come baby, lock me into the shadows of your heart
Come baby, teach me, come baby, reach me, let the music start
I could be dreaming but I keep believing you're the one I'm livin' for
And I will always be emotionally yours

It's like my whole life never happened
When I see you, it's as if I never had a thought
I know this dream, it might be crazy
But it's the only one I've got

Come baby, shake me, come baby, take me, I would be satisfied
Come baby, hold me, come baby, help me, my arms are open wide
I could be unraveling wherever I'm traveling, even to foreign shores
But I will always be emotionally yours

# When the Night Comes Falling from the Sky

Look out across the fields, see me returning
Smoke is in your eye, you draw a smile
From the fireplace where my letters to you are burning
You've had time to think about it for a while

Well, I've walked two hundred miles, now look me over
It's the end of the chase and the moon is high
It won't matter who loves who
You'll love me or I'll love you
When the night comes falling from the sky

I can see through your walls and I know you're hurting
Sorrow covers you up like a cape
Only yesterday I know that you've been flirting
With disaster that you managed to escape

I can't provide for you no easy answers
Who are you that I should have to lie?
You'll know all about it, love
It'll fit you like a glove
When the night comes falling from the sky

I can hear your trembling heart beat like a river
You must have been protecting someone last time I called
I've never asked you for nothing you couldn't deliver
I've never asked you to set yourself up for a fall

I saw thousands who could have overcome the darkness
For the love of a lousy buck, I've watched them die
Stick around, baby, we're not through
Don't look for me, I'll see you
When the night comes falling from the sky

In your teardrops, I can see my own reflection
It was on the northern border of Texas where I crossed the line
I don't want to be a fool starving for affection
I don't want to drown in someone else's wine

For all eternity I think I will remember
That icy wind that's howling in your eye
You will seek me and you'll find me
In the wasteland of your mind
When the night comes falling from the sky

Well, I sent you my feelings in a letter
But you were gambling for support
This time tomorrow I'll know you better
When my memory is not so short

This time I'm asking for freedom
Freedom from a world which you deny
And you'll give it to me now
I'll take it anyhow
When the night comes falling from the sky

# Something's Burning, Baby

Something is burning, baby, are you aware?
Something is the matter, baby, there's smoke in your hair
Are you still my friend, baby, show me a sign
Is the love in your heart for me turning blind?

You've been avoiding the main streets for a long, long while
The truth that I'm seeking is in your missing file
What's your position, baby, what's going on?
Why is the light in your eyes nearly gone?

I know everything about this place, or so it seems
Am I no longer a part of your plans or your dreams?
Well, it is so obvious that something has changed
What's happening, baby, to make you act so strange?

Something is burning, baby, here's what I say
Even the bloodhounds of London couldn't find you today
I see the shadow of a man, baby, makin' you blue
Who is he, baby, and what's he to you?

We've reached the edge of the road, baby, where the pasture begins
Where charity is supposed to cover up a multitude of sins
But where do you live, baby, and where is the light?
Why are your eyes just staring off in the night?

I can feel it in the night when I think of you
I can feel it in the light and it's got to be true
You can't live by bread alone, you won't be satisfied
You can't roll away the stone if your hands are tied

Got to start someplace, baby, can you explain?
Please don't fade away on me, baby, like the midnight train
Answer me, baby, a casual look will do
Just what in the world has come over you?

I can feel it in the wind and it's upside down
I can feel it in the dust as I get off the bus on the outskirts of town
I've had the Mexico City blues since the last hairpin curve
I don't wanna see you bleed, I know what you need but it ain't what you deserve

Something is burning, baby, something's in flames
There's a man going 'round calling names
Ring down when you're ready, baby, I'm waiting for you
I believe in the impossible, you know that I do

# Dark Eyes

Oh, the gentlemen are talking and the midnight moon is on the riverside
They're drinking up and walking and it is time for me to slide
I live in another world where life and death are memorized
Where the earth is strung with lovers' pearls and all I see are dark eyes

A cock is crowing far away and another soldier's deep in prayer
Some mother's child has gone astray, she can't find him anywhere
But I can hear another drum beating for the dead that rise
Whom nature's beast fears as they come and all I see are dark eyes

They tell me to be discreet for all intended purposes
They tell me revenge is sweet and from where they stand, I'm sure it is
But I feel nothing for their game where beauty goes unrecognized
All I feel is heat and flame and all I see are dark eyes

Oh, the French girl, she's in paradise and a drunken man is at the wheel
Hunger pays a heavy price to the falling gods of speed and steel
Oh, time is short and the days are sweet and passion rules the arrow that flies
A million faces at my feet but all I see are dark eyes

# Knocked Out Loaded

Driftin' Too Far from Shore

Maybe Someday

Brownsville Girl

Under Your Spell

*additional lyrics*
Band of the Hand (It's Hell Time, Man!)

505

The empty mirror where all ^(HER) numbers ~~are~~ ^(were) hidden
Empty eyes, ^(disguised by) false pride & false alarms
The empty rooms where her memory ~~is~~ ^(was) forbidden
& all of mankind ~~runnin away~~ from her empty arms
^(With a burning hangover, you fell into her empty arms)

I stumbled & fell, I rode past destruction in the ditches
With the stitches stll mending neath a heart-shaped tatoo
Whinin priests & treacherous young witches
Were handing out the flowers that I'd given to you
^((nailing up))
She wakes him up in some peacefull surroundings
Chained to a tree, near mt laurel & rolling rocks
She's begging to know when will the horns be sounding —
~~H(~~He's pulling her down & she's clutching onto his long golden locks

Peace will come with tranquility & splender
In a shining cloak but will offer no reward
When her idols ~~fixa~~ fall & cruel death surrenders
With it's pale ghost retreating between shadow & sword

# Driftin' Too Far from Shore

I didn't know that you'd be leavin'
Or who you thought you were talkin' to
I figure maybe we're even
Or maybe I'm one up on you

I send you all my money
Just like I did before
I tried to reach you honey
But you're driftin' too far from shore

Driftin' too far from shore
Driftin' too far from shore
Driftin' too far from shore
Driftin' too far from shore

I ain't gonna get lost in this current
I don't like playing cat and mouse
No gentleman likes making love to a servant
Especially when he's in his father's house

I never could guess your weight, baby
Never needed to call you my whore
I always thought you were straight, baby
But you're driftin' too far from shore

Driftin' too far from shore
Driftin' too far from shore
Driftin' too far from shore
Driftin' too far from shore

Well these times and these tunnels are haunted
The bottom of the barrel is too
I waited years sometimes for what I wanted
Everybody can't be as lucky as you

Never no more do I wonder
Why you don't never play with me anymore
At any moment you could go under
'Cause you're driftin' too far from shore

Driftin' too far from shore
Driftin' too far from shore
Driftin' too far from shore
Driftin' too far from shore

You and me we had completeness
I give you all of what I could provide
We weren't on the wrong side, sweetness
We were the wrong side

I've already ripped out the phones, honey
You can't walk the streets in a war
I can finish this alone honey
You're driftin' too far from shore

# Maybe Someday

Maybe someday you'll be satisfied
When you've lost everything you'll have nothing left to hide
When you're through running over things like you're walking 'cross the tracks
Maybe you'll beg me to take you back
Maybe someday you'll find out everybody's somebody's fool
Maybe then you'll realize what it would have taken to keep me cool
Maybe someday when you're by yourself alone
You'll know the love that I had for you was never my own

Maybe someday you'll have nowhere to turn
You'll look back and wonder 'bout the bridges you have burned
You'll look back sometime when the lights grow dim
And you'll see  you look much better with me than you do with him
Through hostile cities and unfriendly towns
Thirty pieces of silver, no money down
Maybe someday, you will understand
That something for nothing is everybody's plan

Maybe someday you'll remember what you felt
When there was blood on the moon in the cotton belt
When both of us, baby, were going through some sort of a test
Neither one of us could do what we do best
I should have known better, baby, I should have called your bluff
I guess I was too off the handle, not sentimental enough
Maybe someday, you'll believe me when I say
That I wanted you, baby, in every kind of way

Maybe someday you'll hear a voice from on high
Sayin', "For whose sake did you live, for whose sake did you die?"
Forgive me, baby, for what I didn't do
For not breakin' down no bedroom door to get at you
Always was a sucker for the right cross
Never wanted to go home 'til the last cent was lost
Maybe someday you will look back and see
That I made it so easy for you to follow me

Maybe someday there'll be nothing to tell
I'm just as happy as you, baby, I just can't say it so well
Never slumbered or slept or waited for lightning to strike
There's no excuse for you to say that we don't think alike
You said you were goin' to Frisco, stay a couple of months
I always like San Francisco, I was there for a party once
Maybe someday you'll see that it's true
There was no greater love than what I had for you

———

# Brownsville Girl

(with Sam Shepard)

Well, there was this movie I seen one time
About a man riding 'cross the desert and it starred Gregory Peck
He was shot down by a hungry kid trying to make a name for himself
The townspeople wanted to crush that kid down and string him up by the neck

Well, the marshal, now he beat that kid to a bloody pulp
As the dying gunfighter lay in the sun and gasped for his last breath
"Turn him loose, let him go, let him say he outdrew me fair and square
I want him to feel what it's like to every moment face his death"

Well, I keep seeing this stuff and it just comes a-rolling in
And you know it blows right through me like a ball and chain
You know I can't believe we've lived so long and are still so far apart
The memory of you keeps callin' after me like a rollin' train

I can still see the day that you came to me on the painted desert
In your busted down Ford and your platform heels
I could never figure out why you chose that particular place to meet
Ah, but you were right. It was perfect as I got in behind the wheel

Well, we drove that car all night into San Anton'
And we slept near the Alamo, your skin was so tender and soft
Way down in Mexico you went out to find a doctor and you never came back
I would have gone on after you but I didn't feel like letting my head get blown off

Well, we're drivin' this car and the sun is comin' up over the Rockies
Now I know she ain't you but she's here and she's got that dark rhythm in her soul
But I'm too over the edge and I ain't in the mood anymore to remember the times
    when I was your only man
And she don't want to remind me. She knows this car would go out of control

Brownsville girl with your Brownsville curls
Teeth like pearls shining like the moon above
Brownsville girl, show me all around the world
Brownsville girl, you're my honey love

Well, we crossed the panhandle and then we headed towards Amarillo
We pulled up where Henry Porter used to live. He owned a wreckin' lot
    outside of town about a mile
Ruby was in the backyard hanging clothes, she had her red hair tied back.
    She saw us come rolling up in a trail of dust
She said, "Henry ain't here but you can come on in, he'll be back in a little while"

510

Then she told us how times were tough and about how she was thinkin' of
    bummin' a ride back to from where she started
But ya know, she changed the subject every time money came up
She said, "Welcome to the land of the living dead."
    You could tell she was so broken hearted
She said, "Even the swap meets around here are getting pretty corrupt"

"How far are y'all going?" Ruby asked us with a sigh
"We're going all the way 'til the wheels fall off and burn
'Til the sun peels the paint and the seat covers fade and the water moccasin dies"
Ruby just smiled and said, "Ah, you know some babies never learn"

Something about that movie though, well I just can't get it out of my head
But I can't remember why I was in it or what part I was supposed to play
All I remember about it was Gregory Peck and the way people moved
And a lot of them seemed to be lookin' my way

Brownsville girl with your Brownsville curls
Teeth like pearls shining like the moon above
Brownsville girl, show me all around the world
Brownsville girl, you're my honey love

Well, they were looking for somebody with a pompadour
I was crossin' the street when shots rang out
I didn't know whether to duck or to run, so I ran
"We got him cornered in the churchyard," I heard somebody shout

Well, you saw my picture in the *Corpus Christi Tribune*. Underneath it,
    it said, "A man with no alibi"
You went out on a limb to testify for me, you said I was with you
Then when I saw you break down in front of the judge and cry real tears
It was the best acting I saw anybody do

Now I've always been the kind of person that doesn't like to trespass
    but sometimes you just find yourself over the line
Oh if there's an original thought out there, I could use it right now
You know, I feel pretty good, but that ain't sayin' much.
    I could feel a whole lot better
If you were just here by my side to show me how

Well, I'm standin' in line in the rain to see a movie starring Gregory Peck
Yeah, but you know it's not the one that I had in mind
He's got a new one out now, I don't even know what it's about
But I'll see him in anything so I'll stand in line

Brownsville girl with your Brownsville curls
Teeth like pearls shining like the moon above
Brownsville girl, show me all around the world
Brownsville girl, you're my honey love

———

You know, it's funny how things never turn out the way you had 'em planned
The only thing we knew for sure about Henry Porter
    is that his name wasn't Henry Porter
And you know there was somethin' about you baby that I liked
    that was always too good for this world
Just like you always said there was somethin' about me you liked
    that I left behind in the French Quarter

Strange how people who suffer together have stronger connections
    than people who are most content
I don't have any regrets, they can talk about me plenty when I'm gone
You always said people don't do what they believe in,
    they just do what's most convenient, then they repent
And I always said, "Hang on to me, baby, and let's hope that the roof stays on"

There was a movie I seen one time, I think I sat through it twice
I don't remember who I was or where I was bound
All I remember about it was it starred Gregory Peck, he wore a gun
    and he was shot in the back
Seems like a long time ago, long before the stars were torn down

Brownsville girl with your Brownsville curls
Teeth like pearls shining like the moon above
Brownsville girl, show me all around the world
Brownsville girl, you're my honey love

# Under Your Spell

(with Carol Bayer Sager)

Somethin' about you that I can't shake
Don't know how much more of this I can take
Baby, I'm under your spell

I was knocked out and loaded in the naked night
When my last dream exploded, I noticed your light
Baby, oh what a story I could tell

It's been nice seeing you, you read me like a book
If you ever want to reach me, you know where to look
Baby, I'll be at the same hotel

I'd like to help you but I'm in a bit of a jam
I'll call you tomorrow if there's phones where I am
Baby, caught between heaven and hell

But I will be back, I will survive
You'll never get rid of me as long as you're alive
Baby, can't you tell

Well it's four in the morning by the sound of the birds
I'm starin' at your picture, I'm hearin' your words
Baby, they ring in my head like a bell

Everywhere you go it's enough to break hearts
Someone always gets hurt, a fire always starts
You were too hot to handle, you were breaking every vow
I trusted you baby, you can trust me now

Turn back baby, wipe your eye
Don't think I'm leaving here without a kiss goodbye
Baby, is there anything left to tell?

I'll see you later when I'm not so out of my head
Maybe next time I'll let the dead bury the dead
Baby, what more can I tell?

Well the desert is hot, the mountain is cursed
Pray that I don't die of thirst
Baby, two feet from the well

# Band of the Hand (It's Hell Time, Man!)

Band of the hand
Band of the hand
Band of the hand
Band of the hand

Down these streets the fools rule
There's no freedom or self respect
A knife's point or a trip to the joint
Is about all you can expect

They kill people here who stand up for their rights
The system's just too damned corrupt
It's always the same, the name of the game
Is who do you know higher up

Band of the hand
Band of the hand
Band of the hand
Band of the hand

The blacks and the whites
Steal the other kids' lives
Wealth is a filthy rag
So erotic so unpatriotic
So wrapped up in the American flag

The witchcraft scum exploiting the dumb
Turns children into crooks and slaves
Whose heroes and healers are real stoned dealers
Who should be put in their graves

Band of the hand
Band of the hand
Band of the hand
Band of the hand

Listen to me Mr. Pusherman
This might be your last night in a bed so soft
There are pimps on the make, politicians on the take
You can't pay us off

We're gonna blow up your home of Voodoo
And watch it burn without any regret
We got the power, we're the new government
You just don't know it yet

Band of the hand
Band of the hand
Band of the hand
Band of the hand

For all of my brothers from Vietnam
And my uncles from World War II
I've got to say that it's countdown time now
We're gonna do what the law should do

And for you pretty baby
I know your story is too painful to share
One day though you'll be talking in your sleep
And when you do, I wanna be there

Band of the hand
Band of the hand
Band of the hand
Band of the hand

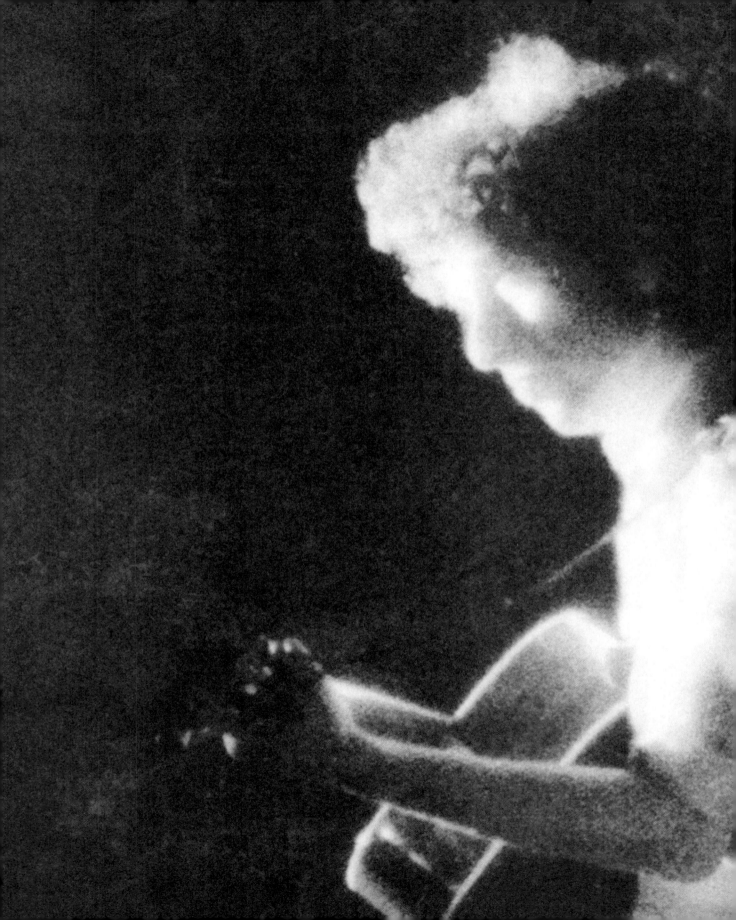

# Down in the Groove

Death Is Not the End

Had a Dream About You, Baby

*additional lyrics*

Night After Night

For days and it turned one sweet day into a vegas storm

ex[d] the ~~book~~ priest was black on the 7th day till the
And waltzed arose a sloping floor                     waltz
whilst in vegas, you couldn't ~~finish~~
And tilted her hat to me                              false
You could [You thought she was a party doll
you
(You fell for) Her personality   and I was I was
                    the true                just along for the
A hound dog tossed beyond the              just along for the ride
That's not the way it happened,            before her at the
                                           Phil X
            I thought you were someone else
            it must 'uv BEEN the mask you wore )    Store

for I figured (I supposed) I've lost you anyway
            ( Why )          — for the silver
            They would be just your voice & mine   free
        (try as to touch each there a was          it must've been because you
You must think I'm someone else / I wish saw your     had to
I hadn't called you for days why, it wasn't becan   had to
I know what we were going to say        you were had to reach
(creeps across the rooftops,        but I hadn't memorized my (goodbye)
            jumping              part of the speech
    I figured I lost you anyway
So I pulled up stakes and went for broke ]   I focused
    It didn't strike me very funny    focus   it
we didn't speak for days and    it must've been the cats had
        put me on a pedestal            got our tongue
    Filled me up with dreams and coke
And I figured I lost you anyway      and when I lost you too
And then you thought it all a joke     it all came clear
But it didn't strike    me very funny       that to

I thought you were typing out you thought it was something
    said   For I figured I lost you anyway          I was so
    So what be the use I wonder if you were loose
    In order to get to you, I am [I'd just have to
    I'd have to use some excuse I come up with some
        It du — fun ( It just struck me     kind of funny )   excuse

After you close down and     you said you
    I didn't call you for days    Cat had my tongue
    (we hadn't talked for
    I didn't talk for days a days    and it wasn't cause the cat
    It was just that everything I said was      had got my tongue
                                            and when the rain came
We didn't talk for days and                        then the
    It Aint my fault nobody ever took the time to teach me      words were
        taught me how to forgive       gone
Blahcuss take me for a fool

# Death Is Not the End

When you're sad and when you're lonely
And you haven't got a friend
Just remember that death is not the end
And all that you've held sacred
Falls down and does not mend
Just remember that death is not the end
Not the end, not the end
Just remember that death is not the end

When you're standing at the crossroads
That you cannot comprehend
Just remember that death is not the end
And all your dreams have vanished
And you don't know what's up the bend
Just remember that death is not the end
Not the end, not the end
Just remember that death is not the end

When the storm clouds gather 'round you
And heavy rains descend
Just remember that death is not the end
And there's no one there to comfort you
With a helpin' hand to lend
Just remember that death is not the end
Not the end, not the end
Just remember that death is not the end

Oh, the tree of life is growing
Where the spirit never dies
And the bright light of salvation shines
In dark and empty skies

When the cities are on fire
With the burning flesh of men
Just remember that death is not the end
And you search in vain to find
Just one law-abiding citizen
Just remember that death is not the end
Not the end, not the end
Just remember that death is not the end

# Had a Dream About You, Baby

I got to see you baby, I don't care
It may be someplace, baby, you say where

I had a dream about you, baby
Had a dream about you, baby
Late last night you come a-rollin' across my mind

You got the crazy rhythm when you walk
You make me nervous when you start to talk

I had a dream about you, baby
Had a dream about you, baby
Late last night you come a-rollin' across my mind

Standin' on the highway, you flag me down
Said, take me Daddy, to the nearest town

I had a dream about you, baby
Had a dream about you, baby
Late last night you come a-rollin' across my mind

The joint is jumpin'
It's really somethin'
The beat is pumpin'
My heart is thumpin'
Spent my money on you honey
My limbs are shakin'
My heart is breakin'

You kiss me, baby, in the coffee shop
You make me nervous, you gotta stop

I had a dream about you, baby
Had a dream about you, baby
Late last night you come a-rollin' across my mind

You got a rag wrapped around your head
Wearing a long dress fire engine red

I had a dream about you, baby
Had a dream about you, baby
Late last night you come a-rollin' across my mind

# Night After Night

Night after night you wander the streets of my mind
Night after night don't know what you think you will find
No place to go, nowhere to turn
Everything around you seems to burn, burn, burn
And there's never any mercy in sight night after night

Night after night
Night after night

Night after night some new plan to blow up the world
Night after night another old man kissing some young girl
You look for salvation, you find none
Just another broken heart, another barrel of a gun
Just another stick of dynamite night after night

Night after night
Night after night

Night after night you drop dead in your bed
Night after night another bottle finds a head
Night after night I think about cutting you loose
But I just can't do it, what would be the use?
So I just keep a-holding you tight night after night

Night after night
Night after night

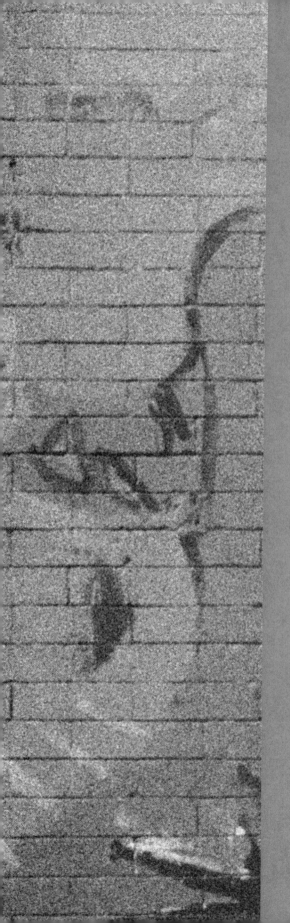

# Oh Mercy

Political World

Where Teardrops Fall

Everything Is Broken

Ring Them Bells

Man in the Long Black Coat

Most of the Time

What Good Am I?

Disease of Conceit

What Was It You Wanted?

Shooting Star

*additional lyrics*

Series of Dreams

Dignity

You were always thinking about her
But she slipped away and you lost her trail
And now that you can't do without her
She's back in town like a nightingale
And there ain't gonna be any next time
By now you better understand
That there ain't gonna be any next time
So hold her and kiss her and love her while you can
– – – – – – – – – – – – – –

# Political World

We live in a political world
Love don't have any place
We're living in times where men commit crimes
And crime don't have a face

We live in a political world
Icicles hanging down
Wedding bells ring and angels sing
Clouds cover up the ground

We live in a political world
Wisdom is thrown into jail
It rots in a cell, is misguided as hell
Leaving no one to pick up a trail

We live in a political world
Where mercy walks the plank
Life is in mirrors, death disappears
Up the steps into the nearest bank

We live in a political world
Where courage is a thing of the past
Houses are haunted, children are unwanted
The next day could be your last

We live in a political world
The one we can see and can feel
But there's no one to check, it's all a stacked deck
We all know for sure that it's real

We live in a political world
In the cities of lonesome fear
Little by little you turn in the middle
But you're never sure why you're here

We live in a political world
Under the microscope
You can travel anywhere and hang yourself there
You always got more than enough rope

We live in a political world
Turning and a-thrashing about
As soon as you're awake, you're trained to take
What looks like the easy way out

We live in a political world
Where peace is not welcome at all
It's turned away from the door to wander some more
Or put up against the wall

We live in a political world
Everything is hers or his
Climb into the frame and shout God's name
But you're never sure what it is

# Where Teardrops Fall

Far away where the soft winds blow
Far away from it all
There is a place you go
Where teardrops fall

Far away in the stormy night
Far away and over the wall
You are there in the flickering light
Where teardrops fall

We banged the drum slowly
And played the fife lowly
You know the song in my heart
In the turning of twilight
In the shadows of moonlight
You can show me a new place to start

I've torn my clothes and I've drained the cup
Strippin' away at it all
Thinking of you when the sun comes up
Where teardrops fall

By rivers of blindness
In love and with kindness
We could hold up a toast if we meet
To the cuttin' of fences
To sharpen the senses
That linger in the fireball heat

Roses are red, violets are blue
And time is beginning to crawl
I just might have to come see you
Where teardrops fall

# Everything Is Broken

Broken lines, broken strings
Broken threads, broken springs
Broken idols, broken heads
People sleeping in broken beds
Ain't no use jiving, ain't no use joking
Everything is broken

Broken bottles, broken plates
Broken switches, broken gates
Broken dishes, broken parts
Streets are filled with broken hearts
Broken words never meant to be spoken
Everything is broken

Seem like every time you stop and turn around
Something else just hit the ground

Broken cutters, broken saws
Broken buckles, broken laws
Broken bodies, broken bones
Broken voices on broken phones
Take a deep breath, feel like you're chokin'
Everything is broken

Every time you leave and go off someplace
Things fall to pieces in my face

Broken hands on broken ploughs
Broken treaties, broken vows
Broken pipes, broken tools
People bending broken rules
Hound dog howling, bullfrog croaking
Everything is broken

# Ring Them Bells

Ring them bells, ye heathen
From the city that dreams
Ring them bells from the sanctuaries
'Cross the valleys and streams
For they're deep and they're wide
And the world's on its side
And time is running backwards
And so is the bride

Ring them bells St. Peter
Where the four winds blow
Ring them bells with an iron hand
So the people will know
Oh it's rush hour now
On the wheel and the plow
And the sun is going down
Upon the sacred cow

Ring them bells Sweet Martha
For the poor man's son
Ring them bells so the world will know
That God is one
Oh the shepherd is asleep
Where the willows weep
And the mountains are filled
With lost sheep

Ring them bells for the blind and the deaf
Ring them bells for all of us who are left
Ring them bells for the chosen few
Who will judge the many when the game is through
Ring them bells, for the time that flies
For the child that cries
When innocence dies

Ring them bells St. Catherine
From the top of the room
Ring them from the fortress
For the lilies that bloom
Oh the lines are long
And the fighting is strong
And they're breaking down the distance
Between right and wrong

# Man in the Long Black Coat

Crickets are chirpin', the water is high
There's a soft cotton dress on the line hangin' dry
Window wide open, African trees
Bent over backwards from a hurricane breeze
Not a word of goodbye, not even a note
She gone with the man
In the long black coat

Somebody seen him hanging around
At the old dance hall on the outskirts of town
He looked into her eyes when she stopped him to ask
If he wanted to dance, he had a face like a mask
Somebody said from the Bible he'd quote
There was dust on the man
In the long black coat

The preacher was a-talkin', there's a sermon he gave
He said, "Every man's conscience is vile and depraved
You cannot depend on it to be your guide
When it's you who must keep it satisfied."
It ain't easy to swallow, it sticks in the throat
She gave her heart to the man
In the long black coat

There are no mistakes in life some people say
And it's true sometimes you can see it that way
I went down to the river but I just missed the boat
She went with the man
In the long black coat

There's smoke on the water, it's been there since June
Tree trunks uprooted, 'neath the high crescent moon
Feel the pulse and vibration and the rumbling force
Somebody is out there beating on a dead horse
She never said nothing, there was nothing she wrote
She went with the man
In the long black coat

# Most of the Time

Most of the time
I'm clear focused all around
Most of the time
I can keep both feet on the ground
I can follow the path, I can read the signs
Stay right with it when the road unwinds
I can handle whatever I stumble upon
I don't even notice she's gone
Most of the time

Most of the time
It's well understood
Most of the time
I wouldn't change it if I could
I can make it all match up, I can hold my own
I can deal with the situation right down to the bone
I can survive, I can endure
And I don't even think about her
Most of the time

Most of the time
My head is on straight
Most of the time
I'm strong enough not to hate
I don't build up illusion 'til it makes me sick
I ain't afraid of confusion no matter how thick
I can smile in the face of mankind
Don't even remember what her lips felt like on mine
Most of the time

Most of the time
She ain't even in my mind
I wouldn't know her if I saw her
She's that far behind
Most of the time
I can't even be sure
If she was ever with me
Or if I was with her

Most of the time
I'm halfway content
Most of the time
I know exactly where it went
I don't cheat on myself, I don't run and hide
Hide from the feelings that are buried inside
I don't compromise and I don't pretend
I don't even care if I ever see her again
Most of the time

# What Good Am I?

What good am I if I'm like all the rest
If I just turn away, when I see how you're dressed
If I shut myself off so I can't hear you cry
What good am I?

What good am I if I know and don't do
If I see and don't say, if I look right through you
If I turn a deaf ear to the thunderin' sky
What good am I?

What good am I while you softly weep
And I hear in my head what you say in your sleep
And I freeze in the moment like the rest who don't try
What good am I?

What good am I then to others and me
If I've had every chance and yet still fail to see
If my hands are tied must I not wonder within
Who tied them and why and where must I have been?

What good am I if I say foolish things
And I laugh in the face of what sorrow brings
And I just turn my back while you silently die
What good am I?

# Disease of Conceit

There's a whole lot of people suffering tonight
From the disease of conceit
Whole lot of people struggling tonight
From the disease of conceit
Comes right down the highway
Straight down the line
Rips into your senses
Through your body and your mind
Nothing about it that's sweet
The disease of conceit

There's a whole lot of hearts breaking tonight
From the disease of conceit
Whole lot of hearts shaking tonight
From the disease of conceit
Steps into your room
Eats your soul
Over your senses
You have no control
Ain't nothing too discreet
About the disease of conceit

There's a whole lot of people dying tonight
From the disease of conceit
Whole lot of people crying tonight
From the disease of conceit
Comes right out of nowhere
And you're down for the count
From the outside world
The pressure will mount
Turn you into a piece of meat
The disease of conceit

Conceit is a disease
That the doctors got no cure
They've done a lot of research on it
But what it is, they're still not sure

There's a whole lot of people in trouble tonight
From the disease of conceit
Whole lot of people seeing double tonight
From the disease of conceit
Give ya delusions of grandeur
And a evil eye
Give you the idea that
You're too good to die
Then they bury you from your head to your feet
From the disease of conceit

# What Was It You Wanted?

What was it you wanted?
Tell me again so I'll know
What's happening in there
What's going on in your show
What was it you wanted
Could you say it again?
I'll be back in a minute
You can get it together by then

What was it you wanted
You can tell me, I'm back
We can start it all over
Get it back on the track
You got my attention
Go ahead, speak
What was it you wanted
When you were kissing my cheek?

Was there somebody looking
When you give me that kiss
Someone there in the shadows
Someone that I might have missed?
Is there something you needed
Something I don't understand
What was it you wanted
Do I have it here in my hand?

Whatever you wanted
Slipped out of my mind
Would you remind me again
If you'd be so kind
Has the record been breaking
Did the needle just skip
Is there somebody waiting
Was there a slip of the lip?

What was it you wanted
I ain't keeping score
Are you the same person
That was here before?
Is it something important?
Maybe not
What was it you wanted?
Tell me again I forgot

Whatever you wanted
What could it be
Did somebody tell you
That you could get it from me
Is it something that comes natural
Is it easy to say
Why do you want it
Who are you anyway?

Is the scenery changing
Am I getting it wrong
Is the whole thing going backwards
Are they playing our song?
Where were you when it started
Do you want it for free
What was it you wanted
Are you talking to me?

# Shooting Star

Seen a shooting star tonight
And I thought of you
You were trying to break into another world
A world I never knew
I always kind of wondered
If you ever made it through
Seen a shooting star tonight
And I thought of you

Seen a shooting star tonight
And I thought of me
If I was still the same
If I ever became what you wanted me to be
Did I miss the mark or overstep the line
That only you could see?
Seen a shooting star tonight
And I thought of me

Listen to the engine, listen to the bell
As the last fire truck from hell
Goes rolling by
All good people are praying
It's the last temptation, the last account
The last time you might hear the sermon on the mount
The last radio is playing

Seen a shooting star tonight
Slip away
Tomorrow will be
Another day
Guess it's too late to say the things to you
That you needed to hear me say
Seen a shooting star tonight
Slip away

# Series of Dreams

I was thinking of a series of dreams
Where nothing comes up to the top
Everything stays down where it's wounded
And comes to a permanent stop
Wasn't thinking of anything specific
Like in a dream, when someone wakes up and screams
Nothing too very scientific
Just thinking of a series of dreams

Thinking of a series of dreams
Where the time and the tempo fly
And there's no exit in any direction
'Cept the one that you can't see with your eyes
Wasn't making any great connection
Wasn't falling for any intricate scheme
Nothing that would pass inspection
Just thinking of a series of dreams

Dreams where the umbrella is folded
Into the path you are hurled
And the cards are no good that you're holding
Unless they're from another world

In one, numbers were burning
In another, I witnessed a crime
In one, I was running, and in another
All I seemed to be doing was climb
Wasn't looking for any special assistance
Not going to any great extremes
I'd already gone the distance
Just thinking of a series of dreams

# Dignity

Fat man lookin' in a blade of steel
Thin man lookin' at his last meal
Hollow man lookin' in a cottonfield
For dignity

Wise man lookin' in a blade of grass
Young man lookin' in the shadows that pass
Poor man lookin' through painted glass
For dignity

Somebody got murdered on New Year's Eve
Somebody said dignity was the first to leave
I went into the city, went into the town
Went into the land of the midnight sun

Searchin' high, searchin' low
Searchin' everywhere I know
Askin' the cops wherever I go
Have you seen dignity?

Blind man breakin' out of a trance
Puts both his hands in the pockets of chance
Hopin' to find one circumstance
Of dignity

I went to the wedding of Mary Lou
She said, "I don't want nobody see me talkin' to you"
Said she could get killed if she told me what she knew
About dignity

I went down where the vultures feed
I would've gone deeper, but there wasn't any need
Heard the tongues of angels and the tongues of men
Wasn't any difference to me

Chilly wind sharp as a razor blade
House on fire, debts unpaid
Gonna stand at the window, gonna ask the maid
Have you seen dignity?

Drinkin' man listens to the voice he hears
In a crowded room full of covered-up mirrors
Lookin' into the lost forgotten years
For dignity

Met Prince Phillip at the home of the blues
Said he'd give me information if his name wasn't used
He wanted money up front, said he was abused
By dignity

Footprints runnin' 'cross the silver sand
Steps goin' down into tattoo land
I met the sons of darkness and the sons of light
In the bordertowns of despair

Got no place to fade, got no coat
I'm on the rollin' river in a jerkin' boat
Tryin' to read a note somebody wrote
About dignity

Sick man lookin' for the doctor's cure
Lookin' at his hands for the lines that were
And into every masterpiece of literature
For dignity

Englishman stranded in the blackheart wind
Combin' his hair back, his future looks thin
Bites the bullet and he looks within
For dignity

Someone showed me a picture and I just laughed
Dignity never been photographed
I went into the red, went into the black
Into the valley of dry bone dreams

So many roads, so much at stake
So many dead ends, I'm at the edge of the lake
Sometimes I wonder what it's gonna take
To find dignity

# Under the Red Sky

handy dandy   *who was the*
              *the last time ya Look*

1/ handy dandy contrversy always surrounds him   *vry*
   wherefer he goes too bad for him something back ~~there always hounds him~~
   *"c'mn there*
   *hounding ~~pressing~~ him*

2. handy dandy he *is* ~~was~~ in a room all ~~just~~ pacing the floor that supports him
   in better times anyghing he desired would have just kept walking on
         of power  pushing towrd   towrds him  *still he lose*
                        covering   power   his respectability dont bother

3. handy dandy a tower of strenght & stability
   he does it with mirrors but he doesnt really, do actually
   *acceseessable*  *humnot it*  he dont need to lie cause he's so full of humility
                               *about*

2handy da, compulsive & healty, plausible obsesive automatic
  bloin g his horn for the girls & bringing them up tothe attic
       for the girl ~~niggers~~ running them up *somed*
  *does he wear ~~dark~~ sunglasses ~~~~*        *Does he know that he's so stupid*
5. handy..... will well yeal maybble                *ignorant & blind will ~~~~*
   he ~~looks~~ how much do you weigh  *sto*            *dumb Scholar*

  *~~She~~ ~~somehow ~~ says "try off this" He says not ~~~~ baby*
6. he's in a rom full ov people and somuddeny theres' nobody cheering
   ~~it xxinxxxxxmxxhim~~he says c'mon baby lets both take the wheel to this
              car it dont matter ~~xtexxm~~ who is steering

# Wiggle Wiggle

Wiggle, wiggle, wiggle like a gypsy queen
Wiggle, wiggle, wiggle all dressed in green
Wiggle, wiggle, wiggle 'til the moon is blue
Wiggle 'til the moon sees you

Wiggle, wiggle, wiggle in your boots and shoes
Wiggle, wiggle, wiggle, you got nothing to lose
Wiggle, wiggle, wiggle like a swarm of bees
Wiggle on your hands and knees

Wiggle to the front, wiggle to the rear
Wiggle 'til you wiggle right out of here
Wiggle 'til it opens, wiggle 'til it shuts
Wiggle 'til it bites, wiggle 'til it cuts

Wiggle, wiggle, wiggle like a bowl of soup
Wiggle, wiggle, wiggle like a rolling hoop
Wiggle, wiggle, wiggle like a ton of lead
Wiggle—you can raise the dead

Wiggle 'til you're high, wiggle 'til you're higher
Wiggle 'til you vomit fire
Wiggle 'til it whispers, wiggle 'til it hums
Wiggle 'til it answers, wiggle 'til it comes

Wiggle, wiggle, wiggle like satin and silk
Wiggle, wiggle, wiggle like a pail of milk
Wiggle, wiggle, wiggle, rattle and shake
Wiggle like a big fat snake

# Under the Red Sky

There was a little boy and there was a little girl
And they lived in an alley under the red sky
There was a little boy and there was a little girl
And they lived in an alley under the red sky

There was an old man and he lived in the moon
One summer's day he came passing by
There was an old man and he lived in the moon
And one day he came passing by

Someday little girl, everything for you is gonna be new
Someday little girl, you'll have a diamond as big as your shoe

Let the wind blow low, let the wind blow high
One day the little boy and the little girl were both baked in a pie
Let the wind blow low, let the wind blow high
One day the little boy and the little girl were both baked in a pie

This is the key to the kingdom and this is the town
This is the blind horse that leads you around

Let the bird sing, let the bird fly
One day the man in the moon went home and the river went dry
Let the bird sing, let the bird fly
The man in the moon went home and the river went dry

# Unbelievable

It's unbelievable, it's strange but true
It's inconceivable it could happen to you
You go north and you go south
Just like bait in the fish's mouth
Ya must be livin' in the shadow of some kind of evil star
It's unbelievable it would get this far

It's undeniable what they'd have you to think
It's indescribable, it can drive you to drink
They said it was the land of milk and honey
Now they say it's the land of money
Who ever thought they could ever make that stick
It's unbelievable you can get this rich this quick

Every head is so dignified
Every moon is so sanctified
Every urge is so satisfied as long as you're with me
All the silver, all the gold
All the sweethearts you can hold
That don't come back with stories untold
Are hanging on a tree

It's unbelievable like a lead balloon
It's so impossible to even learn the tune
Kill that beast and feed that swine
Scale that wall and smoke that vine
Feed that horse and saddle up the drum
It's unbelievable, the day would finally come

Once there was a man who had no eyes
Every lady in the land told him lies
He stood beneath the silver sky and his heart began to bleed
Every brain is civilized
Every nerve is analyzed
Everything is criticized when you are in need

It's unbelievable, it's fancy-free
So interchangeable, so delightful to see
Turn your back, wash your hands
There's always someone who understands
It don't matter no more what you got to say
It's unbelievable it would go down this way

# Born in Time

In the lonely night
In the blinking stardust of a pale blue light
You're comin' thru to me in black and white
When we were made of dreams

You're blowing down the shaky street
You're hearing my heart beat
In the record-breaking heat
Where we were born in time

Not one more night, not one more kiss
Not this time baby, no more of this
Takes too much skill, takes too much will
It's revealing
You came, you saw, just like the law
You married young, just like your ma
You tried and tried, you made me slide
You left me reelin' with this feelin'

On the rising curve
Where the ways of nature will test every nerve
You won't get anything you don't deserve
Where we were born in time

You pressed me once, you pressed me twice
You hang the flame, you'll pay the price
Oh babe, that fire
Is still smokin'
You were snow, you were rain
You were striped, you were plain
Oh babe, truer words
Have not been spoken or broken

In the hills of mystery
In the foggy web of destiny
You can have what's left of me
Where we were born in time

# T.V. Talkin' Song

One time in London I'd gone out for a walk
Past a place called Hyde Park where people talk
'Bout all kinds of different gods, they have their point of view
To anyone passing by, that's who they're talking to

There was someone on a platform talking to the folks
About the T.V. god and all the pain that it invokes
"It's too bright a light," he said, "for anybody's eyes
If you've never seen one it's a blessing in disguise"

I moved in closer, got up on my toes
Two men in front of me were coming to blows
The man was saying something 'bout children when they're young
Being sacrificed to it while lullabies are being sung

"The news of the day is on all the time
All the latest gossip, all the latest rhyme
Your mind is your temple, keep it beautiful and free
Don't let an egg get laid in it by something you can't see"

"Pray for peace!" he said. You could feel it in the crowd
My thoughts began to wander. His voice was ringing loud
"It will destroy your family, your happy home is gone
No one can protect you from it once you turn it on"

"It will lead you into some strange pursuits
Lead you to the land of forbidden fruits
It will scramble up your head and drag your brain about
Sometimes you gotta do like Elvis did and shoot the damn thing out"

"It's all been designed," he said, "to make you lose your mind
And when you go back to find it, there's nothing there to find
Every time you look at it, your situation's worse
If you feel it grabbing out for you, send for the nurse"

The crowd began to riot and they grabbed hold of the man
There was pushing, there was shoving and everybody ran
The T.V. crew was there to film it, they jumped right over me
Later on that evening, I watched it on T.V.

# 10,000 Men

Ten thousand men on a hill
Ten thousand men on a hill
Some of 'm goin' down, some of 'm gonna get killed

Ten thousand men dressed in oxford blue
Ten thousand men dressed in oxford blue
Drummin' in the morning, in the evening they'll be coming for you

Ten thousand men on the move
Ten thousand men on the move
None of them doing nothin' that your mama wouldn't disapprove

Ten thousand men digging for silver and gold
Ten thousand men digging for silver and gold
All clean shaven, all coming in from the cold

Hey! Who could your lover be?
Hey! Who could your lover be?
Let me eat off his head so you can really see!

Ten thousand women all dressed in white
Ten thousand women all dressed in white
Standin' at my window wishing me goodnight

Ten thousand men looking so lean and frail
Ten thousand men looking so lean and frail
Each one of 'm got seven wives, each one of 'm just out of jail

Ten thousand women all sweepin' my room
Ten thousand women all sweepin' my room
Spilling my buttermilk, sweeping it up with a broom

Ooh, baby, thank you for my tea!
Baby, thank you for my tea!
It's so sweet of you to be so nice to me

# 2 × 2

One by one, they followed the sun
One by one, until there were none
Two by two, to their lovers they flew
Two by two, into the foggy dew
Three by three, they danced on the sea
Four by four, they danced on the shore
Five by five, they tried to survive
Six by six, they were playing with tricks

How many paths did they try and fail?
How many of their brothers and sisters lingered in jail?
How much poison did they inhale?
How many black cats crossed their trail?

Seven by seven, they headed for heaven
Eight by eight, they got to the gate
Nine by nine, they drank the wine
Ten by ten, they drank it again

How many tomorrows have they given away?
How many compared to yesterday?
How many more without any reward?
How many more can they afford?

Two by two, they stepped into the ark
Two by two, they step in the dark
Three by three, they're turning the key
Four by four, they turn it some more

One by one, they follow the sun
Two by two, to another rendezvous

# God Knows

God knows you ain't pretty
God knows it's true
God knows there ain't anybody
Ever gonna take the place of you

God knows it's a struggle
God knows it's a crime
God knows there's gonna be no more water
But fire next time

God don't call it treason
God don't call it wrong
It was supposed to last a season
But it's been so strong for so long

God knows it's fragile
God knows everything
God knows it could snap apart right now
Just like putting scissors to a string

God knows it's terrifying
God sees it all unfold
There's a million reasons for you to be crying
You been so bold and so cold

God knows that when you see it
God knows you've got to weep
God knows the secrets of your heart
He'll tell them to you when you're asleep

God knows there's a river
God knows how to make it flow
God knows you ain't gonna be taking
Nothing with you when you go

God knows there's a purpose
God knows there's a chance
God knows you can rise above the darkest hour
Of any circumstance

God knows there's a heaven
God knows it's out of sight
God knows we can get all the way from here to there
Even if we've got to walk a million miles by candlelight

# Handy Dandy

Handy Dandy, controversy surrounds him
He been around the world and back again
Something in the moonlight still hounds him
Handy Dandy, just like sugar and candy

Handy Dandy, if every bone in his body was broken he would never admit it
He got an all-girl orchestra and when he says
"Strike up the band," they hit it
Handy Dandy, Handy Dandy

You say, "What are ya made of?"
He says, "Can you repeat what you said?"
You'll say, "What are you afraid of?"
He'll say, "Nothin'! Neither 'live nor dead."

Handy Dandy, he got a stick in his hand and a pocket full of money
He says, "Darling, tell me the truth, how much time I got?"
She says, "You got all the time in the world, honey"
Handy Dandy, Handy Dandy

He's got that clear crystal fountain
He's got that soft silky skin
He's got that fortress on the mountain
With no doors, no windows, no thieves can break in

Handy Dandy, sitting with a girl named Nancy in a garden feelin' kind of lazy
He says, "Ya want a gun? I'll give ya one." She says, "Boy, you talking crazy"
Handy Dandy, just like sugar and candy
Handy Dandy, pour him another brandy

Handy Dandy, he got a basket of flowers and a bag full of sorrow
He finishes his drink, he gets up from the table, he says
"Okay, boys, I'll see you tomorrow"
Handy Dandy, Handy Dandy, just like sugar and candy
Handy Dandy, just like sugar and candy

# Cat's in the Well

The cat's in the well, the wolf is looking down
The cat's in the well, the wolf is looking down
He got his big bushy tail dragging all over the ground

The cat's in the well, the gentle lady is asleep
Cat's in the well, the gentle lady is asleep
She ain't hearing a thing, the silence is a-stickin' her deep

The cat's in the well and grief is showing its face
The world's being slaughtered and it's such a bloody disgrace

The cat's in the well, the horse is going bumpety bump
The cat's in the well, and the horse is going bumpety bump
Back alley Sally is doing the American jump

The cat's in the well, and Papa is reading the news
His hair's falling out and all of his daughters need shoes

The cat's in the well and the barn is full of bull
The cat's in the well and the barn is full of bull
The night is so long and the table is oh, so full

The cat's in the well and the servant is at the door
The drinks are ready and the dogs are going to war

The cat's in the well, the leaves are starting to fall
The cat's in the well, leaves are starting to fall
Goodnight, my love, may the Lord have mercy on us all

# Time Out of Mind

Love Sick

Dirt Road Blues

Standing in the Doorway

Million Miles

Tryin' to Get to Heaven

'Til I Fell in Love with You

Not Dark Yet

Cold Irons Bound

Make You Feel My Love

Can't Wait

Highlands

*additional lyrics*

Things Have Changed

Red River Shore

My heart's in the highlands at the break of day
Over the hills and far away
I'm not there yet)
(There's a way to get there and I'll figure it out somehow
I'm there in my mind. That's good enough for now

# Love Sick

I'm walking through streets that are dead
Walking, walking with you in my head
My feet are so tired, my brain is so wired
And the clouds are weeping

Did I hear someone tell a lie?
Did I hear someone's distant cry?
You thrilled me to my heart, then you ripped it all apart
You went through my pockets when I was sleeping

I'm sick of love . . . but I'm in the thick of it
This kind of love . . . I'm so sick of it

I see lovers in the meadow
I see silhouettes in the window
I watch them 'til they're gone and they leave me hanging on
To a shadow

I'm sick of love . . . I hear the clock tick
I'm sick of love . . . I'm love sick

Sometimes the silence can be like the thunder
Sometimes I feel like I'm being plowed under
Could you ever be true? I think of you
And I wonder

I'm sick of love . . . I wish I'd never met you
I'm sick of love . . . I'm trying to forget you

Just don't know what to do
I'd give anything to just be with you

# Dirt Road Blues

Gon' walk down that dirt road, 'til someone lets me ride
Gon' walk down that dirt road, 'til someone lets me ride
If I can't find my baby, I'm gonna run away and hide

I been pacing around the room hoping maybe she'd come back
Pacing 'round the room hoping maybe she'd come back
Well, I been praying for salvation laying 'round in a one-room country shack

Gon' walk down that dirt road until my eyes begin to bleed
Gon' walk down that dirt road until my eyes begin to bleed
'Til there's nothing left to see, 'til the chains have been shattered and I've been freed

I been lookin' at my shadow, I been watching the colors up above
Lookin' at my shadow, watching the colors up above
Rolling through the rain and hail, looking for the sunny side of love

Gon' walk on down that dirt road 'til I'm right beside the sun
Gon' walk on down until I'm right beside the sun
I'm gonna have to put up a barrier to keep myself away from everyone

# Standing in the Doorway

I'm walking through the summer nights
Jukebox playing low
Yesterday everything was going too fast
Today, it's moving too slow
I got no place left to turn
I got nothing left to burn
Don't know if I saw you, if I would kiss you or kill you
It probably wouldn't matter to you anyhow
You left me standing in the doorway crying
I got nothing to go back to now

The light in this place is so bad
Making me sick in the head
All the laughter is just making me sad
The stars have turned cherry red
I'm strumming on my gay guitar
Smoking a cheap cigar
The ghost of our old love has not gone away
Don't look like it will anytime soon
You left me standing in the doorway crying
Under the midnight moon

Maybe they'll get me and maybe they won't
But not tonight and it won't be here
There are things I could say but I don't
I know the mercy of God must be near
I've been riding the midnight train
Got ice water in my veins
I would be crazy if I took you back
It would go up against every rule
You left me standing in the doorway crying
Suffering like a fool

When the last rays of daylight go down
Buddy, you'll roll no more
I can hear the church bells ringing in the yard
I wonder who they're ringing for
I know I can't win
But my heart just won't give in
Last night I danced with a stranger
But she just reminded me you were the one
You left me standing in the doorway crying
In the dark land of the sun

I'll eat when I'm hungry, drink when I'm dry
And live my life on the square
And even if the flesh falls off of my face
I know someone will be there to care
It always means so much
Even the softest touch
I see nothing to be gained by any explanation
There are no words that need to be said
You left me standing in the doorway crying
Blues wrapped around my head

# Million Miles

You took a part of me that I really miss
I keep asking myself how long it can go on like this
You told yourself a lie, that's all right mama I told myself one too
I'm tryin' to get closer but I'm still a million miles from you

You took the silver, you took the gold
You left me standing out in the cold
People asked about you, I didn't tell them everything I knew
Well, I'm tryin' to get closer but I'm still a million miles from you

I'm drifting in and out of dreamless sleep
Throwing all my memories in a ditch so deep
Did so many things I never did intend to do
Well, I'm tryin' to get closer but I'm still a million miles from you

I need your love so bad, turn your lamp down low
I need every bit of it for the places that I go
Sometimes I wonder just what it's all coming to
Well, I'm tryin' to get closer but I'm still a million miles from you

Well, I don't dare close my eyes and I don't dare wink
Maybe in the next life I'll be able to hear myself think
Feel like talking to somebody but I just don't know who
Well, I'm tryin' to get closer but I'm still a million miles from you

The last thing you said before you hit the street
"Gonna find me a janitor to sweep me off my feet"
I said, "That's all right, you do what you gotta do"
Well, I'm tryin' to get closer, I'm still a million miles from you

Rock me, pretty baby, rock me 'til everything gets real
Rock me for a little while, rock me 'til there's nothing left to feel
And I'll rock you too
I'm tryin' to get closer but I'm still a million miles from you

Well, there's voices in the night trying to be heard
I'm sitting here listening to every mind-polluting word
I know plenty of people who would put me up for a day or two
Yes, I'm tryin' to get closer but I'm still a million miles from you

# Tryin' to Get to Heaven

The air is getting hotter
There's a rumbling in the skies
I've been wading through the high muddy water
With the heat rising in my eyes
Every day your memory grows dimmer
It doesn't haunt me like it did before
I've been walking through the middle of nowhere
Trying to get to heaven before they close the door

When I was in Missouri
They would not let me be
I had to leave there in a hurry
I only saw what they let me see
You broke a heart that loved you
Now you can seal up the book and not write anymore
I've been walking that lonesome valley
Trying to get to heaven before they close the door

People on the platforms
Waiting for the trains
I can hear their hearts a-beatin'
Like pendulums swinging on chains
I tried to give you everything
That your heart was longing for
I'm just going down the road feeling bad
Trying to get to heaven before they close the door

I'm going down the river
Down to New Orleans
They tell me everything is gonna be all right
But I don't know what "all right" even means
I was riding in a buggy with Miss Mary-Jane
Miss Mary-Jane got a house in Baltimore
I been all around the world, boys
Now I'm trying to get to heaven before they close the door

Gonna sleep down in the parlor
And relive my dreams
I'll close my eyes and I wonder
If everything is as hollow as it seems
When you think that you've lost everything
You find out you can always lose a little more
I been to Sugar Town, I shook the sugar down
Now I'm trying to get to heaven before they close the door

# 'Til I Fell in Love with You

Well, my nerves are exploding and my body's tense
I feel like the whole world got me pinned up against the fence
I've been hit too hard, I've seen too much
Nothing can heal me now, but your touch
I don't know what I'm gonna do
I was all right 'til I fell in love with you

Well, my house is on fire, burning to the sky
I thought it would rain but the clouds passed by
Now I feel like I'm coming to the end of my way
But I know God is my shield and he won't lead me astray
Still I don't know what I'm gonna do
I was all right 'til I fell in love with you

Boys in the street beginning to play
Girls like birds flying away
When I'm gone you will remember my name
I'm gonna win my way to wealth and fame
I don't know what I'm gonna do
I was all right 'til I fell in love with you

Junk is piling up, taking up space
My eyes feel like they're falling off my face
Sweat falling down, I'm staring at the floor
I'm thinking about that girl who won't be back no more
I don't know what I'm gonna do
I was all right 'til I fell in love with you

Well, I'm tired of talking, I'm tired of trying to explain
My attempts to please you were all in vain
Tomorrow night before the sun goes down
If I'm still among the living, I'll be Dixie bound
I just don't know what I'm gonna do
I was all right 'til I fell in love with you

# Not Dark Yet

Shadows are falling and I've been here all day
It's too hot to sleep, time is running away
Feel like my soul has turned into steel
I've still got the scars that the sun didn't heal
There's not even room enough to be anywhere
It's not dark yet, but it's getting there

Well, my sense of humanity has gone down the drain
Behind every beautiful thing there's been some kind of pain
She wrote me a letter and she wrote it so kind
She put down in writing what was in her mind
I just don't see why I should even care
It's not dark yet, but it's getting there

Well, I've been to London and I've been to gay Paree
I've followed the river and I got to the sea
I've been down on the bottom of a world full of lies
I ain't looking for nothing in anyone's eyes
Sometimes my burden seems more than I can bear
It's not dark yet, but it's getting there

I was born here and I'll die here against my will
I know it looks like I'm moving, but I'm standing still
Every nerve in my body is so vacant and numb
I can't even remember what it was I came here to get away from
Don't even hear a murmur of a prayer
It's not dark yet, but it's getting there

# Cold Irons Bound

I'm beginning to hear voices and there's no one around
Well, I'm all used up and the fields have turned brown
I went to church on Sunday and she passed by
My love for her is taking such a long time to die

I'm waist deep, waist deep in the mist
It's almost like, almost like I don't exist
I'm twenty miles out of town in cold irons bound

The walls of pride are high and wide
Can't see over to the other side
It's such a sad thing to see beauty decay
It's sadder still to feel your heart torn away

One look at you and I'm out of control
Like the universe has swallowed me whole
I'm twenty miles out of town in cold irons bound

There's too many people, too many to recall
I thought some of 'm were friends of mine, I was wrong about 'm all
Well, the road is rocky and the hillside's mud
Up over my head nothing but clouds of blood

I found my world, found my world in you
But your love just hasn't proved true
I'm twenty miles out of town in cold irons bound
Twenty miles out of town in cold irons bound

Oh, the winds in Chicago have torn me to shreds
Reality has always had too many heads
Some things last longer than you think they will
There are some kind of things you can never kill

It's you and you only I been thinking about
But you can't see in and it's hard lookin' out
I'm twenty miles out of town in cold irons bound

Well the fat's in the fire and the water's in the tank
The whiskey's in the jar and the money's in the bank
I tried to love and protect you because I cared
I'm gonna remember forever the joy that we shared

Looking at you and I'm on my bended knee
You have no idea what you do to me
I'm twenty miles out of town in cold irons bound
Twenty miles out of town in cold irons bound

# Make You Feel My Love

When the rain is blowing in your face
And the whole world is on your case
I could offer you a warm embrace
To make you feel my love

When the evening shadows and the stars appear
And there is no one there to dry your tears
I could hold you for a million years
To make you feel my love

I know you haven't made your mind up yet
But I would never do you wrong
I've known it from the moment that we met
No doubt in my mind where you belong

I'd go hungry, I'd go black and blue
I'd go crawling down the avenue
There's nothing that I wouldn't do
To make you feel my love

The storms are raging on the rollin' sea
And on the highway of regret
Put your hand in mine and come with me
I'll see that you don't get wet

I could make you happy, make your dreams come true
Nothing that I wouldn't do
Go to the ends of the earth for you
To make you feel my love

# Can't Wait

I can't wait, wait for you to change your mind
It's late, I'm trying to walk the line
Well, it's way past midnight and there are people all around
Some on their way up, some on their way down
The air burns and I'm trying to think straight
And I don't know how much longer I can wait

I'm your man, I'm trying to recover the sweet love that we knew
You understand that my heart can't go on beating without you
Well, your loveliness has wounded me, I'm reeling from the blow
I wish I knew what it was keeps me loving you so
I'm breathing hard, standing at the gate
But I don't know how much longer I can wait

Skies are grey, I'm looking for anything that will bring a happy glow
Night or day, it doesn't matter where I go anymore, I just go
If I ever saw you coming I don't know what I would do
I'd like to think I could control myself, but it isn't true
That's how it is when things disintegrate
And I don't know how much longer I can wait

I'm doomed to love you, I've been rolling through stormy weather
I'm thinking of you and all the places we could roam together

It's mighty funny, the end of time has just begun
Oh, honey, after all these years you're still the one
While I'm strolling through the lonely graveyard of my mind
I left my life with you somewhere back there along the line
I thought somehow that I would be spared this fate
But I don't know how much longer I can wait

# Highlands

Well my heart's in the Highlands, gentle and fair
Honeysuckle blooming in the wildwood air
Bluebells blazing where the Aberdeen waters flow
Well my heart's in the Highlands
I'm gonna go there when I feel good enough to go

Windows were shakin' all night in my dreams
Everything was exactly the way that it seems
Woke up this morning and I looked at the same old page
Same ol' rat race
Life in the same ol' cage

I don't want nothing from anyone, ain't that much to take
Wouldn't know the difference between a real blonde and a fake
Feel like a prisoner in a world of mystery
I wish someone would come
And push back the clock for me

Well my heart's in the Highlands wherever I roam
That's where I'll be when I get called home
The wind, it whispers to the buck-eyed trees in rhyme
Well my heart's in the Highlands
I can only get there one step at a time

I'm listening to Neil Young, I gotta turn up the sound
Someone's always yelling turn it down
Feel like I'm drifting
Drifting from scene to scene
I'm wondering what in the devil could it all possibly mean?

Insanity is smashing up against my soul
You can say I was on anything but a roll
If I had a conscience, well, I just might blow my top
What would I do with it anyway
Maybe take it to the pawn shop

My heart's in the Highlands at the break of dawn
By the beautiful lake of the Black Swan
Big white clouds like chariots that swing down low
Well my heart's in the Highlands
Only place left to go

I'm in Boston town, in some restaurant
I got no idea what I want
Well, maybe I do but I'm just really not sure
Waitress comes over
Nobody in the place but me and her

It must be a holiday, there's nobody around
She studies me closely as I sit down
She got a pretty face and long white shiny legs
She says, "What'll it be?"
I say, "I don't know, you got any soft boiled eggs?"

She looks at me, says, "I'd bring you some
But we're out of 'm, you picked the wrong time to come"
Then she says, "I know you're an artist, draw a picture of me!"
I say, "I would if I could, but
I don't do sketches from memory"

"Well," she says, "I'm right here in front of you, or haven't you looked?"
I say, "All right, I know, but I don't have my drawing book!"
She gives me a napkin, she says, "You can do it on that"
I say, "Yes I could, but
I don't know where my pencil is at!"

She pulls one out from behind her ear
She says, "All right now, go ahead, draw me, I'm standing right here"
I make a few lines and I show it for her to see
Well she takes the napkin and throws it back
And says, "That don't look a thing like me!"

I said, "Oh, kind Miss, it most certainly does"
She says, "You must be jokin'." I say, "I wish I was!"
Then she says, "You don't read women authors, do you?"
Least that's what I think I hear her say
"Well," I say, "how would you know and what would it matter anyway?"

"Well," she says, "you just don't seem like you do!"
I said, "You're way wrong"
She says, "Which ones have you read then?" I say, "I read Erica Jong!"
She goes away for a minute
And I slide up out of my chair
I step outside back to the busy street but nobody's going anywhere

Well my heart's in the Highlands with the horses and hounds
Way up in the border country, far from the towns
With the twang of the arrow and a snap of the bow
My heart's in the Highlands
Can't see any other way to go

Every day is the same thing out the door
Feel further away than ever before
Some things in life, it gets too late to learn
Well, I'm lost somewhere
I must have made a few bad turns

I see people in the park forgetting their troubles and woes
They're drinking and dancing, wearing bright-colored clothes
All the young men with their young women looking so good
Well, I'd trade places with any of them
In a minute, if I could

I'm crossing the street to get away from a mangy dog
Talking to myself in a monologue
I think what I need might be a full-length leather coat
Somebody just asked me
If I registered to vote

The sun is beginning to shine on me
But it's not like the sun that used to be
The party's over and there's less and less to say
I got new eyes
Everything looks far away

Well, my heart's in the Highlands at the break of day
Over the hills and far away
There's a way to get there and I'll figure it out somehow
But I'm already there in my mind
And that's good enough for now

# Things Have Changed

A worried man with a worried mind
No one in front of me and nothing behind
There's a woman on my lap and she's drinking champagne
Got white skin, blood in my eyes
I'm looking up into the sapphire-tinted skies
I'm well dressed, waiting on the last train

Standing on the gallows with my head in a noose
Any minute now I'm expecting all hell to break loose

People are crazy and times are strange
I'm locked in tight, I'm out of range
I used to care, but things have changed

This place ain't doing me any good
I'm in the wrong town, I should be in Hollywood
Just for a second there I thought I saw something move
Gonna take dancing lessons, do the jitterbug rag
Ain't no shortcuts, gonna dress in drag
Only a fool in here would think he's got anything to prove

Lot of water under the bridge, lot of other stuff too
Don't get up gentlemen, I'm only passing through

People are crazy and times are strange
I'm locked in tight, I'm out of range
I used to care, but things have changed

I've been walking forty miles of bad road
If the Bible is right, the world will explode
I've been trying to get as far away from myself as I can
Some things are too hot to touch
The human mind can only stand so much
You can't win with a losing hand

Feel like falling in love with the first woman I meet
Putting her in a wheelbarrow and wheeling her down the street

People are crazy and times are strange
I'm locked in tight, I'm out of range
I used to care, but things have changed

I hurt easy, I just don't show it
You can hurt someone and not even know it
The next sixty seconds could be like an eternity
Gonna get low down, gonna fly high
All the truth in the world adds up to one big lie
I'm in love with a woman who don't even appeal to me

Mr. Jinx and Miss Lucy, they jumped in the lake
I'm not that eager to make a mistake

People are crazy and times are strange
I'm locked in tight, I'm out of range
I used to care, but things have changed

# Red River Shore

Some of us turn off the lights and we lay
Up in the moonlight shooting by
Some of us scare ourselves to death in the dark
To be where the angels fly
Pretty maids all in a row lined up
Outside my cabin door
I've never wanted any of 'em wanting me
'Cept the girl from the Red River shore

Well I sat by her side and for a while I tried
To make that girl my wife
She gave me her best advice when she said
Go home and lead a quiet life
Well I been to the East and I been to the West
And I been out where the black winds roar
Somehow, though, I never did get that far
With the girl from the Red River shore

Well I knew when I first laid eyes on her
I could never be free
One look at her and I knew right away
She should always be with me
Well the dream dried up a long time ago
Don't know where it is anymore
True to life, true to me
Was the girl from the Red River shore

Well I'm wearing the cloak of misery
And I've tasted jilted love
And the frozen smile upon my face
Fits me like a glove
But I can't escape from the memory
Of the one that I'll always adore
All those nights when I lay in the arms
Of the girl from the Red River shore

Well we're livin' in the shadows of a fading past
Trapped in the fires of time
I tried not to ever hurt anybody
And to stay out of a life of crime
And when it's all been said and done
I never did know the score
One more day is another day away
From the girl from the Red River shore

Well I'm a stranger here in a strange land
But I know this is where I belong
I ramble and gamble for the one I love
And the hills will give me a song
Though nothing looks familiar to me
I know I've stayed here before
Once a thousand nights ago
With the girl from the Red River shore

Well I went back to see about her once
Went back to straighten it out
Everybody that I talked to had seen us there
Said they didn't know who I was talkin' about
Well the sun went down a long time ago
And doesn't seem to shine anymore
I wish I could have spent every hour of my life
With the girl from the Red River shore

Now I heard of a guy who lived a long time ago
A man full of sorrow and strife
That if someone around him died and was dead
He knew how to bring him on back to life
Well I don't know what kind of language he used
Or if they do that kind of thing anymore
Sometimes I think nobody ever saw me here at all
'Cept the girl from the Red River shore

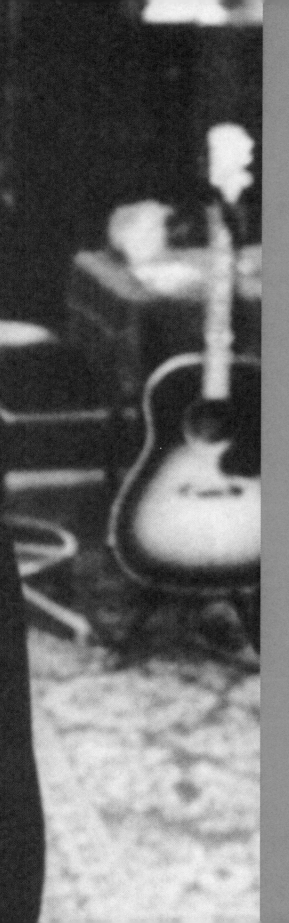

# "Love and Theft"

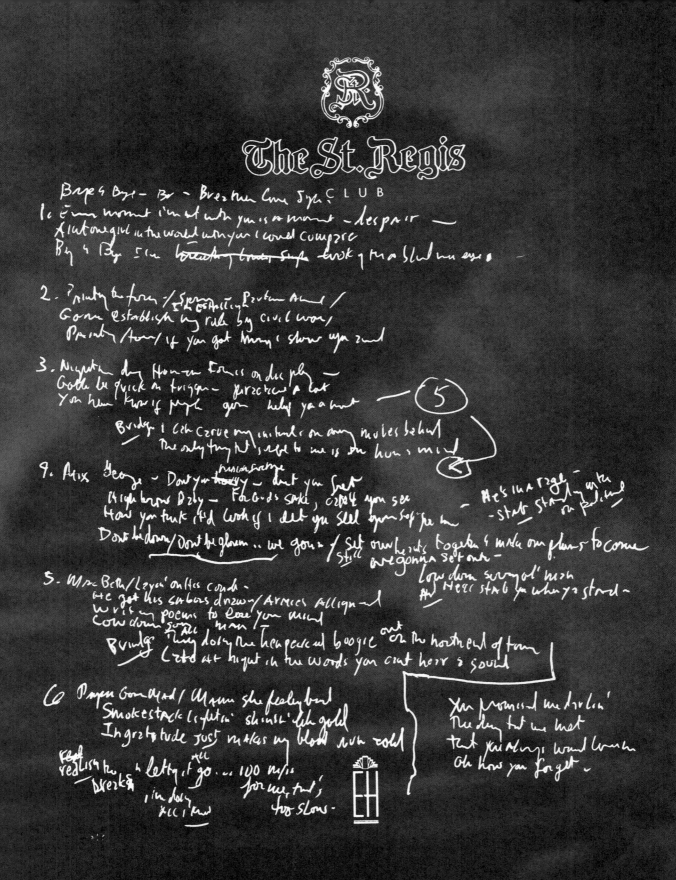

# Tweedle Dee & Tweedle Dum

Tweedle-dee Dum and Tweedle-dee Dee
They're throwing knives into the tree
Two big bags of dead man's bones
Got their noses to the grindstones
Living in the Land of Nod
Trustin' their fate to the hands of God
They pass by so silently
Tweedle-dee Dum and Tweedle-dee Dee

Well, they're going to the country, they're gonna retire
They're taking a street car named Desire
Looking in the window at the pecan pie
Lot of things they'd like they would never buy
Neither one gonna turn and run
They're making a voyage to the sun
"His Master's voice is calling me,"
Says Tweedle-dee Dum to Tweedle-dee Dee

Tweedle-dee Dee and Tweedle-dee Dum
All that and more and then some
They walk among the stately trees
They know the secrets of the breeze
Tweedle-dee Dum says to Tweedle-dee Dee
"Your presence is obnoxious to me."
They're like babies sittin' on a woman's knee
Tweedle-dee Dum and Tweedle-dee Dee

Well, they're living in a happy harmony
Tweedle-dee Dum and Tweedle-dee Dee
They're one day older and a dollar short
They've got a parade permit and a police escort
Tweedle-dee Dee—he's on his hands and his knees
Saying, "Throw me somethin', Mister, please."
"What's good for you is good for me,"
Says Tweedle-dee Dum to Tweedle-dee Dee

Well a childish dream is a deathless need
And a noble truth is a sacred creed
They're lying low and they're makin' hay
They seem determined to go all the way
One is a lowdown, sorry old man
The other will stab you where you stand
"I've had too much of your company,"
Says Tweedle-dee Dum to Tweedle-dee Dee

# Mississippi

Every step of the way we walk the line
Your days are numbered, so are mine
Time is pilin' up, we struggle and we scrape
We're all boxed in, nowhere to escape
City's just a jungle, more games to play
Trapped in the heart of it, trying to get away
I was raised in the country, I been workin' in the town
I been in trouble ever since I set my suitcase down
Got nothing for you, I had nothing before
Don't even have anything for myself anymore
Sky full of fire, pain pourin' down
Nothing you can sell me, I'll see you around
All my powers of expression and thoughts so sublime
Could never do you justice in reason or rhyme
Only one thing I did wrong
Stayed in Mississippi a day too long

Well, the devil's in the alley, mule's in the stall
Say anything you wanna, I have heard it all
I was thinkin' about the things that Rosie said
I was dreaming I was sleeping in Rosie's bed
Walking through the leaves, falling from the trees
Feeling like a stranger nobody sees
So many things that we never will undo
I know you're sorry, I'm sorry too
Some people will offer you their hand and some won't
Last night I knew you, tonight I don't
I need somethin' strong to distract my mind
I'm gonna look at you 'til my eyes go blind
Well I got here following the southern star
I crossed that river just to be where you are
Only one thing I did wrong
Stayed in Mississippi a day too long

Well my ship's been split to splinters and it's sinking fast
I'm drownin' in the poison, got no future, got no past
But my heart is not weary, it's light and it's free
I've got nothin' but affection for all those who've sailed with me
Everybody movin' if they ain't already there
Everybody got to move somewhere
Stick with me baby, stick with me anyhow
Things should start to get interesting right about now
My clothes are wet, tight on my skin
Not as tight as the corner that I painted myself in
I know that fortune is waitin' to be kind
So give me your hand and say you'll be mine
Well, the emptiness is endless, cold as the clay
You can always come back, but you can't come back all the way
Only one thing I did wrong
Stayed in Mississippi a day too long

# Summer Days

Summer days, summer nights are gone
Summer days and the summer nights are gone
I know a place where there's still somethin' going on

I got a house on a hill, I got hogs all out in the mud
I got a house on a hill, I got hogs out lying in the mud
Got a long haired woman, she got royal Indian blood

Everybody get ready—lift up your glasses and sing
Everybody get ready to lift up your glasses and sing
Well, I'm standin' on the table, I'm proposing a toast to the King

Well, I'm drivin' in the flats in a Cadillac car
The girls all say, "You're a worn out star."
My pockets are loaded and I'm spending every dime
How can you say you love someone else when you know it's me all the time?

Well, the fog's so thick you can't spy the land
The fog is so thick that you can't even spy the land
What good are you anyway, if you can't stand up to some old business man?

Wedding bells ringin', the choir is beginning to sing
Yes, the wedding bells are ringing and the choir is beginning to sing
What looks good in the day, at night is another thing

She's looking into my eyes, she's holding my hand
She's looking into my eyes, she's holding my hand
She says, "You can't repeat the past." I say, "You can't? What do you mean, you
    can't? Of course you can."

Where do you come from? Where do you go?
Sorry that's nothin' you would need to know
Well, my back has been to the wall for so long, it seems like it's stuck
Why don't you break my heart one more time just for good luck

I got eight carburetors, boys, I'm using 'em all
Well, I got eight carburetors and boys, I'm using 'em all
I'm short on gas, my motor's starting to stall

My dogs are barking, there must be someone around
My dogs are barking, there must be someone around
I got my hammer ringin', pretty baby, but the nails ain't goin' down

———

You got something to say, speak or hold your peace
Well, you got something to say, speak now or hold your peace
If it's information you want you can go get it from the police

Politician got on his jogging shoes
He must be running for office, got no time to lose
You been suckin' the blood out of the genius of generosity
You been rolling your eyes—you been teasing me

Standing by God's river, my soul is beginnin' to shake
Standing by God's river, my soul is beginnin' to shake
I'm countin' on you love, to give me a break

Well, I'm leaving in the morning as soon as the dark clouds lift
Yes, I'm leaving in the morning just as soon as the dark clouds lift
Gonna break in the roof—set fire to the place as a parting gift

Summer days, summer nights are gone
Summer days, summer nights are gone
I know a place where there's still somethin' going on

# Bye and Bye

Bye and bye, I'm breathin' a lover's sigh
I'm sittin' on my watch so I can be on time
I'm singin' love's praises with sugar-coated rhyme
Bye and bye, on you I'm casting my eye

I'm paintin' the town—swinging my partner around
I know who I can depend on, I know who to trust
I'm watchin' the roads, I'm studying the dust
I'm paintin' the town making my last go-round

Well, I'm slippin' and slidin', walkin' on briars
To get to the one that my heart desires

I'm rollin' slow—I'm doing all I know
I'm tellin' myself I found true happiness
That I've still got a dream that hasn't been repossessed
I'm rollin' slow, goin' where the wild red roses grow

Well the future for me is already a thing of the past
You were my first love and you will be my last

Papa gone mad, mama, she's feeling sad
I'll establish my rule through civil war
Bring it on up from the ocean's floor
I'll take you higher just so you can see the fire

# Lonesome Day Blues

Well, today has been a sad ol' lonesome day
Yeah, today has been a sad ol' lonesome day
I'm just sittin' here thinking
With my mind a million miles away

Well, they're doing the double shuffle, throwin' sand on the floor
They're doing the double shuffle, they're throwin' sand on the floor
When I left my long-time darlin'
She was standing in the door

Well, my pa he died and left me, my brother got killed in the war
Well, my pa he died and left me, my brother got killed in the war
My sister, she ran off and got married
Never was heard of any more

Samantha Brown lived in my house for about four or five months
Samantha Brown lived in my house for about four or five months
Don't know how it looked to other people
I never slept with her even once

The road's washed out—weather not fit for man or beast
Yeah, the road's washed out—weather not fit for man or beast
Funny how the things you have the hardest time parting with
Are the things you need the least

I'm forty miles from the mill—I'm droppin' it into overdrive
I'm forty miles from the mill—I'm droppin' it into overdrive
Got my dial set on the radio
I'm telling myself I'm still alive

I see your lover-man comin'—comin' 'cross the barren field
I see your lover-man comin'—comin' 'cross the barren field
He's not a gentleman at all—he's rotten to the core
He's a coward and he steals

Well my captain he's decorated—he's well schooled and he's skilled
My captain, he's decorated—he's well schooled and he's skilled
He's not sentimental—don't bother him at all
How many of his pals have been killed

Last night the wind was whisperin', I was trying to make out what it was
Last night the wind was whisperin' somethin'—I was trying to make out what it was
I tell myself something's comin'
But it never does

I'm gonna spare the defeated—I'm gonna speak to the crowd
I'm gonna spare the defeated, boys, I'm going to speak to the crowd
I am goin' to teach peace to the conquered
I'm gonna tame the proud

Well the leaves are rustlin' in the wood—things are fallin' off of the shelf
Leaves are rustlin' in the wood—things are fallin' off the shelf
You gonna need my help, sweetheart
You can't make love all by yourself

# Floater (Too Much to Ask)

Down over the window
Comes the dazzling sunlit rays
Through the back alleys—through the blinds
Another one of them endless days
Honey bees are buzzin'
Leaves begin to stir
I'm in love with my second cousin
I tell myself I could be happy forever with her
I keep listenin' for footsteps
But I ain't hearing any
From the boat I fish for bullheads
I catch a lot, sometimes too many
A summer breeze is blowing
A squall is settin' in
Sometimes it's just plain stupid
To get into any kind of wind

The old men 'round here, sometimes they get
On bad terms with the younger men
But old, young, age don't carry weight
It doesn't matter in the end
One of the boss' hangers-on
Comes to call at times you least expect
Try to bully ya—strong arm you—inspire you with fear
It has the opposite effect
There's a new grove of trees on the outskirts of town
The old one is long gone
Timber two-foot six across
Burns with the bark still on
They say times are hard, if you don't believe it
You can just follow your nose
It don't bother me—times are hard everywhere
We'll just have to see how it goes

My old man, he's like some feudal lord
Got more lives than a cat
Never seen him quarrel with my mother even once
Things come alive or they fall flat
You can smell the pinewood burnin'
You can hear the school bell ring
Gotta get up near the teacher if you can
If you wanna learn anything
Romeo, he said to Juliet, "You got a poor complexion.
It doesn't give your appearance a very youthful touch!"
Juliet said back to Romeo, "Why don't you just shove off
If it bothers you so much."
They all got out of here any way they could
The cold rain can give you the shivers
They went down the Ohio, the Cumberland, the Tennessee
All the rest of them rebel rivers

If you ever try to interfere with me or cross my path again
You do so at the peril of your own life
I'm not quite as cool or forgiving as I sound
I've seen enough heartaches and strife
My grandfather was a duck trapper
He could do it with just dragnets and ropes
My grandmother could sew new dresses out of old cloth
I don't know if they had any dreams or hopes
I had 'em once though, I suppose, to go along
With all the ring dancin' Christmas carols on all of the Christmas Eves
I left all my dreams and hopes
Buried under tobacco leaves
It's not always easy kicking someone out
Gotta wait a while—it can be an unpleasant task
Sometimes somebody wants you to give something up
And tears or not, it's too much to ask

# High Water (For Charley Patton)

High water risin'—risin' night and day
All the gold and silver are being stolen away
Big Joe Turner lookin' east and west
From the dark room of his mind
He made it to Kansas City
Twelfth Street and Vine
Nothing standing there
High water everywhere

High water risin', the shacks are slidin' down
Folks lose their possessions—folks are leaving town
Bertha Mason shook it—broke it
Then she hung it on a wall
Says, "You're dancin' with whom they tell you to
Or you don't dance at all."
It's tough out there
High water everywhere

I got a cravin' love for blazing speed
Got a hopped up Mustang Ford
Jump into the wagon, love, throw your panties overboard
I can write you poems, make a strong man lose his mind
I'm no pig without a wig
I hope you treat me kind
Things are breakin' up out there
High water everywhere

High water risin', six inches 'bove my head
Coffins droppin' in the street
Like balloons made out of lead
Water pourin' into Vicksburg, don't know what I'm going to do
"Don't reach out for me," she said
"Can't you see I'm drownin' too?"
It's rough out there
High water everywhere

Well, George Lewis told the Englishman, the Italian and the Jew
"Don't open up your mind, boys,
To every conceivable point of view."
They got Charles Darwin trapped out there on Highway Five
Judge says to the High Sheriff
"I want him dead or alive
Either one, I don't care."
High water everywhere

The Cuckoo is a pretty bird, she warbles as she flies
I'm preachin' the word of God
I'm puttin' out your eyes
I asked Fat Nancy for something to eat, she said, "Take it off the shelf—
As great as you are, man,
You'll never be greater than yourself."
I told her I didn't really care
High water everywhere

I'm gettin' up in the morning—I believe I'll dust my broom
Keeping away from the women
I'm givin' 'em lots of room
Thunder rolling over Clarksdale, everything is looking blue
I just can't be happy, love
Unless you're happy too
It's bad out there
High water everywhere

# Moonlight

The seasons they are turnin'
And my sad heart is yearnin'
To hear again the songbird's sweet melodious tone
Meet me in the moonlight alone

The dusky light, the day is losing
Orchids, poppies, black-eyed Susan
The earth and sky that melts with flesh and bone
Meet me in the moonlight alone

The air is thick and heavy
All along the levee
Where the geese into the countryside have flown
Meet me in the moonlight alone

Well, I'm preachin' peace and harmony
The blessings of tranquility
Floating like a dream across the floor
I'll take you 'cross the river dear
You've no need to linger here
Draw the blinds, step outside the door

The clouds are turnin' crimson
The leaves fall from the limbs an'
The branches cast their shadows over stone
Meet me in the moonlight alone

The boulevards of Cypress trees
The masquerades of birds and bees
The petals, pink and white, the wind has blown
Meet me in the moonlight alone

The trailing moss and mystic glow
Purple blossoms soft as snow
Step up and drop the coin right into the slot
The fading light of sunset glowed
It's crowded on the narrow road
Who cares whether you forgive me or not

My pulse is runnin' through my palm
The sharp hills are rising from
The yellow fields with twisted oaks that groan
Meet me in the moonlight alone

# Honest with Me

Well, I'm stranded in the city that never sleeps
Some of these women they just give me the creeps
I'm avoidin' the Southside the best I can
These memories I got, they can strangle a man
Well, I came ashore in the dead of the night
Lot of things can get in the way when you're tryin' to do what's right
You don't understand it—my feelings for you
You'd be honest with me if only you knew

I'm not sorry for nothin' I've done
I'm glad I fought—I only wish we'd won
The Siamese twins are comin' to town
People can't wait—they're gathered around
When I left my home the sky split open wide
I never wanted to go back there—I'd rather have died
You don't understand it—my feelings for you
You'd be honest with me if only you knew

My woman got a face like a teddy bear
She's tossin' a baseball bat in the air
The meat is so tough you can't cut it with a sword
I'm crashin' my car, trunk first into the boards
You say my eyes are pretty and my smile is nice
Well, I'll sell it to ya at a reduced price
You don't understand it—my feelings for you
You'd be honest with me if only you knew

Some things are too terrible to be true
I won't come here no more if it bothers you
The Southern Pacific leaving at nine forty-five
I'm having a hard time believin' some people were ever alive
I'm stark naked, but I don't care
I'm going off into the woods, I'm huntin' bare
You don't understand it—my feelings for you
Well, you'd be honest with me if only you knew

I'm here to create the new imperial empire
I'm going to do whatever circumstances require
I care so much for you—didn't think that I could
I can't tell my heart that you're no good
Well, my parents they warned me not to waste my years
And I still got their advice oozing out of my ears
You don't understand it—my feelings for you
Well, you'd be honest with me if only you knew

---

# Po' Boy

Man comes to the door—I say, "For whom are you looking?"
He says, "Your wife." I say, "She's busy in the kitchen cookin'."
Poor boy, where you been?
I already tol' you—won't tell you again

I say, "How much you want for that?" I go into the store
The man says, "Three dollars." "All right," I say, "Will you take four?"
Poor boy, never say die
Things will be all right by and by

Been workin' on the mainline—workin' like the devil
The game is the same—it's just up on a different level
Poor boy, dressed in black
Police at your back

Poor boy in a red hot town
Out beyond the twinklin' stars
Ridin' first class trains—making the rounds
Tryin' to keep from fallin' between the cars

Othello told Desdemona, "I'm cold, cover me with a blanket.
By the way, what happened to that poison wine?" She says, "I gave it to you, you
    drank it."
Poor boy, layin' 'em straight
Pickin' up the cherries fallin' off the plate

Time and love has branded me with its claws
Had to go to Florida, dodgin' them Georgia laws
Poor boy, sitting in the gloom
Calls down to room service, says, "Send up a room."

My mother was a daughter of a wealthy farmer
My father was a traveling salesman, I never met him
When my mother died, my uncle took me in—he ran a funeral parlor
He did a lot of nice things for me and I won't forget him

All I know is that I'm thrilled by your kiss
I don't know any more than this
Poor boy, pickin' up sticks
Build ya a house out of mortar and bricks

Knockin' on the door, I say, "Who is it and where are you from?"
Man says, "Freddy!" I say, "Freddy who?" He says, "Freddy or not here I come."
Poor boy, 'neath the stars that shine
Washin' them dishes, feedin' them swine

———

# Cry a While

Well, I had to go down and see a guy named Mr. Goldsmith
A nasty, dirty, double-crossin', back-stabbin' phony I didn't wanna have to be dealin' with
But I did it for you and all you gave me was a smile
Well, I cried for you—now it's your turn to cry awhile

I don't carry dead weight—I'm no flash in the pan
All right, I'll set you straight, can't you see I'm a union man?
I'm lettin' the cat out of the cage, I'm keeping a low profile
Well, I cried for you—now it's your turn, you can cry awhile

Feel like a fighting rooster—feel better than I ever felt
But the Pennsylvania line's in an awful mess and the Denver road is about to melt
I went to the church house, every day I go an extra mile
Well, I cried for you—now it's your turn, you can cry awhile

Last night 'cross the alley there was a pounding on the walls
It must have been Don Pasqualli makin' a two A.M. booty call
To break a trusting heart like mine was just your style
Well, I cried for you—now it's your turn to cry awhile

I'm on the fringes of the night, fighting back tears that I can't control
Some people they ain't human, they got no heart or soul
Well, I'm crying to the Lord—I'm tryin' to be meek and mild
Yes, I cried for you—now it's your turn, you can cry awhile

Well, there's preachers in the pulpits and babies in the cribs
I'm longin' for that sweet fat that sticks to your ribs
I'm gonna buy me a barrel of whiskey—I'll die before I turn senile
Well, I cried for you—now it's your turn, you can cry awhile

Well, you bet on a horse and it ran on the wrong way
I always said you'd be sorry and today could be the day
I might need a good lawyer, could be your funeral, my trial
Well, I cried for you—now it's your turn, you can cry awhile

# Sugar Baby

I got my back to the sun 'cause the light is too intense
I can see what everybody in the world is up against
You can't turn back—you can't come back, sometimes we push too far
One day you'll open up your eyes and you'll see where we are

Sugar Baby get on down the road
You ain't got no brains, no how
You went years without me
Might as well keep going now

Some of these bootleggers, they make pretty good stuff
Plenty of places to hide things here if you wanna hide 'em bad enough
I'm staying with Aunt Sally, but you know, she's not really my aunt
Some of these memories you can learn to live with and some of them you can't

Sugar Baby get on down the line
You ain't got no brains, no how
You went years without me
You might as well keep going now

The ladies in Darktown, they're doing the Darktown Strut
You always got to be prepared but you never know for what
There ain't no limit to the amount of trouble women bring
Love is pleasing, love is teasing, love's not an evil thing

Sugar Baby, get on down the road
You ain't got no brains, no how
You went years without me
You might as well keep going now

Every moment of existence seems like some dirty trick
Happiness can come suddenly and leave just as quick
Any minute of the day the bubble could burst
Try to make things better for someone, sometimes you just end up making it a
    thousand times worse

Sugar Baby, get on down the road
You ain't got no brains, no how
You went years without me
Might as well keep going now

Your charms have broken many a heart and mine is surely one
You got a way of tearing a world apart, love, see what you done
Just as sure as we're living, just as sure as you're born
Look up, look up—seek your Maker—'fore Gabriel blows his horn

Sugar Baby, get on down the line
You ain't got no sense, no how
You went years without me
Might as well keep going now

# 'Cross the Green Mountain

(from the film *Gods and Generals*)

I crossed the green mountain, I slept by the stream
Heaven blazin' in my head, I dreamt a monstrous dream
Something came up out of the sea
Swept through the land of the rich and the free

I look into the eyes of my merciful friend
And then I ask myself, is this the end?
Memories linger, sad yet sweet
And I think of the souls in heaven who will meet

Altars are burning with flames falling wide
The foe has crossed over from the other side
They tip their caps from the top of the hill
You can feel them come, more brave blood to spill

Along the dim Atlantic line
The ravaged land lies for miles behind
The light's comin' forward and the streets are broad
All must yield to the avenging God

The world is old, the world is gray
Lessons of life can't be learned in a day
I watch and I wait and I listen while I stand
To the music that comes from a far better land

Close the eyes of our Captain, peace may he know
His long night is done, the great leader is laid low
He was ready to fall, he was quick to defend
Killed outright he was by his own men

It's the last day's last hour of the last happy year
I feel that the unknown world is so near
Pride will vanish and glory will rot
But virtue lives and cannot be forgot

The bells of evening have rung
There's blasphemy on every tongue
Let them say that I walked in fair nature's light
And that I was loyal to truth and to right

Serve God and be cheerful, look upward beyond
Beyond the darkness that masks the surprises of dawn
In the deep green grasses of the blood stained wood
They never dreamed of surrendering. They fell where they stood

Stars fell over Alabama, I saw each star
You're walkin' in dreams whoever you are
Chilled are the skies, keen is the frost
The ground's froze hard and the morning is lost

A letter to mother came today
Gunshot wound to the breast is what it did say
But he'll be better soon he's in a hospital bed
But he'll never be better, he's already dead

I'm ten miles outside the city and I'm lifted away
In an ancient light that is not of day
They were calm, they were blunt, we knew 'em all too well
We loved each other more than we ever dared to tell

# Waitin' for You

(from the film *Divine Secrets of the Ya-Ya Sisterhood*)

I never dreamed there could be someone made just for me
I'm not letting her have her way
I come here to see what she has to say
Oh, the poor gal always wins the day
I'm staying ahead of the game, she's doing the same
And the whiskey's flying into my head
The fiddler's arm has gone dead
And talk is beginning to spread

When did our love go bad?
Whatever happened to the best friend that I had?
Been so long since I held you tight
Been so long since we said goodnight
The taste of tears is bittersweet
When you're near me, my heart forgets to beat
You're there every night among the good and the true
And I'll be around, waitin' for you

The king of them all is starting to fall
I lost my gal at the boatman's ball
The night has a thousand hearts and eyes
Hope may vanish but it never dies
I'll see you tomorrow when freedom rings
I'm gonna stay on top of things
It's the middle of the summer and the moon is blue
I'll be around waitin' for you

Another deal gone down, another man done gone
You put up with it all and you carry on
Something holding you back but you'll come through
I'd bet the world and everything in it on you
Happiness is but a state of mind
Anytime you want you can cross the state line
You don't need to be rich or well-to-do
I'll be around waitin' for you

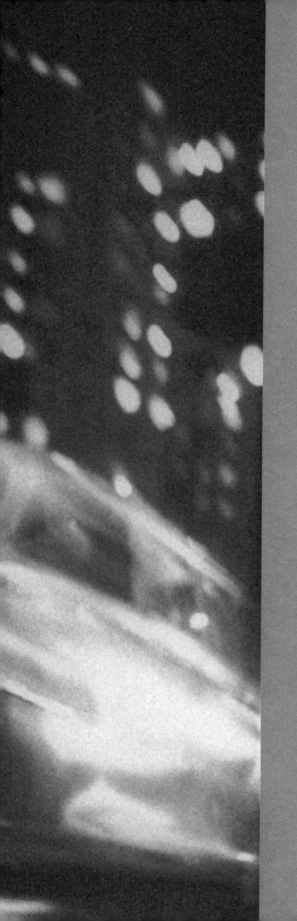

# Modern Times

1. Lost John, sitting on the railroad track / Country's out of whack
   Blues this morning falling down like hail
   Gonna leave a greasy trail

2. Gonna travel the world is what I'm going to do / then come back and see you
   Days creep by, each one feels like a year   ( many the years)
   So many things come to nothing 'round here

3. I'm the oldest son of a crazy man / I'm in a cowboy band
   Got a pile of sins to pay for and i aint got time to hide
   I'd walk thru a blazing fire baby if I knew you was on the other side

4. Going where the Southern crosses the yellow Dog / to get away from those demagogues
   And these bad luck women that stick (to you) like glue
   Always getting in the way when there's work to do        let's go down   (stopping all my thoughts before
                                                                              they start to run all
                                                                              cooking at em (all) one by one)

5. Dr. Frankenstein's        (let's go down to Jacksonville)   went psycho-billy        She's a
   still up there at his castle on the hill / up there still (with his moonshine still)   cathouse woman I had --
   Al there in the graveyard, Frankie's raising hell                      to Jacksonville)   saucy all day
   I'm beginning to believe (empty tub) what the scriptures tell                                (on)

6. She says "(look out Daddy, dont want ya to tear your pants! / you could get wrecked in this deuce"
   They say that whiskey'll kill ya but i dont think it will
   You went away and left me but i believe you love me still

7. It's getting light outside, the temperature dropping / i think the rain has stopped        (been)
   I'm going to make you come to grips with fate                    It's been too late
   When I'm thru with you, you'll learn how to keep your business straight    It ever since the world
                                                                                   begun
                                                                              fn A C

8. the judge is coming, all rise / lift up your eyes
   i went to the river, threw away my dice
   Before you call me any dirty names, you better think twice

9. Dont know why my baby never looked so good before / i dont have to wonder no more
   She been cookin' all day and it's gonna take her all night
   I cant eat it all (up) in a single bite

10. Today i'll stand in faith and raise / the voice of praise     (You've made all my
    My heart would never go astray ( my eyes would never go astray )   Every kind of grief gives way --
    A lifetime with you is like some heavenly day    i could never go away
                                                     couldnt be any other way
                                                                        your sweet love
                                                                        has eternal (way)

11. Everything I've ever known to be right has been proven wrong / I'll be driftin' along   A cathouse
    i went to the dance / wore out my shoes                                                 woman is
    She says "dont worry ('bout it) Daddy, dont you know you cant lose "   showered my sight   go hand in hand --
                                                                          day

12. The bright spark of the steady lights / has veiled the day's distracting sights / (nowhere in sight)
    i know you'd never throw me down (I'll be lovin' you when my whiskers touch the ground)   I've lived many lives - (you never threw
                                                                             i was born on high ground   you down)
    When you die, I'll keep hanging around — (HAS                          I'm stuck with you cher --
    dimm)

13. Lost John — 1st verse —

# Thunder on the Mountain

Thunder on the mountain, fires on the moon
There's a ruckus in the alley and the sun will be here soon
Today's the day, gonna grab my trombone and blow
Well, there's hot stuff here and it's everywhere I go
I was thinkin' 'bout Alicia Keys, couldn't keep from crying
When she was born in Hell's Kitchen, I was living down the line
I'm wondering where in the world Alicia Keys could be
I been looking for her even clear through Tennessee
Feel like my soul is beginning to expand
Look into my heart and you will sort of understand
You brought me here, now you're trying to run me away
The writing's on the wall, come read it, come see what it say

Thunder on the mountain, rolling like a drum
Gonna sleep over there, that's where the music coming from
I don't need any guide, I already know the way
Remember this, I'm your servant both night and day
The pistols are poppin' and the power is down
I'd like to try somethin' but I'm so far from town
The sun keeps shinin' and the North Wind keeps picking up speed
Gonna forget about myself for a while, gonna go out and see what others need
I've been sitting down studying the art of love
I think it will fit me like a glove
I want some real good woman to do just what I say
Everybody got to wonder what's the matter with this cruel world today

Thunder on the mountain rolling to the ground
Gonna get up in the morning walk the hard road down
Some sweet day I'll stand beside my king
I wouldn't betray your love or any other thing
Gonna raise me an army, some tough sons of bitches
I'll recruit my army from the orphanages
I been to St. Herman's church and I've said my religious vows
I've sucked the milk out of a thousand cows
I got the porkchops, she got the pie
She ain't no angel and neither am I
Shame on your greed, shame on your wicked schemes
I'll say this, I don't give a damn about your dreams

Thunder on the mountain heavy as can be
Mean old twister bearing down on me
All the ladies of Washington scrambling to get out of town
Looks like something bad gonna happen, better roll your airplane down
Everybody's going and I want to go too
Don't wanna take a chance with somebody new
I did all I could and I did it right there and then
I've already confessed—no need to confess again
Gonna make a lot of money, gonna go up north
I'll plant and I'll harvest what the earth brings forth
The hammer's on the table, the pitchfork's on the shelf
For the love of God, you ought to take pity on yourself

# Spirit on the Water

Spirit on the water
Darkness on the face of the deep
I keep thinking about you baby
I can't hardly sleep
I'm traveling by land
Traveling through the dawn of day
You're always on my mind
I can't stay away
I'd forgotten about you
Then you turned up again
I always knew
That we were meant to be more than friends
When you are near
It's just as plain as it can be
I'm wild about you, gal
You ought to be a fool about me

Can't explain
The sources of this hidden pain
You burned your way into my heart
You got the key to my brain
I've been trampling through mud
Praying to the powers above
I'm sweating blood
You got a face that begs for love
Life without you
Doesn't mean a thing to me
If I can't have you
I'll throw my love into the deep blue sea
Sometimes I wonder
Why you can't treat me right
You do good all day
Then you do wrong all night

When you're with me
I'm a thousand times happier than I could ever say
What does it matter
What price I pay
They brag about your sugar
Brag about it all over town
Put some sugar in my bowl
I feel like laying down
I'm pale as a ghost
Holding a blossom on a stem
You ever seen a ghost? No
But you have heard of them
I hear your name
Ringing up and down the line
I'm saying it plain
These ties are strong enough to bind

I been in a brawl
Now I'm feeling the wall
I'm going away baby
I won't be back 'til fall
High on the hill
You can carry all my thoughts with you
You've numbed my will
This love could tear me in two
I wanna be with you in paradise
And it seems so unfair
I can't go back to paradise no more
I killed a man back there
You think I'm over the hill
You think I'm past my prime
Let me see what you got
We can have a whoppin' good time

# Rollin' and Tumblin'

I rolled and I tumbled, I cried the whole night long
I rolled and I tumbled, I cried the whole night long
Woke up this mornin', I must have bet my money wrong

I got troubles so hard, I can't stand the strain
I got troubles so hard, I just can't stand the strain
Some young lazy slut has charmed away my brains

The landscape is glowin', gleamin' in the golden light of day
The landscape is glowin', gleamin' in the gold light of day
I ain't holding nothin' back now, I ain't standin' in anybody's way

I'm flat out spent, this woman been drivin' me to tears
I'm flat out spent, this woman she been drivin' me to tears
This woman so crazy, I swear I ain't gonna touch another one for years

Well, the warm weather is comin' and the buds are on the vine
The warm weather's comin', the buds are on the vine
Ain't nothing so depressing as trying to satisfy this woman of mine

I got up this mornin', saw the rising sun return
Well, I got up this mornin', seen the rising sun return
Sooner or later you too shall burn

The night's filled with shadows, the years are filled with early doom
The night's filled with shadows, the years are filled with early doom
I've been conjuring up all these long dead souls from their crumblin' tombs

Let's forgive each other darlin', let's go down to the greenwood glen
Let's forgive each other darlin', let's go down to the greenwood glen
Let's put our heads together, let's put old matters to an end

Now I rolled and I tumbled and I cried the whole night long
Ah, I rolled and I tumbled, I cried the whole night long
I woke up this morning, I think I must be travelin' wrong

# When the Deal Goes Down

In the still of the night, in the world's ancient light
Where wisdom grows up in strife
My bewildering brain, toils in vain
Through the darkness on the pathways of life
Each invisible prayer is like a cloud in the air
Tomorrow keeps turning around
We live and we die, we know not why
But I'll be with you when the deal goes down

We eat and we drink, we feel and we think
Far down the street we stray
I laugh and I cry and I'm haunted by
Things I never meant nor wished to say
The midnight rain follows the train
We all wear the same thorny crown
Soul to soul, our shadows roll
And I'll be with you when the deal goes down

The moon gives light and shines by night
I scarcely feel the glow
We learn to live and then we forgive
O'er the road we're bound to go
More frailer than the flowers, these precious hours
That keep us so tightly bound
You come to my eyes like a vision from the skies
And I'll be with you when the deal goes down

I picked up a rose and it poked through my clothes
I followed the winding stream
I heard the deafening noise, I felt transient joys
I know they're not what they seem
In this earthly domain, full of disappointment and pain
You'll never see me frown
I owe my heart to you, and that's sayin' it true
And I'll be with you when the deal goes down

# Someday Baby

I don't care what you do, I don't care what you say
I don't care where you go or how long you stay
Someday baby, you ain't gonna worry po' me anymore

Well you take my money and you turn me out
You fill me up with nothin' but self doubt
Someday baby, you ain't gonna worry po' me anymore

When I was young, driving was my crave
You drive me so hard, almost to the grave
Someday baby, you ain't gonna worry po' me anymore

Something is the matter, my mind tied up in knots
I keep recycling the same old thoughts
Someday baby, you ain't gonna worry po' me anymore

So many good things in life I overlooked
I don't know what to do now, you got me so hooked
Someday baby, you ain't gonna worry po' me anymore

Gonna get myself together, I'm gonna ring your neck
When all else fails I'll make it a matter of self-respect
Someday baby, you ain't gonna worry po' me anymore

You can take your clothes, put 'm in a sack
You goin' down the road, baby and you can't come back
Someday baby, you ain't gonna worry po' me anymore

I try to be friendly, I try to be kind
Now I'm gonna drive you from your home, just like I was driven from mine
Someday baby, you ain't gonna worry po' me anymore

# Workingman's Blues #2

There's an evening's haze settling over the town
Starlight by the edge of the creek
The buying power of the proletariat's gone down
Money's getting shallow and weak
The place I love best is a sweet memory
It's a new path that we trod
They say low wages are a reality
If we want to compete abroad

My cruel weapons been laid back on the shelf
Come and sit down on my knee
You are dearer to me than myself
As you yourself can see
I'm listening to the steel rails hum
Got both eyes tight shut
I'm just trying to keep the hunger from
Creepin' its way into my gut

Meet me at the bottom, don't lag behind
Bring me my boots and shoes
You can hang back or fight your best on the front line
Sing a little bit of these workingman's blues

I'm sailing on back getting ready for the long haul
Leaving everything behind
If I stay here I'll lose it all
The bandits will rob me blind
I'm trying to feed my soul with thought
Gonna sleep off the rest of the day
Sometimes nobody wants what you got
Sometimes you can't give it away

I woke up this morning and sprang to my feet
Went into town on a whim
I saw my father there in the street
At least I think it was him
In the dark I hear the night birds call
The hills are rugged and steep
I sleep in the kitchen with my feet in the hall
If I told you my whole story you'd weep

Meet me at the bottom, don't lag behind
Bring me my boots and shoes
You can hang back or fight your best on the front line
Sing a little bit of these workingman's blues

They burned my barn and they stole my horse
I can't save a dime
It's a long way down and I don't want to be forced
Into a life of continual crime
I can see for myself that the sun is sinking
O'er the banks of the deep blue sea
Tell me, am I wrong in thinking
That you have forgotten me

Now they worry and they hurry and they fuss and they fret
They waste your nights and days
Them, I will forget
You, I'll remember always
It's a cold black night and it's midsummer's eve
And the stars are spinning around
I still find it so hard to believe
That someone would kick me when I'm down

Meet me at the bottom, don't lag behind
Bring me my boots and shoes
You can hang back or fight your best on the front line
Sing a little bit of these workingman's blues

I'll be back home in a month or two
When the frost is on the vine
I'll punch my spear right straight through
Half-ways down your spine
I'll lift up my arms to the starry skies
And pray the fugitive's prayer
I'm guessing tomorrow the sun will rise
I hope the final judgment's fair

The battle is over up in the hills
And the mist is closing in
Look at me, with all of my spoils
What did I ever win?
Gotta brand new suit and a brand new wife
I can live on rice and beans
Some people never worked a day in their life
They don't know what work even means

Meet me at the bottom, don't lag behind
Bring me my boots and shoes
You can hang back or fight your best on the front line
Sing a little bit of these workingman's blues

# Beyond the Horizon

Beyond the horizon, behind the sun
At the end of the rainbow life has only begun
In the long hours of twilight 'neath the stardust above
Beyond the horizon it is easy to love
I'm staring out the window
Of an ancient town
Petals from flowers
Falling to the ground
Beyond the horizon, in the springtime or fall
Love waits forever, for one and for all

Beyond the horizon, across the divide
'Round about midnight, we'll be on the same side
Down in the valley the water runs cold
Beyond the horizon someone's prayin' for your soul
I lost my true lover
In the dusk, in the dawn
I have to recover
Get up and go on
Beyond the horizon, beyond love's burning game
Every step that you take, I'm walking the same

Beyond the horizon, the night winds blow
The theme of a melody from many moons ago
The bells of St. Mary, how sweetly they chime
Beyond the horizon I found you just in time
Slipping and sliding
Too late to stop
Riding and gliding
It's lonely at the top
Beyond the horizon, the sky is so blue
I've got more than a lifetime to live lovin' you

# Nettie Moore

Lost John sittin' on a railroad track
Something's out of whack
Blues this morning falling down like hail
Gonna leave a greasy trail

Gonna travel the world is what I'm gonna do
Then come back and see you
All I ever do is struggle and strive
If I don't do anybody any harm, I might make it back home alive

I'm the oldest son of a crazy man
I'm in a cowboy band
Got a pile of sins to pay for and I ain't got time to hide
I'd walk through a blazing fire, baby, if I knew you was on the other side

Oh, I miss you Nettie Moore
And my happiness is o'er
Winter's gone, the river's on the rise
I loved you then and ever shall
But there's no one here that's left to tell
The world has gone black before my eyes

The world of research has gone berserk
Too much paperwork
Albert's in the graveyard, Frankie's raising hell
I'm beginning to believe what the scriptures tell

I'm going where the Southern crosses the Yellow Dog
Get away from all these demagogues
And these bad luck women stick like glue
It's either one or the other or neither of the two

She says, "Look out daddy, don't want you to tear your pants.
You can get wrecked in this dance."
They say whiskey will kill ya, but I don't think it will
I'm riding with you to the top of the hill

Oh, I miss you Nettie Moore
And my happiness is o'er
Winter's gone, the river's on the rise
I loved you then and ever shall
But there's no one here that's left to tell
The world has gone black before my eyes

———

Don't know why my baby never looked so good before
I don't have to wonder no more
She been cooking all day and it's gonna take me all night
I can't eat all that stuff in a single bite

The Judge is coming in, everybody rise
Lift up your eyes
You can do what you please, you don't need my advice
Before you call me any dirty names you better think twice

Getting light outside, the temperature dropped
I think the rain has stopped
I'm going to make you come to grips with fate
When I'm through with you, you'll learn to keep your business straight

Oh, I miss you Nettie Moore
And my happiness is o'er
Winter's gone, the river's on the rise
I loved you then and ever shall
But there's no one here that's left to tell
The world has gone black before my eyes

The bright spark of the steady lights
Has dimmed my sights
When you're around all my grief gives 'way
A lifetime with you is like some heavenly day

Everything I've ever known to be right has been proven wrong
I'll be drifting along
The woman I'm lovin', she rules my heart
No knife could ever cut our love apart

Today I'll stand in faith and raise
The voice of praise
The sun is strong, I'm standing in the light
I wish to God that it were night

Oh, I miss you Nettie Moore
And my happiness is o'er
Winter's gone, the river's on the rise
I loved you then and ever shall
But there's no one here that's left to tell
The world has gone black before my eyes

# The Levee's Gonna Break

If it keep on rainin' the levee gonna break
If it keep on rainin' the levee gonna break
Everybody saying this is a day only the Lord could make

Well I worked on the levee Mama, both night and day
Well I worked on the levee Mama, both night and day
I got to the river and I threw my clothes away

I paid my time and now I'm as good as new
I paid my time and now I'm as good as new
They can't take me back, not unless I want them to

If it keep on rainin' the levee gonna break
If it keep on rainin' the levee gonna break
Some of these people gonna strip you of all they can take

I can't stop here, I ain't ready to unload
I can't stop here, I ain't ready to unload
Riches and salvation can be waiting behind the next bend in the road

I picked you up from the gutter and this is the thanks I get
I picked you up from the gutter and this is the thanks I get
You say you want me to quit ya, I told you no, not just yet

I look in your eyes, I see nobody else but me
I look in your eyes, I see nobody other than me
I see all that I am and all I hope to be

If it keep on rainin' the levee gonna break
If it keep on rainin' the levee gonna break
Some of these people don't know which road to take

When I'm with you I forget I was ever blue
When I'm with you I forget I was ever blue
Without you there's no meaning in anything I do

Some people on the road carrying everything that they own
Some people on the road carrying everything that they own
Some people got barely enough skin to cover their bones

Put on your cat clothes, Mama, put on your evening dress
Put on your cat clothes, Mama, put on your evening dress
A few more years of hard work then there'll be a thousand years of happiness

If it keep on rainin' the levee gonna break
If it keep on rainin' the levee gonna break
I tried to get you to love me, but I won't repeat that mistake

If it keep on rainin' the levee gonna break
If it keep on rainin' the levee gonna break
Plenty of cheap stuff out there still around to take

I woke up this morning, butter and eggs in my bed
I woke up this morning, butter and eggs in my bed
I ain't got enough room to even raise my head

Come back, baby, say we never more will part
Come back, baby, say we never more will part
Don't be a stranger without a brain or heart

If it keep on rainin' the levee gonna break
If it keep on rainin' the levee gonna break
Some people still sleepin', some people are wide awake

# Ain't Talkin'

As I walked out tonight in the mystic garden
The wounded flowers were dangling from the vines
I was passing by yon cool and crystal fountain
Someone hit me from behind

Ain't talkin', just walkin'
Through this weary world of woe
Heart burnin', still yearnin'
No one on earth would ever know

They say prayer has the power to help
So pray for me mother
In the human heart an evil spirit can dwell
I'm trying to love my neighbor and do good unto others
But oh, mother, things ain't going well

Ain't talkin', just walkin'
I'll burn that bridge before you can cross
Heart burnin', still yearnin'
They'll be no mercy for you once you've lost

Now I'm all worn down by weepin'
My eyes are filled with tears, my lips are dry
If I catch my opponents ever sleepin'
I'll just slaughter them where they lie

Ain't talkin', just walkin'
Through a world mysterious and vague
Heart burnin', still yearnin'
Walking through the cities of the plague

The whole world is filled with speculation
The whole wide world which people say is round
They will tear your mind away from contemplation
They will jump on your misfortune when you're down

Ain't talkin', just walkin'
Eatin' hog-eyed grease in hog-eyed town
Heart burnin', still yearnin'
Someday you'll be glad to have me around

They will crush you with wealth and power
Every waking moment you could crack
I'll make the most of one last extra hour
I'll avenge my father's death then I'll step back

Ain't talkin', just walkin'
Hand me down my walkin' cane
Heart burnin', still yearnin'
Got to get you out of my miserable brain

It's bright in the heavens and the wheels are flying
Fame and honor never seem to fade
The fire's gone out but the light is never dying
Who says I can't get heavenly aid?

Ain't talkin', just walkin'
Carrying a dead man's shield
Heart burnin', still yearnin'
Walkin' with a toothache in my heel

The suffering is unending
Every nook and cranny has its tears
I'm not playing, I'm not pretending
I'm not nursing any superfluous fears

Ain't talkin', just walkin'
Walkin' ever since the other night
Heart burnin', still yearnin'
Walkin' 'til I'm clean out of sight

As I walked out in the mystic garden
On a hot summer day, hot summer lawn
Excuse me, ma'am, I beg your pardon
There's no one here, the gardener is gone

Ain't talkin', just walkin'
Up the road around the bend
Heart burnin', still yearnin'
In the last outback, at the world's end

# Can't Escape from You

Oh the evening train is rolling
All along the homeward way
All my hopes are over the horizon
All my dreams have gone astray
The hillside darkly shaded
Stars fall from above
All the joys of earth have faded
The nights untouched by love
I'll be here 'til tomorrow
Beneath a shroud of gray
I'll pretend I'm free from sorrow
My heart is miles away
The dead bells are ringing
My train is overdue
To your memory I'm clinging
I can't escape from you

Well I hear the sound of thunder
Roaring loud and long
Sometimes you've got to wonder
God knows I've done no wrong
You've wasted all your power
You threw out the Christmas pie
You'll wither like a flower
And play the fool and die
I'm neither sad nor sorry
I'm all dressed up in black
I fought for fame and glory
You tried to break my back
In the far off sweet forever
The sunshine breaking through
We should have walked together
I can't escape from you

I cannot grasp the shadows
That gather near the door
Rain fall 'round my window
I wish I'd seen you more
The path is ever winding
The stars they never age
The morning light is blinding
All the world's a stage
Should be the time of gladness
Happy faces everywhere
But the mystery of madness
Is propagating in the air
I don't like the city
Not like some folks do
Isn't it a pity
I can't escape from you?

# Huck's Tune

Well I wandered alone
Through a desert of stone
And I dreamt of my future wife
My sword's in my hand
And I'm next in command
In this version of death called life
My plate and my cup
Are right straight up
I took a rose from the hand of a child
When I kiss your lips
The honey drips
But I'm gonna have to put you down for a while

Every day we meet
On any old street
And you're in your girlish prime
The short and the tall
Are coming to the ball
I go there all the time
Behind every tree
There's something to see
The river is wider than a mile
I tried you twice
You couldn't be nice
I'm gonna have to put you down for a while

Here come the nurse
With money in her purse
Here come the ladies and men
You push it all in
And you've no chance to win
You play 'em on down to the end
I'm laying in the sand
Getting a sunshine tan
Moving along, riding in style
From my toes to my head
You knock me dead
I'm gonna have to put you down for a while

I count the years
And I shed no tears
I'm blinded to what might have been
Nature's voice
Makes my heart rejoice
Play me the wild song of the wind
I found hopeless love
In the room above
When the sun and the weather were mild
You're as fine as wine
I ain't handing you no line
But I'm gonna have to put you down for a while

All the merry little elves
Can go hang themselves
My faith is as cold as can be
I'm stacked high to the roof
And I'm not without proof
If you don't believe me, come see
You think I'm blue
I think so too
In my words, you'll find no guile
The game's gotten old
The deck's gone cold
And I'm gonna have to put you down for a while

The game's gotten old
The deck's gone cold
I'm gonna have to put you down for a while

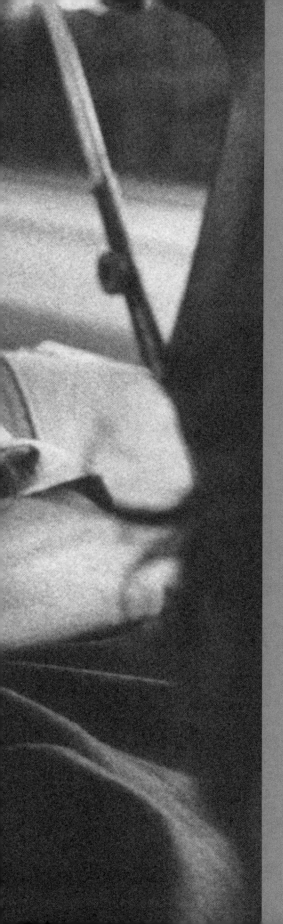

# Together Through Life

Beyond Here Lies Nothin'
Life Is Hard
My Wife's Home Town
If You Ever Go to Houston
Forgetful Heart
Jolene
This Dream of You
Shake Shake Mama
I Feel a Change Comin' On
It's All Good

Life is for love — all they say that comes Blind
If you want to live Easy baby — mine —

What the use of all my dreaming / I must have better
Ya ~~~~~ dreame wen do for me sorry things to do
, thy

You just as whore that's Ever — baby you could start
I must losing my mind

(Pleading) James Joyce (For
People —

Everybody got all the money / Even beautiful clothes
Everybody got flowers i don't even a single rose

# Beyond Here Lies Nothin'

(with Robert Hunter)

I love you pretty baby
You're the only love I've ever known
Just as long as you stay with me
The whole world is my throne
Beyond here lies nothin'
Nothin' we can call our own

I'm movin' after midnight
Down boulevards of broken cars
Don't know what I'd do without it
Without this love that we call ours
Beyond here lies nothin'
Nothin' but the moon and stars

Down every street there's a window
And every window made of glass
We'll keep on lovin' pretty baby
For as long as love will last
Beyond here lies nothin'
But the mountains of the past

My ship is in the harbor
And the sails are spread
Listen to me pretty baby
Lay your hand upon my head
Beyond here lies nothin'
Nothin' done and nothin' said

# Life Is Hard

(with Robert Hunter)

The evening winds are still
I've lost the way and will
Can't tell you where they went
I just know what they meant
I'm always on my guard
Admitting life is hard
Without you near me

The friend you used to be
So near and dear to me
You slipped so far away
Where did we go astray
I pass the old schoolyard
Admitting life is hard
Without you near me

Ever since the day
The day you went away
I felt that emptiness so wide
I don't know what's wrong or right
I just know I need strength to fight
Strength to fight that world outside

Since we've been out of touch
I haven't felt that much
From day to barren day
My heart stays locked away
I walk the boulevard
Admitting life is hard
Without you near me

The sun is sinking low
I guess it's time to go
I feel a chilly breeze
In place of memories
My dreams are locked and barred
Admitting life is hard
Without you near me

# My Wife's Home Town

(with Robert Hunter)

Well I didn't come here to deal with a doggone thing
I just came here to hear the drummer's cymbal ring
There ain't no way you can put me down
I just want to say that Hell's my wife's home town

Well there's reasons for that and reasons for this
I can't think of any just now, but I know they exist
I'm sitting in the sun 'til my skin turns brown
I just want to say that Hell's my wife's home town
Home town, home town

She can make you steal, make you rob
Give you the hives, make you lose your job
Make things bad, she can make things worse
She got stuff more potent than a gypsy curse

One of these days, I'll end up on the run
I'm pretty sure, she'll make me kill someone
I'm going inside, roll the shutters down
I just want to say that Hell's my wife's home town

Well there's plenty to remember, plenty to forget
I still can remember the day we met
I lost my reason long ago
My love for her is all I know

State gone broke, the county's dry
Don't be looking at me with that evil eye
Keep on walking, don't be hanging around
I'm telling you again that Hell's my wife's home town
Home town, home town

# If You Ever Go to Houston

(with Robert Hunter)

If you ever go to Houston
Better walk right
Keep your hands in your pockets
And your gun-belt tight
You'll be asking for trouble
If you're lookin' for a fight
If you ever go to Houston
Boy, you better walk right

If you're ever down there
On Bagby and Lamar
You better watch out for
The man with the shining star
Better know where you're going
Or stay where you are
If you're ever down there
On Bagby and Lamar

I know these streets
I've been here before
I nearly got killed here
During the Mexican war
Something always
Keeps me coming back for more
I know these streets
I've been here before

If you ever go to Dallas
Say hello to Mary Anne
Say I'm still pullin' on the trigger
Hangin' on the best that I can
If you see her sister Lucy
Say I'm sorry I'm not there
Tell her other sister Betsy
To pray the sinner's prayer

I got a restless fever
Burnin' in my brain
Got to keep ridin' forward
Can't spoil the game
The same way I leave here
Will be the way that I came
Got a restless fever
Burnin' in my brain

If you ever go to Austin
Fort Worth or San Antone
Find the bar rooms I got lost in
And send my memories home
Put my tears in a bottle
Screw the top on tight
If you ever go to Houston
You better walk right

# Forgetful Heart

(with Robert Hunter)

Forgetful heart
Lost your power of recall
Every little detail
You don't remember at all
The times we knew
Who would remember better than you

Forgetful heart
We laughed and had a good time, you and I
It's been so long
Now you're content to let the days go by
When you were there
You were the answer to my prayer

Forgetful heart
We loved with all the love that life can give
What can I say
Without you it's so hard to live
Can't take much more
Why can't we love like we did before

Forgetful heart
Like a walking shadow in my brain
All night long
I lay awake and listen to the sound of pain
The door has closed forevermore
If indeed there ever was a door

# Jolene

(with Robert Hunter)

Well you're comin' down High Street, walkin' in the sun
You make the dead man rise and holler she's the one
Jolene, Jolene
Baby, I am the king and you're the queen

Well it's a long old highway, don't ever end
I've got a Saturday night special, I'm back again
I'll sleep by your door, lay my life on the line
You probably don't know, but I'm gonna make you mine
Jolene, Jolene
Baby, I am the king and you're the queen

I keep my hands in my pocket, I'm movin' along
People think they know, but they're all wrong
You're something nice, I'm gonna grab my dice
If I can do it once, I can do it twice
Jolene, Jolene
Baby, I am the king and you're the queen

Well I found out the hard way, I've had my fill
You can't find somebody with his back to a hill
Those big brown eyes, they set off a spark
When you hold me in your arms things don't look so dark
Jolene, Jolene
Baby, I am the king and you're the queen

# This Dream of You

How long can I stay in this nowhere café
'Fore night turns into day
I wonder why I'm so frightened of dawn
All I have and all I know
Is this dream of you
Which keeps me living on

There's a moment when all old things
Become new again
But that moment might have been here and gone
All I have and all I know
Is this dream of you
Which keeps me living on

I look away, but I keep seeing it
I don't want to believe, but I keep believing it
Shadows dance upon the wall
Shadows that seem to know it all

Am I too blind to see?
Is my heart playing tricks on me?
Too late to stop now even though all my friends are gone
All I have and all I know
Is this dream of you
Which keeps me living on

Everything I touch seems to disappear
Everywhere I turn you are always here
I'll run this race until my earthly death
I'll defend this place with my dying breath

From a cheerless room in a curtained gloom
I saw a star from heaven fall
I turned and looked again but it was gone
All I have and all I know
Is this dream of you
Which keeps me living on

# Shake Shake Mama

(with Robert Hunter)

I get the blues for you baby when I look up at the sun
I get the blues for you baby when I look up at the sun
Come back here we can have some real fun

Well it's early in the evening and everything is still
Well it's early in the evening and everything is still
One more time, I'm walking up on Heartbreak Hill

Shake, shake mama, like a ship goin' out to sea
Shake, shake mama, like a ship goin' out to sea
You took all my money and you give it to Richard Lee

Down by the river Judge Simpson walkin' around
Down by the river Judge Simpson walkin' around
Nothing shocks me more than that old clown

Some of you women you really know your stuff
Some of you women you really know your stuff
But your clothes are all torn and your language is a little too rough

Shake, shake mama, shake it 'til the break of day
Shake, shake mama, shake it 'til the break of day
I'm right here baby, I'm not that far away

I'm motherless, fatherless, almost friendless too
I'm motherless, fatherless, almost friendless too
It's Friday morning on Franklin Avenue

Shake, shake mama, raise your voice and pray
Shake, shake mama, raise your voice and pray
If you're goin' on home, better go the shortest way

# I Feel a Change Comin' On

(with Robert Hunter)

Well I'm looking the world over
Looking far off into the East
And I see my baby coming
She's walking with the village priest
I feel a change coming on
And the last part of the day is already gone

We got so much in common
We strive for the same old ends
And I just can't wait
Wait for us to become friends
I feel a change coming on
And the fourth part of the day is already gone

Life is for love
And they say that love is blind
If you want to live easy
Baby pack your clothes with mine
I feel a change coming on
And the fourth part of the day is already gone

Ain't no use in dreamin'
I got better things to do
Dreams never worked anyway
Even when they did come true

You're as whorish as ever
It ain't no surprise
We see the meaning of life
In each other's eyes
I feel a change coming on
And the fourth part of the day is already gone

I'm hearing Billy Joe Shaver
And I'm reading James Joyce
Some people they tell me
I got the blood of the land in my voice

Everybody got all the money
Everybody got all the beautiful clothes
Everybody got all the flowers
I don't have one single rose
I feel a change coming on
And the fourth part of the day is already gone

---

# It's All Good

(with Robert Hunter)

Talk about me babe, if you must
Throw on the dirt, pile on the dust
I'd do the same thing if I could
You've heard what they say—they say it's all good
All good
It's all good

Big politician telling lies
Restaurant kitchen, all full of flies
Don't make a bit of difference, don't see why it should
I'll tell ya somethin'—it's all good
It's all good
It's all good

Wives are leavin' their husbands, they beginning to roam
They leave the party and they never get home
I wouldn't change it, even if I could
Same ol' story—it's all good
It's all good
All good

Brick by brick, they tear you down
A teacup of water is enough to drown
Check your oil, look under the hood
Whatever you see, it's all good
All good
Say it's all good

People in the country, people on the land
Some so sick, they can hardly stand
Everybody would move away, if they could
It's hard to believe but it's all good
Yeah

The widow's cry, the orphan's plea
Everywhere you look, more misery
Come 'long with me, babe, I wish you would
You know what I'm sayin', it's all good
All good, I said it's all good
All good

Cold blooded killer, stalking the town
Cop cars blinking, something bad going down
Buildings are crumbling in the neighborhood
No doubt about it, it's all good
It's all good
They say it's all good

I'll pluck off your beard and blow it in your face
This time tomorrow I'll be rolling in your place
I'm going out back, get some firewood
It is what it is, and it's all good
It's all good

# Tempest

6.   Set 'm up Joe, play Walkin' the Floor
It's not like nobody's ever asked you before
With check the liquor and you make Amends
while the smile of Heaven descends
If love is a sin, then beauty's a crime
All things are beautiful in their time
The black white, the yellow and brown
It's all right here for you in Scarlet Town

They tell me that
The Law's the Law

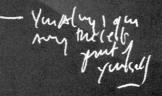

— Yesterday i gave        — the ... are
away myself             would a friend-
pant of            ud rude
yourself

Some fernodays
crosses the
Line
Faded the quality
pretend      i'llspend
the
schoolboy plays

Thedoors Are chained

# Duquesne Whistle

(with Robert Hunter)

Listen to that Duquesne whistle blowin'
Blowin' like it's gonna sweep my world away
I'm gonna stop in Carbondale and keep on going
That Duquesne train gonna ride me night and day

You say I'm a gambler, you say I'm a pimp
But I ain't neither one

Listen to that Duquesne whistle blowin'
Sound like it's on a final run

Listen to that Duquesne whistle blowin'
Blowin' like she never blowed before
Blue light blinkin', red light glowin'
Blowin' like she's at my chamber door

You smiling through the fence at me
Just like you always smiled before

Listen to that Duquesne whistle blowin'
Blowin' like she ain't gonna blow no more

Can't you hear that Duquesne whistle blowin'
Blowin' like the sky's gonna blow apart
You're the only thing alive that keeps me goin'
You're like a time bomb in my heart

I can hear a sweet voice gently calling
Must be the Mother of our Lord

Listen to that Duquesne whistle blowin'
Blowin' like my woman's on board

Listen to that Duquesne whistle blowin'
Blowin' like it's gonna blow my blues away
You ole rascal, I know exactly where you're goin'
I'll lead you there myself at the break of day

I wake up every morning with that woman in my bed
Everybody telling me she's gone to my head

Listen to that Duquesne whistle blowin'
Blowin' like it's gonna kill me dead

Can't you hear that Duquesne whistle blowin'
Blowin' through another no-good town
The lights of my native land are glowin'
I wonder if they'll know me next time around

I wonder if that old oak tree's still standing
That old oak tree, the one we used to climb

Listen to that Duquesne whistle blowin'
Blowin' like she's blowin' right on time

———

# Soon After Midnight

I'm searching for phrases to sing your praises
I need to tell someone
It's soon after midnight and my day has just begun

A gal named Honey took my money
She was passing by
It's soon after midnight and the moon is in my eye

My heart is cheerful, it's never fearful
I been down on the killing floors
I'm in no great hurry, I'm not afraid of your fury
I've faced stronger walls than yours

Charlotte's a harlot, dresses in scarlet
Mary dresses in green
It's soon after midnight and I've got a date with a fairy queen

They chirp and they chatter, what does it matter
They're lying there dying in their blood
Two Timing Slim, who's ever heard of him?
I'll drag his corpse through the mud

It's now or never, more than ever
When I met you I didn't think you would do
It's soon after midnight and I don't want nobody but you

# Narrow Way

I'm gonna walk across the desert 'til I'm in my right mind
I won't even think about what I left behind
Nothin' back there anyway I can call my own
Go back home, leave me alone

It's a long road, it's a long and narrow way
If I can't work up to you
You'll have to work down to me someday

Ever since the British burned the white house down
There's a bleeding wound in the heart of town
I saw you drinking from an empty cup
I saw you buried and I saw you dug up

It's a long road, it's a long and narrow way
If I can't work up to you
You'll have to work down to me someday

Look down angel, from the skies
Help my weary soul to rise
I kissed your cheek, I dragged your plow
You broke my heart, I was your friend 'til now

It's a long road, it's a long and narrow way
If I can't work up to you
You'll have to work down to me someday

In the courtyard of the golden sun
You stand and fight or you break and run
You went and lost your lovely head
For a drink of wine and a crust of bread

It's a long road, it's a long and narrow way
If I can't work up to you
You'll have to work down to me someday

We looted and we plundered on distant shores
Why is my share not equal to yours?
Your father left you, your mother too
Even death has washed his hands of you

It's a long road, it's a long and narrow way
If I can't work up to you
You'll have to work down to me someday

———

This is hard country to stay alive in
Blades are everywhere and they're breaking my skin
I'm armed to the hilt and I'm struggling hard
You won't get out of here unscarred

It's a long road, it's a long and narrow way
If I can't work up to you
You'll have to work down to me someday

You got too many lovers waiting at the wall
If I had a thousand tongues I couldn't count them all
Yesterday I could have thrown them all in the sea
Today, even one may be too much for me

It's a long road, it's a long and narrow way
If I can't work up to you
You'll have to work down to me someday

Cake walking baby, you can do no wrong
Put your arms around me where they belong
I want to take you on a roller coaster ride
Lay my hands all over you, tie you to my side

It's a long road, it's a long and narrow way
If I can't work up to you
You'll have to work down to me someday

I got a heavy stacked woman with a smile on her face
And she has crowned my soul with grace
I'm still hurting from an arrow that pierced my chest
I'm gonna have to take my head and bury it between your breasts

It's a long road, it's a long and narrow way
If I can't work up to you
You'll have to work down to me someday

Been dark all night, but now it's dawn
The moving finger is moving on
You can guard me while I sleep
Kiss away the tears I weep

It's a long road, it's a long and narrow way
If I can't work up to you
You'll have to work down to me someday

I love women and she loves men
We've been to the West and we going back again
I heard a voice at the dusk of day
Saying, "Be gentle brother, be gentle and pray"

It's a long road, it's a long and narrow way
If I can't work up to you
You'll have to work down to me someday

# Long and Wasted Years

It's been such a long, long time
Since we loved each other and our hearts were true
One time, for one brief day
I was the man for you

Last night I heard you talking in your sleep
Saying things you shouldn't say
Oh, baby
You just might have to go to jail some day

Is there a place we can go?
Is there anybody we can see?
Maybe what's right for you
Isn't really right for me

I ain't seen my family in twenty years
That ain't easy to understand
They may be dead by now
I lost track of them after they lost their land

Shake it up baby, twist and shout
You tell me what it's all about
What you doing out in the sun anyway?
Don't you know the sun can burn your brains right out?

My enemy slammed into the earth
I don't know what he was worth
But he lost it all, everything and more
What a blithering fool he took me for

I wear dark glasses to cover my eyes
There're secrets in them I can't disguise
Come back, baby
If I hurt your feelings, I apologize

Two trains running side by side
Forty miles wide down the Eastern line
You don't have to go, I just came to you
Because you're a friend of mine

I think when my back was turned
The whole world behind me burned
Maybe today, if not today, maybe tomorrow
Maybe there'll be a limit on all my sorrow

We cried on a cold and frosty morn'
We cried because our souls were torn
So much for tears
So much for those long and wasted years

# Pay in Blood

Well I'm grinding my life away, steady and sure
Nothing more wretched than what I must endure
I'm drenched in the light that shines from the sun
I could stone you to death for the wrongs that you done

Sooner or later you'll make a mistake
I'll put you in a chain that you never can break
Legs and arms and body and bone
I pay in blood, but not my own

Night after night, day after day
They strip your useless hopes away
The more I take, the more I give
The more I die, the more I live

I got something in my pocket make your eyeballs swim
I got dogs that could tear you limb to limb
I'm circling around in the southern zone
I pay in blood, but not my own

Another politician pumping out his piss
Another ragged beggar blowin' ya a kiss
Life is short and it don't last long
They'll hang you in the morning and sing ya a song

Someone must have slipped a drug in your wine
You gulped it down and you lost your mind
My head so hard, it must be made of stone
I pay in blood, but not my own

How I made it back home nobody knows
Or how I survived so many blows
I been through hell, what good did it do?
My conscience is clear, what about you?

I'll give you justice, I'll fatten your purse
Show me your moral virtues first
Hear me holler, hear me moan
I pay in blood but not my own

You bit your lover in the bed
Come here I'll break your lousy head
Our nation must be saved and freed
You been accused of murder, how do you plead?

This is how I spend my days
I came to bury not to praise
I'll drink my fill and sleep alone
I pay in blood, but not my own

# Scarlet Town

In Scarlet Town where I was born
There's ivy leaf and silver thorn
The streets have names you can't pronounce
Gold is down to a quarter of an ounce

The music starts and the people sway
Everybody says, are you going my way?
Uncle Tom still working for Uncle Bill
Scarlet Town is under the hill

Scarlet Town in the month of May
Sweet William on his deathbed lay
Mistress Mary by the side of the bed
Kissing his face, heaping prayers on his head

So brave, so true, so gentle is he
I'll weep for him as he'd weep for me
Little Boy Blue come blow your horn
In Scarlet Town where I was born

Scarlet Town in the hot noon hours
There's palm leaf shadows and scattered flowers
Beggars crouching at the gate
Help comes but it comes too late

On marble slabs and in fields of stone
You make your humble wishes known
I touched the garment but the hem was torn
In Scarlet Town where I was born

In Scarlet Town the end is near
The seven wonders of the world are here
The evil and the good living side by side
All human forms seem glorified

Put your heart on a platter and see who'll bite
See who'll hold you and kiss you good night
There's walnut groves and maple wood
In Scarlet Town crying won't do you no good

In Scarlet Town you fight your father's foes
Up on the hill a chilly wind blows
You fight 'em on high and you fight 'em down in
You fight 'em with whisky, morphine and gin

You got legs that can drive men mad
A lot of things we didn't do that I wish we had
In Scarlet Town the sky is clear
You'll wish to God that you stayed right here

Set 'em up Joe, play Walking The Floor
Play it for my flat chested junkie whore
I'm staying up late and I'm making amends
While the smile of heaven descends

If love is a sin then beauty is a crime
All things are beautiful in their time
The black and the white, the yellow and the brown
It's all right there for ya in Scarlet Town

# Early Roman Kings

All the early Roman Kings in their sharkskin suits
Bowties and buttons, high top boots
Driving the spikes in, blazing the rails
Nailed in their coffins in top hats and tails
Fly away little bird, fly away, flap your wings
Fly by night like the early Roman Kings

All the early Roman Kings in the early, early morn'
Coming down the mountain, distributing the corn
Speeding through the forest, racing down the track
You try to get away, they drag you back
Tomorrow is Friday, we'll see what it brings
Everybody's talking 'bout the early Roman Kings

They're peddlers and they're meddlers, they buy and they sell
They destroyed your city, they'll destroy you as well
They're lecherous and treacherous, hell bent for leather
Each of them bigger than all men put together
Sluggers and muggers wearing fancy gold rings
All the women going crazy for the early Roman Kings

I'll dress up your wounds with a blood clotted rag
I ain't afraid to make love to a bitch or a hag
If you see me coming and you're standing there
Wave your handkerchief in the air
I ain't dead yet, my bell still rings
I keep my fingers crossed like the early Roman Kings

I'll strip you of life, strip you of breath
Ship you down to the house of death
One day you will ask for me
There'll be no one else that you'll want to see
Bring down my fiddle, tune up my strings
Gonna break it wide open like the early Roman Kings

I was up on black mountain the day Detroit fell
They killed them all off and they sent them to hell
Ding Dong Daddy, you're coming up short
Gonna put you on trial in a Sicilian court
I've had my fun, I've had my flings
Gonna shake 'em all down like the early Roman Kings

# Tin Angel

It was late last night when the boss came home
To a deserted mansion and a desolate throne
Servant said, "Boss, the lady's gone
She left this morning just 'fore dawn."

"You got something to tell me, tell it to me, man.
Come to the point as straight as you can."
"Old Henry Lee, chief of the clan,
Came riding through the woods and took her by the hand."

The boss he laid back flat on his bed
He cursed the heat and he clutched his head
He pondered the future of his fate
To wait another day would be far too late

"Go fetch me my coat and my tie
And the cheapest labor that money can buy
Saddle me up my buckskin mare
If you see me go by, put up a prayer."

Well, they rode all night and they rode all day
Eastward long on the broad highway
His spirit was tired and his vision was bent
His men deserted him and onward he went

He came to a place where the light was dull
His forehead pounding in his skull
Heavy heart was wracked with pain
Insomnia raging in his brain

Well he threw down his helmet and his cross-handled sword
He renounced his faith, he denied his Lord
Crawled on his belly, put his ear to the wall
One way or another he'd put an end to it all

He leaned down, cut the electric wire
Stared into the flames and he snorted the fire
Peered through the darkness, caught a glimpse of the two
It was hard to tell for certain who was who

He lowered himself down on a golden chain
His nerves were quaking in every vein
His knuckles were bloody, he sucked in the air
He ran his fingers through his greasy hair

They looked at each other and their glasses clinked
One single unit inseparably linked
"Got a strange premonition there's a man close by."
"Don't worry about him, he wouldn't harm a fly."

From behind the curtain the boss crossed the floor
He moved his feet and he bolted the door
Shadows hiding the lines in his face
With all the nobility of an ancient race

She turned, she was startled with a look of surprise
With a hatred that could hit the skies
"You're a reckless fool, I can see it in your eyes.
To come this way was by no means wise."

"Get up, stand up, you greedy lipped wench
And cover your face or suffer the consequence.
You are making my heart full sick.
Put your clothes back on double quick."

"Silly boy, you think me a saint.
I'll listen no more to your words of complaint.
You've given me nothing but the sweetest lies.
Now hold your tongue and feed your eyes."

"I'd have given you the stars and the planets too
But what good would these things do you?
Bow the heart, if not the knee
Or never again this world you'll see."

"Oh, please let not your heart be cold.
This man is dearer to me than gold."
"Oh my dear, you must be blind.
He's a gutless ape with a worthless mind."

"You had your way too long with me.
Now it's me who'll determine how things shall be.
Try to escape," he cussed and cursed
"You'll have to try to get past me first."

"I dare not let your passion rule.
You think my heart, the heart of a fool.
And you sir, you cannot deny
You made a monkey of me, what and for why?"

"I'll have no more of this insulting chat.
The devil can have you, I'll see to that.
Look sharp or step aside,
Or in the cradle you'll wish you died."

———

The gun went boom and the shot rang clear
First bullet grazed his ear
Second ball went right straight in
And he bent in the middle like a twisted pin

He crawled to the corner and he lowered his head
He gripped the chair and he grabbed the bed
It would take more than needle and thread
Bleeding from the mouth, he's as good as dead

"You shot my husband down, you fiend."
"Husband, what husband, what the hell do you mean?
He was a man of strife, a man of sin.
I cut him down and I'll throw him to the wind."

"Hear this," she said, with angry breath
"You too shall meet the lord of death.
It was I who brought your soul to life."
And she raised her robe and she drew out a knife

His face was hard and caked with sweat
His arms ached and his hands were wet
"You're a murderous queen and a bloody wife.
If you don't mind, I'll have the knife."

"We're two of a kind and our blood runs hot.
But we're no way similar in body and thought.
All husbands are good men, as all wives know."
Then she pierced him to the heart and his blood did flow

His knees went limp and he reached for the door
His doom was sealed, he slid to the floor
He whispered in her ear, "This is all your fault.
My fighting days have come to a halt."

She touched his lip and kissed his cheek
He tried to speak, but his breath was weak
"You died for me, now I'll die for you."
She put the blade to her heart and she ran it through

All three lovers together in a heap
Thrown into the grave forever to sleep
Funeral torches blazed away
Through the towns and the villages all night and all day

# Tempest

The pale moon rose in its glory
Out on the western town
She told a sad, sad story
Of the great ship that went down

'Twas the fourteen day of April
Over the waves she rode
Sailing into tomorrow
To a golden age foretold

The night was bright with starlight
The seas were sharp and clear
Moving through the shadows
The promised hour was near

Lights were holding steady
Gliding over the foam
All the lords and ladies
Heading for their eternal home

The chandeliers were swaying
From the balustrades above
The orchestra was playing
Songs of faded love

The watchman he lay dreaming
As the ballroom dancers twirled
He dreamed the Titanic was sinking
Into the underworld

Leo took his sketchbook
He was often so inclined
He closed his eyes and painted
The scenery in his mind

Cupid struck his bosom
And broke it with a snap
The closest woman to him
He fell into her lap

He heard a loud commotion
Something sounded wrong
His inner spirit was saying
That he couldn't stand here long

He staggered to the quarterdeck
No time now to sleep
Water on the quarterdeck
Already three foot deep

Smokestack leaning sideways
Heavy feet began to pound
He walked into the whirlwind
Sky spinning all around

The ship was going under
The universe opened wide
The roll was called up yonder
The angels turned aside

Lights down in the hallway
Flickering dim and dull
Dead bodies already floating
In the double bottomed hull

The engines then exploded
Propellers they failed to start
The boilers overloaded
The ship's bow split apart

Passengers were flying
Backward, forward, far and fast
They mumbled, fumbled, tumbled
Each one more weary than the last

The veil was torn asunder
'Tween the hours of twelve and one
No change, no sudden wonder
Could undo what had been done

The watchman lay there dreaming
At forty-five degrees
He dreamed the Titanic was sinking
Dropping to her knees

Wellington, he was sleeping
His bed began to slide
His valiant heart was beating
He pushed the tables aside

Glass of shattered crystal
Lay scattered 'round about
He strapped on both his pistols
How long could he hold out?

His men and his companions
Were nowhere to be seen
In silence there he waited for
Time and space to intervene

The passageway was narrow
There was blackness in the air
He saw every kind of sorrow
Heard voices everywhere

Alarm bells were ringing
To hold back the swelling tide
Friends and lovers clinging
To each other side by side

Mothers and their daughters
Descending down the stairs
Jumped into the icy waters
Love and pity sent their prayers

The rich man, Mr. Astor
Kissed his darling wife
He had no way of knowing
Be the last trip of his life

Calvin, Blake and Wilson
Gambled in the dark
Not one of them would ever live to
Tell the tale of disembark

Brother rose up against brother
In every circumstance
They fought and slaughtered each other
In a deadly dance

They lowered down the lifeboats
From the sinking wreck
There were traitors, there were turncoats
Broken backs and broken necks

The bishop left his cabin
To help all those in need
Turned his eyes up to the heavens
Said, "The poor are yours to feed."

Davey the brothel keeper
Came out, dismissed his girls
Saw the water getting deeper
Saw the changing of his world

Jim Dandy smiled
He'd never learned to swim
Saw the little crippled child
And he gave his seat to him

He saw the starlight shining
Streaming from the East
Death was on the rampage
But his heart was now at peace

They battened down the hatches
But the hatches wouldn't hold
They drowned upon the staircase
Of brass and polished gold

Leo said to Cleo
"I think I'm going mad."
But he'd lost his mind already
Whatever mind he had

He tried to block the doorway
To save all those from harm
Blood from an open wound
Pouring down his arm

Petals fell from flowers
'Til all of them were gone
In the long and dreadful hours
The wizard's curse played on

The host was pouring brandy
He was going down slow
He stayed right 'til the end
He was the last to go

There were many, many others
Nameless here forevermore
They'd never sailed the ocean
Or left their homes before

The watchman, he lay dreaming
The damage had been done
He dreamed the Titanic was sinking
And he tried to tell someone

The captain, barely breathing
Kneeling at the wheel
Above him and beneath him
Fifty thousand tons of steel

He looked over at his compass
And he gazed into its face
Needle pointing downward
He knew he lost the race

In the dark illumination
He remembered bygone years
He read the Book of Revelation
And he filled his cup with tears

When the Reaper's task had ended
Sixteen hundred had gone to rest
The good, the bad, the rich, the poor
The loveliest and the best

They waited at the landing
And they tried to understand
But there is no understanding
On the judgment of God's hand

News came over the wires
And struck with deadly force
Love had lost its fires
All things had run their course

The watchman he lay dreaming
Of all things that can be
He dreamed the Titanic was sinking
Into the deep blue sea

# Roll on John

Doctor, doctor, tell me the time of day
Another bottle's empty, another penny spent
He turned around and he slowly walked away
They shot him in the back and down he went

Shine your light
Move it on
You burned so bright
Roll on, John

From the Liverpool docks to the red light Hamburg streets
Down in the quarry with the Quarrymen
Playing to the big crowds, playing to the cheap seats
Another day in the life on your way to your journey's end

Shine your light
Move it on
You burned so bright
Roll on, John

Sailing through the trade winds bound for the South
Rags on your back just like any other slave
They tied your hands and they clamped your mouth
Wasn't no way out of that deep, dark cave

Shine your light
Move it on
You burned so bright
Roll on, John

I heard the news today, oh boy
They hauled your ship up on the shore
Now the city gone dark, there is no more joy
They tore the heart right out and cut it to the core

Shine your light
Move it on
You burned so bright
Roll on, John

Put down your bags and get 'em packed
Leave right now, you won't be far from wrong
The sooner you go, the quicker you'll be back
You been cooped up on an island far too long

Shine your light
Move it on
You burned so bright
Roll on, John

Slow down, you're moving way too fast
Come together right now over me
Your bones are weary, you're about to breathe your last
Lord, you know how hard that it can be

Shine your light
Move it on
You burned so bright
Roll on, John

Roll on John, roll through the rain and snow
Take the right hand road and go where the buffalo roam
They'll trap you in an ambush 'fore you know
Too late now to sail back home

Shine your light
Move it on
You burned so bright
Roll on, John

Tyger, tyger, burning bright
I pray the Lord my soul to keep
In the forest of the night
Cover him over, and let him sleep

Shine your light
Move it on
You burned so bright
Roll on, John

# Index of Publishers and Copyright Dates